Read, Rhyme, and Romp

READ, RHYME, AND ROMP

Early Literacy Skills and Activities for Librarians, Teachers, and Parents

Heather McNeil

LIBRARIES UNLIMITED

AN IMPRINT OF ABC-CLIO, LLC
Santa Barbara, California • Denver, Colorado • Oxford, England

Copyright 2012 by Heather McNeil

Library of Congress Cataloging-in-Publication Data

McNeil, Heather, author.
  Read, rhyme, and romp : early literacy skills and activities for librarians, teachers, and parents / Heather McNeil.
     pages cm
  Includes bibliographical references and index.
  ISBN 978-1-59884-956-1 (hardcopy : alk. paper)—ISBN 978-1-59884-957-8 (ebook)   1. Children's libraries—Activity programs—United States
2. Libraries and preschool children—United States.   3. Reading—Parent participation—United States.   4. Children—Books and reading—United States.
5. Reading (Early childhood)—United States.   6. Reading promotion—United States.   7. Children's literature—Bibliography.   8. Best books—United States.   I. Title.
  Z718.3.M36   2012
  027.62'5—dc23   2012014171

ISBN: 978-1-59884-956-1   *1958*
EISBN: 978-1-59884-957-8

16   15   14   13   12   1   2   3   4   5

This book is also available on the World Wide Web as an eBook.
Visit www.abc-clio.com for details.

Libraries Unlimited
An Imprint of ABC-CLIO, LLC

ABC-CLIO, LLC
130 Cremona Drive, P.O. Box 1911
Santa Barbara, California 93116-1911

This book is printed on acid-free paper ∞

Manufactured in the United States of America

To all the wonderful, silly, creative, and dedicated children's librarians I have had the joy of working with, including Sharon, Caroline, Joan, Jane, Rhoda, Nancy, Cheryl, Jo, Sandy, Chandra, Paige, Josie, Julie, Sheila…

To my daughter, whom I love like crazy cakes…

Most of all, to my mother, who made this book possible by giving me encouragement, time, and memories of the best childhood with books anyone could wish for.

CONTENTS

ACKNOWLEDGMENTS

I want to thank the parents of Emma, Gina, Jack, Lily, Emily, and Jack for allowing me to use precious photographs of their children. I also want to thank Leaetta Mitchell for spending a morning at Toddlin' Tales taking pictures of me and the lively crowd.

I also want to thank the children's librarians at Deschutes Public Library for helping me find titles when I couldn't remember them, or recommending titles I hadn't thought of. You are all wonderful at what you do!

Finally, a huge THANK YOU to Todd Parr, who is gracious, generous, and a good friend as well as one of my favorite children's authors and illustrators.

Introduction

FROM PICKLED PEACHES TO THE MOON: THE LIFELONG POWER OF READING, RHYMING, AND ROMPING

My journey toward the writing of this book began as a daughter, the child of a military family that moved every two years. Born in Germany, then off to army posts in the United States, then to Turkey, then back to the United States. Different homes, different schools, different friends. I had amazing opportunities to experience other cultures and perspectives. I learned about adapting, like a chameleon, to whatever situation was now called "home." Through all the changes, my parents saw to it that we had traditions and pastimes that bound us together as a family. Catching lightning bugs in jars while camping in Canada, braving the chilling waters of Rapid Creek during summer vacations at our cabin in the Black Hills, pulling taffy until it was hard enough to seriously remove teeth, cutting out paper dolls (remember the Campbell's Soup girls?), swimming with jellyfish in the Aegean Sea, reading aloud every night.

Through all the moves, my mother made sure there were books in our lives, which always made those moves just that much heavier. But the books came along, and some I still have today. *Three Little Bunnies* by Ruth Dixon, published in 1950, features Maximilian, a bunny who is often in trouble, and amazing photos by Dale Rooks of real rabbits dressed in human clothes. There were the poems and songs by A. A. Milne. My mother says my favorite was "Rice Pudding": "What is the matter with Mary Jane?/She's crying with all her might and main,/And she won't eat her dinner—rice pudding again—/What is the matter with Mary Jane?" I have a 1924 edition of *Raggedy Ann and Andy and the Camel with the Wrinkled Knees* by Johnny Gruelle; I was sure the Raggedy Ann and Andy dolls my Aunt Harriet made for me were up and about at night, having adventures just like those in the book. My brother and I absolutely adored *Thidwick the Big-Hearted Moose* by Dr. Seuss, and the phrase "For a host, above all, must be nice to his guest" is often repeated in our family. We wore out a record (remember those?) listening to *The Elephant's Child,* produced by Columbia Records in 1956, and read by Gary Moore. *The Fairy Tale Book,* published in 1958, was an oversized volume of 28 stories from around the world, translated by Marie Ponsot. I remember first hearing the stories, later reading them on my own, and always being fascinated by the glorious and lavish illustrations by Adrienne Segur. I have had the joy in recent years of reading some of the stories to my daughter. *The Better Homes and Gardens Storybook* had many favorites, including "The Little Red Hen" done as a rebus with small pictures inserted into the text. *My Bookhouse: In the Nursery* belonged to my mother before me, and is now falling apart, but I clearly remember "The Gingerbread Man" and "Wynken, Blynken, and Nod" by Eugene Field as the ones I chose most often. Of course, I had Little Golden Books, such as *Nursery Songs* by Leah Gale, *Little Gray Donkey* by Alice Lunt, and *The Shy Little Kitten* by Cathleen Schurr and Gustaf Tenggren—all of them now fragile with age, but still holding a place in my heart.

My mother's rule was that my brother, Rod, and I each got to pick every other book, so he was introduced to the sweetness of *Little Women* by Louisa May Alcott, and I was given the high adventures of *Treasure Island* by Robert Louis Stevenson. My brother was especially fond of the Oz books, and now collects them (somehow I managed to keep *Ozma of Oz*). I believe that my most poignant memory is that of reading aloud *Girl of the Limberlost* by Gene Stratton Porter, while Mom was pickling peaches in the crisp and crunchy autumn. I can vividly remember sitting on the kitchen stool while steam and the smell of cloves and cinnamon surrounded me. Perhaps those aromas are still in the pages of the book in the glass-covered bookshelf that belonged to my grandfather and is now gracing the entrance hall of my house.

There was also storytelling. My grandfather, a Shakespeare professor, recited the cowboy poetry of Badger Clark: "'Way high up the Mogollons,/ Among the mountain tops,/A lion cleaned a yearlin's bones/And licked his thankful chops..." He repeated the chilling, mesmerizing words of the great bard himself, snarling "Out, out, damned spot!" as he washed his hands, which terrified, and fascinated, his grandchildren. My mother told of the wee folk and convinced me that dandelion seeds were fairies who would grant the wishes I wished for as I blew them away. My aunt, a spellbinding storyteller (and librarian), walked the streets of Sheridan, Wyoming, gathering up children to listen to her tales. She knew, long before it was confirmed with research, that songs, rhymes, and stories were essential to build a reader.

There was also writing. My maternal grandmother wrote poetry, such as this one to her husband in 1965:

Remember when our girls were little girls?
It was your humor that would save the day;
Your busy hours that found time to play,
Have noise and fun, and tell the stories, too.
(How we'd all laugh with you!)
I'd get the supper—do the humdrum things,
You'd make the willow whistles—and give us wings!

She later wrote a book for her family about our family, a collection of recipes combined with stories of pioneers, ranchers, strong women, and hardships. My mother followed her example and wrote a book for all of us about all the houses she lived in and the memories that made each of them a home.

Reading aloud, writing, and storytelling began my life, and continued to enchant and empower me throughout childhood.

Next came the beginnings of my life as a librarian. Much to my surprise and horror, I discovered that many children did not have someone who told stories, or wrote poems, or read aloud with passion in their voice. So I brought that to my story times and storytelling, bringing literature alive through puppet shows, creative interpretation, dialects and character voices, and much, much love of books. Like all children's librarians, I read books, recommended books, read aloud books, and designed programs around books. We even did overnights at the Bemis Public Library in Littleton, Colorado, where children age 6–11 *and their parents* spent the night at the library celebrating books. We began with three hours of creative activities, including reader's theatre by library staff, family crafts, storytelling, and songs around the campfire. Then we climbed into sleeping bags sprinkled throughout the children's area. Everyone was allowed to read by flashlight as long as it didn't disturb others. In the morning, there was orange juice, coffee, doughnuts, and bleary-eyed good-byes.

Over the years, there have been deep connections with special children. Through mutual fun at story time, sharing what's going on at school, and exploring shelves together to make recommendations for the next good book, I have memories of special interactions and discoveries that have touched my heart or tickled my funny bone. In this book, you'll meet several of them; I'll begin with Jeff.

Jeff was a regular attendee at my story times in Littleton. He was full of questions and curiosity, and we shared a very special friendship. If Jeff came to the library and I had the audacity not to be at the public desk, one of the staff members would come to my office and simply say, "Jeff is here." Nothing more need be said. I stopped whatever I was doing, and went out to the children's room to sit on the floor and talk with Jeff.

At age five, Jeff decided he wanted to be an astronaut. Each week, after story time, I gave him a book about the planets or the space shuttle or how a telescope works. One day he requested a book about Venus, and, as I searched for an appropriate one, he explained, "You know what? When I'm an astronaut, I'm going to Venus. I'll tell you about it when I get back."

"Oh, goodness, Jeff, that's a long journey, I probably won't be here when you get back."

The next week he requested a book about the moon. I gave him one by Seymour Simon. He left my side to go play with his younger, quieter sister, Krista. His mother leaned over and said to me, "You know why Jeff wanted a book about the moon? Because he knows the moon is closer, and you'll still be here when he gets back."

The next stage began when I became a "better late than never" parent at age 47. I was able to continue my passion for books with my adopted daughter. When she was one, her favorite was a cardboard book of *Barnyard Dance* by Sandra Boynton. I sang and mooed, she giggled and bounced. At age two, she asked for *Papa's Song* by Kate McMullan every night. I think it was because of the different voices I used for each of the family members who are trying to lull the baby bear to sleep with words such as "I'm your mama, up since dawn./How I wish that you would yawn." When she was three, *Aki and the Fox* by Akiko Hayashi was read over and over. I was attracted to the story because the Asian girl looks so much like Jamie. I think Jamie loved it because of the simplicity and gentleness of the story about a beloved stuffed fox who keeps insisting, "I'm fine. I'm fine," even after his many misadventures. She enjoyed the song "Pickin' peas, landin' on my knees!" and the wily rabbit in *Pickin' Peas,* retold by Margaret Read MacDonald, and admired the naughtiness of the zebra in *Naughty* by Caroline Castle. *The Ornery Morning* by Patricia Brennan Demuth was read aloud so many times she could repeat with me the cumulative chant, "If rooster won't crow morning,/Cow won't give milk,/Hen won't lay egg,/ Horse won't pull rake,/Dog won't herd Sheep,/Sheep won't give wool,/Cat won't case Rat,/I'm in a pack of wacky trouble." Bedtime favorites, even though she is now beginning her teen years, are still *Sleepytime Rhyme* by Remy Charlip and *If I Could: A Mother's Promise* by Susan Milord, both of which I sing with a lullaby tune.

Of course, now she reads on her own, but we still read aloud together: *To Kill a Mockingbird* by Harper Lee; all the Harry Potter series by J. K. Rowling; *Chicken Soup for the Adopted Soul* by Jack Canfield, Mark Victor

> Reading can make raising your baby that much more wonderful. At its best, it's a chance to snuggle in tightly and quietly enter another world together. At the very least, it's a distraction from a difficult moment or a difficult day. Sometimes it's a last-ditch way to provide entertainment when you simply haven't got another creative thing left to give.
>
> Straub, Susan, and K. J. Dell'Antonia. *Reading with Babies, Toddlers and Twos: A Guide to Choosing, Reading and Loving Books Together,* p. 3. Naperville, IL: Sourcebooks, Inc., 2006. Used with permission.

Hansen, and LeAnn Thieman; and, currently, *Raven Speak* by Diane Lee Wilson (perfect for horse lovers). Story time is our favorite time.

Stage four began with "Every Child Ready to Read @ Your Library" (ECRR). In 2005, the Public Library Association and the American Library Services Children Division of the American Library Association teamed up to create a program to promote early literacy through story times at libraries. It spread across the nation slowly at first, some librarians reluctant to provide tips to parents, or be perceived as reading teachers. But from the first training I attended, I knew that ECRR is about teaching exactly what I have loved, and believed, and passed on—stories, songs, rhymes, and playing with your child are what make the difference in creating memories, close bonds, and a love of books. I am honored to be certified as a master trainer in ECRR through Portland State University.

ECRR originally based their program on six early literacy skills that have been identified by experts as necessary for a child to be ready to read. It isn't about teaching reading, it's about knowing and loving books and language. It's about using playtime and story time to enhance a child's ability to understand what makes up a story, how letters sound, what happens when you move around parts of words, and being aware that print has meaning and purpose. The six skills, in the order they usually develop in a young child, are:

- Print motivation. A child loves books, asks for books, finds himself and his feelings, and interests in books.
- Vocabulary. This is about knowing the names of things. The more language skills a child already has before learning to read, the easier it is to sound out and determine the word.
- Print awareness. Print is everywhere, and it means something. We read print, not pictures. We use print to communicate important things, like stories, rules, directions, jokes, information, and more.

- Narrative skills. What is a story? How does a story begin and end? What might happen during a story? A child who can tell a parent what she did at the park has narrative skills, as well as the child who plays dress up, or makes up a story with his robots that transform into vehicles and weapons.

- Phonological awareness. Singing and rhyming are not only fun, but also functional because they teach phonological awareness. That includes determining whether words rhyme (log/frog), putting together chunks of words to make another word (pea and nut make peanut), and saying one-syllable words with the first sound (art with "c" becomes cart).

- Letter knowledge. Most children know the alphabet song, but they also need to know the sound of each of the letters and how to identify it in words.

The second edition of ECRR is organized around the concepts of talking, singing, reading, writing, and playing with your child(ren), with the same six skills as the first edition woven throughout. The kit and manual include everything needed for workshops with staff, parents, and community, from handouts to script, from bookmarks to a DVD.

And now I'm at the fifth phase, which is writing this book, the result of a lifetime of early literacy. Based on almost 35 years of producing weekly story times, 12 years of being a parent, 3 years of teaching about early literacy, and more years than I can believe of reading children's books, I have compiled more than 450 recommendations for books that have touched me or others. I explain about the early literacy skills, as well as describe a variety of creative activities you can do at a preschool, at the library, or at home, to enhance those skills in your child(ren). You'll find bits of research that might be useful for you if asking for administrative or financial support. If you're a librarian or preschool teacher, be sure to read the sections for parents so you can offer those ideas at story times, workshops, or family gatherings. You'll find testimonials from parents, teachers, and librarians about how books, songs, and rhymes have influenced their lives. Most of all, I hope you'll find reassurance that what matters is simply bringing a young child and books together.

Here's what I hope this book will encourage you to do. Tuck a child into your arms and read a story that gives him wings. Gather a group of children together and teach them a song that opens their hearts to harmony. Play a game with a child that brings giggles of delight and forever memories of time together. When you introduce a child to the wonders of stories, the charm of lyrics, the enchantment of rhymes, you have given him more joy than any screen can provide, more lasting memories than any electronic gizmo will create, and more assurance of trust and care than any wallet can buy.

Reading aloud is a timeless gift of love. Learning to read is an endless gift of possibility and dreams come true, even the dream of going to the moon and back in time for another story.

Another story about Jeff. Just before Thanksgiving, I was shelving books that had been left lying helter-skelter about the room. In came ebullient Jeff and thoughtful Krista. I gave Jeff a new book we had just received about outer space, and then we sat down to visit.

"You know what?" asked Jeff.

"No, what?"

"We're going to Pueblo for Thanksgiving. And you know what?"

"No, what?"

"My grandparents will be there, and Uncle Jim, and my cousins. And we're having turkey and stuffing and apple pie"—here he licked his lips and rubbed his tummy, so I would know how he felt about turkey and stuffing and apple pie—"And you know what else?"

"No, what?"

Suddenly, Jeff leaned forward, and whispered into my ear, "I love you."

Reading aloud is an intimate sharing of one's heart and time that creates lifelong memories. Jamie's grandmother, Mara, read aloud *Little Women* by Louisa May Alcott to both me as a young girl and Jamie.

BIBLIOGRAPHY

Alcott, Louisa May. *Little Women*. Boston, MA: Little Brown & Co., 1896.

Baum, L. Frank. *Ozma of Oz*. Chicago, IL: The Reilly & Lee Co., 1907.

Beaupre, Olive, ed. *My Bookhouse: In the Nursery*. Chicago, IL: The Bookhouse for Children, 1925.

Boynton, Sandra. *Barnyard Dance*. New York: Workman Publishing Company, 1993.

Canfield, Jack. *Chicken Soup for the Adopted Soul*. Deerfield Beach, FL: HCI Books, 2008.

Castle, Caroline. *Naughty*. New York: Knopf Books for Young Readers, 2001.

Charlip, Remy. *Sleepytime Rhyme*. New York: Scholastic, 2000.

Clark, Badger. *Sun and Saddle Leather*. Stockton, CA: The Westerners Foundation, affiliated with University of the Pacific, 1962.

Demuth, Patricia Brennan. *The Ornery Morning*. New York: Dutton Juvenile, 1991.

Dixon, Ruth. *Three Little Bunnies*. Chicago, IL: Rand McNally & Company, 1956.

Gale, Leah. *Nursery Songs*. A Little Golden Book. New York: Simon & Schuster, 1946.

Gruelle, Johnny. *Raggedy Ann and Andy and the Camel with the Wrinkled Knees*, Joliet, IL: P. F. Volland Company, 1924.

Hayashi, Akiko. *Aki and the Fox*. New York: Doubleday, 1991.

Lee, Harper. *To Kill a Mockingbird*. New York: Harper Perennial, 2007.

Lunt, Alice. *Little Gray Donkey*. New York: Simon & Schuster, 1954.

MacDonald, Margaret Read. *Pickin' Peas*. New York: HarperCollins, 1998.

McMullan, Kate. *Papa's Song*. New York: Farrar, Straus and Giroux, 2003.

Milne, A. A. *The World of Christopher Robin*. New York: E. P. Dutton, Inc., 1958.

Milord, Susan. *If I Could: A Mother's Promise*. Somerville, MA: Candlewick Press, 2008.

O'Connor, Betty, compiler. *The Better Homes and Gardens Storybook*. Des Moines, IA: Meredith Publishing Company, 1950.

Ponsot, Marie, translator. *The Fairy Tale Book: A Selection of Twenty-Eight Traditional Stories from the French, German, Danish, Russian and Japanese by Hans Christian Andersen, the Brothers Grimm, Madame d'Aulnoy, Madame Leprince de Beaumont, Madame la Comtesse de Segur, and Charles Perrault*. New York: Simon & Schuster, 1958.

Porter, Gene Stratton. *Girl of the Limberlost*. New York: Grosset & Dunlap, 1909.

Rowling, J. K. *Harry Potter and the Sorcerer's Stone*. New York: Scholastic, · 1997.

Rowling, J. K. *Harry Potter and the Chamber of Secrets.* New York: Scholastic, 1999.

Rowling, J. K. *Harry Potter and the Goblet of Fire.* New York: Scholastic, 2000.

Rowling, J. K. *Harry Potter and the Prisoner of Azkaban.* New York: Scholastic, 2001.

Rowling, J. K. *Harry Potter and the Order of the Phoenix.* New York: Scholastic, 2003.

Rowling, J. K. *Harry Potter and the Half-Blood Prince.* New York: Scholastic, 2005.

Rowling, J. K. *Harry Potter and the Deathly Hallows.* New York: Scholastic, 2007.

Schurr, Cathleen, and Gustaf Tenggren. *The Shy Little Kitten.* A Little Golden Book. New York: Simon & Schuster, 1946.

Seuss, Dr. *Thidwick, the Big-Hearted Moose.* New York: Random House Books for Young Readers, 1948.

Simon, Seymour. *The Moon.* New York: Simon and Schuster Books for Young Readers, 1984.

Stevenson, Robert Louis. *Treasure Island.* New York: Charles Scribner's Sons, 1911.

Straub, Susan, and K. J. Dell'Antonia. *Reading with Babies, Toddlers and Twos: A Guide to Choosing, Reading and Loving Books Together.* Naperville, IL: Sourcebooks, Inc., 2006.

Wilson, Diane Lee. *Raven Speak.* New York: Margaret K. McElderry Books, 2011.

Chapter One

"I FOUND JUST WHAT I WANTED!": BEGIN WITH BOOKS

It is a simple circle—if the adult reading the story loves the story, that adult will love reading it aloud, and because he or she is having such a positive experience, the child experiences love for the story, and by extension, love for the person reading it. And when this happens, a space is created—a holy space, if you will—where the book, the child, and the adult are under a spell together. It may be a quiet, dramatic, or wildly raucous spell, but it is a spell nonetheless.

Johnston, Allyn, and Marla Frazee, "Why We're Still in Love with Picture Books (Even Though They're Supposed To Be Dead)." Reprinted from the May/June, 2011 issues of *The Horn Book* Magazine by permission of The Horn Book, Inc., www.hbook.com.

One average day at the library, I was approached by a five-year-old. "I want a book about dinosaurs," he mumbled.

"We have lots of books about dinosaurs," I replied. "Follow me."

We walked across the room and down the aisle, until we arrived at the location for Tyrannosaurus Rex and all his gargantuous buddies. "Here they are," I said. "Was there any particular dinosaur you wanted?"

He shook his head, mutely staring at the three shelves full of prehistoric wonder. I pulled out a couple of titles I thought would particularly intrigue him, and then left him to explore on his own. I hadn't walked more than 20 feet when he yelled out in a voice loud enough to make any rampaging triceratops proud, "MOM! I FOUND JUST WHAT I WANTED! DINO-SAURS! LOTS AND LOTS OF DINOSAURS!"

He was ecstatic, and I made no attempt to squelch that enthusiasm with a reminder to be quiet in the library. Instead, I just walked back to the desk, wearing a smile and relishing those words, "just what I wanted." In books. At the library. I imagine him in the years ahead asking for superheroes, volcanoes, silly jokes, and how to draw aliens. He believed in books.

Children who become readers start by loving books, wanting books, asking for books, and finding in books just what he or she feels, fears, loves, wants, and needs. Books are easily available to her in the house, and she is read to every day, right from birth. Books are given as gifts, phrases from favorite stories are repeated in the family, and he sees his care providers also making time in each day to read what they love, whether it's a book on how to start a business at home or a don't-interrupt-me-now-I-can't-put-this-book-down adventure. It means books are important.

Reading aloud to a child is guaranteed to build bonds of intimacy, encourage curiosity, expand vocabulary, improve academic success, and develop the brain. It's absolutely free, since public libraries are free. No electronic equipment, batteries, or expensive packaged programs are necessary. When reading aloud begins at birth, it automatically becomes a treasured time that both child and parent will value, whether shared at the library or at home. In fact, it will become the best kind of addiction. "Read another one, Daddy!" "Is today library story time, Mommy?" "I don't want to watch TV; I want a story in your lap." Gasp!

Is there proof? Oh, yes! Reach Out and Read is a national program that encourages pediatricians to give families quality books during well visits and to actively promote the importance of reading aloud. On their website is an excellent article entitled, "Reading Aloud to Children: The Evidence," from the *British Medical Journal*'s Archives of Disease in Childhood. Co-authors E. Duursma, M. Augustyn, and B. Zuckerman summarize all the reasons why reading aloud is essential for encouraging the early literacy skills a child needs in order to be ready to read and cite the studies that prove its importance. Among the many reasons are the following:

1. During shared reading, children learn letters, begin to understand print, and recognize how to use a book.

2. Children learn grammar from well-written books.

3. Rhyming words in books teach children about phonological awareness, a prerequisite for reading.

4. Children's books contain "50% more rare words than prime-time television or even college students' conversations." The more

words a child knows when he or she begins school, the easier it will be to learn to read.

5. The earlier the age a child hears books read aloud, the higher the scores on language measures in school.

6. Reading aloud can help with wake-and-sleep patterns when it is part of bedtime routines.

7. Children learn from books and begin to understand concepts such as "coping strategies, building self-esteem and general world knowledge."

8. Asking questions and encouraging the child to have a conversation about the story and the pictures, and making connections to the child's world (a technique known as dialogic reading) result in more advanced vocabulary, story comprehension, and emergent literacy.

The article, an excellent source for statistical evidence, makes it clear that reading aloud from the beginning of a child's life and having books readily available at home assure a positive difference in a child's ability to learn to read (http://www.reachoutandread.org/FileRepository/ReadingAloudtoChildren_ADC_July2008.pdf).

As if that isn't enough, there's also all the magic that's going on inside the brain of a young child while she cuddles with a parent or engages in motor skill activities at story time. I'm certainly not an expert on brain development, nor is it necessary for a librarian, preschool teacher, or parent to know everything about neurons, dendrites, or synaptic pruning. Yikes! But a basic understanding of how a baby learns is helpful, so here are key points to consider, as they relate to emergent literacy and reading aloud.

The most important fact is that studies no longer support the idea that the brain develops on a predetermined schedule. Instead, it develops according to experiences that change, or rewire, the brain. According to Alison Gopnik, Andrew N. Meltzoff, and Patricia K. Kuhl, coauthors of *The Scientist in the Crib: Minds, Brains, and How Children Learn,* "Everything a baby sees, hears, tastes, touches and smells influences the way the brain gets hooked up" (p. 181). The environment plays a vital role in determining brain development, and each brain is unique.

To begin with, a baby's brain contains all the nerve cells, or neurons, it will ever have. How many? About 100 billion neurons, say Gopnik et al., "the same number as the number of stars in the Milky Way" (p. 183). As the baby experiences his world, the wiring or connections between cells change, reliant on activity and stimulation. When permanent connections (synapses) are made between one cell's branches (axons) and another cell's branches (dendrites), there is neurotransmission, a communication that allows cells to talk to one another. The more the child discovers with all his senses, the more the cells connect, and the more the brain grows. Children's brains are considerably more active than adult brains with all this wiring, continuing at a frantic pace until age 9 or 10, then gradually declining and reaching the adult level by age 18. Synapses increase from 2,500 at birth to 15,000 per neuron by age two or three. All this wiring is what allows the child to learn and remember.

But brains don't continue making more and more connections forever. Unneeded or weak connections are deleted (pruned), allowing for the frequently used connections to grow stronger. This is an important process since it results in a brain that is adapted to the world of the child. So a baby learns that crying in the middle of the night brings food, and a toddler learns that asking for a quacker brings food, and a preschooler learns that dipping a spoon into oatmeal brings food.

What does this mean in relation to early literacy? Basically, the more you know, the more you grow. Every time a child hears a song, or a rhyme, or a story, synapses are happening. When the child hears it again, the connection is stronger. Repeated words are remembered. Illustrations begin to have names—rabbit, truck, blanket. Stories develop meaning and can progress from text as simple as "One duck. Two horses. Three cows" to "The night Max wore his wolf suit…" Language increases from "Meow meow" to "Can we read *Bad Kitty*? It's my favorite!"

There's another important attribute about reading aloud to a child that affects brain development, and that is the fact that cuddling with a child while reading, and having hilarious fun together at library story time are positive experiences that release serotonin into the brain. Serotonin is what makes us happy. Serotonin tells our brains, "This activity is one I want to repeat again and again." As a result, the child begins to associate books with feeling good (assuming that the experience with the books was relaxed and mutually enjoyable, not punitive or harsh). Later, when a child has the early literacy skills necessary to learn to read, she *wants* to read because she *loves* books. And wanting is more than half the battle.

WHAT CAN YOU DO?: AT THE PRESCHOOL

If you are reading this book, the assumption is that you care about literacy, so you are probably already reading aloud to the children in your preschool. Hopefully, the books are of the best quality, not just donations or paperbacks parents no longer want, or favorite television characters that have didactic lessons and pedestrian vocabulary. Children need to hear books that invite conversation, challenge perceptions, introduce new ideas, and offer excellent vocabulary. When a child laughs uproariously each time he gets to yell out "Chicken butt!" in the book with the same title by Erica S. Perl, he is embracing the fact that books can be just downright silly. When the class guinea pig dies, everyone can learn about grieving and remembering loved ones by talking about *Badger's Parting Gift* by Susan Varley. When you're preparing for a field trip to the local public library, they can get ready with Judy Sierra's *Wild about Books*. What you're doing is connecting their world to literature, so that they will welcome any opportunity to hear a story and, eventually, read on their own.

If a child already loves books and identifies books as being fun, exciting, interesting, or relevant, then learning to read will be ever so much easier. But if the child has never found himself in a book, there is a much bigger barrier to overcome.

The other recommendation I make is that story time be a special time set aside every day with a memorable routine and in a space free from distractions. Sometimes, you'll just grab a book to fill in five extra minutes or to calm down the energy. But there also needs to be a time that has a ritual at the beginning and ending; has stories that invite participation through repetition, rhythm, and rhyme; and is at the same time and location so that the children eagerly anticipate the glory of it all. Here are some general tips of a successful read-aloud time in a preschool or day care:

1. Avoid distractions. For instance, if it's just before lunch or snack, make sure the children are not facing the tables where the food is being set out because that is what will catch their attention. Don't plan on having story time just when parents are picking up children. That's a fine time for a quick story, but not for story time.

2. Begin with an opening that tells them, "This is listening time." It might be a puppet singing, "The More We Get Together," or it might be a clapping rhyme, or it might be an action song that invites wiggles and jumps, but ends with quietly sitting and listening. You'll find examples of openings and closings in Chapter Seven.

3. Select books that are sure to appeal to almost everyone, and that include children of different ethnicities and lifestyles. Ask your public librarian for recommendations of books that are favorites at library story times.

4. Tie in at least one of the books with what is happening around them. If you're studying numbers, read a counting book such as *One More Bunny: Adding from One to Ten* by Rick Walton. If it's the first week with the children, and it's obvious some are feeling

anxious, share *Off to School, Baby Duck* by Amy Hest. If sharing seems to be a reoccurring problem, try *The Delicious Bug* by Janet Perlman, and follow with a discussion about what the chameleons learned about resolving their conflict. You're making books relevant to their lives and motivating them to want more.

WHAT CAN YOU DO?: AT THE LIBRARY

Librarians know their stuff. They know the books, the children, and the best rhymes and songs. Using all that knowledge, they can put together a story time that is filled with giggles, energy, enthusiasm, and participation. They can role model simple early literacy concepts, and read aloud from books that are not as well known, while also choosing longtime favorites. Chapter Seven will go into more detail about designing story time, but right now I want to talk about the power of books.

Books teach in a nonthreatening way, or they make us laugh or cry, or they open our minds to new worlds and ideas. When you read aloud *Pouch!* by David Ezra Stein. you will find that, on the surface, it's just a clever story about a toddler kangaroo starting to explore his world. But it also contains the following concepts:

- When I go out on my own, it might be scary.
- When I go out on my own, I might make new friends.
- Mommy will always be there to comfort me.
- Other kids feel like I do.
- A baby kangaroo is called a joey.
- I'm braver than Joey. He's silly!

At some level, each of these revelations is nestling into the child's brain and heart, preparing him for new adventures and feelings. But it's also just a well-written and simple story about growing up. Plus, it allows everyone to call out "Pouch!" each time Joey returns home.

One of the most successful programs I've ever organized was a series of puppet shows starring Tumbleweed the coyote. Once a month, another staff member would join me to do story time. One of us was the puppeteer, and the other was out in front of the stage, interacting with the children. Tumbleweed was a bumbling coyote who always seemed to have a problem. Through silly conversation with other puppets, reading aloud a couple of books on the subject, and talking with the children, Tumbleweed was able to at least identify his trouble and begin working toward a solution. Some of the topics included staying with a babysitter, best friend moving away, death of a pet, new baby, and good manners. The latter involved Penelope Pig, who ate loudly and greedily, grabbed what she wanted, and talked with her mouth full. One mother came in the next week and said, "I have tried over and over to get my son to have good table manners. Then he heard Tumbleweed and Penelope, and now he's telling us how to behave!"

A puppet show might not be your cup of tea, or you might not have another staff member available to assist. (How about a parent volunteer?) At the very least, occasionally use books to address issues, in a fun and positive way, and allow some time for conversation. Books such as *Llama Llama Mad at Mama* by Anna Dewdney and *Chicken Chickens* by Valeri Gorbachev present to children that others have the same feelings they have, such as being tired of going shopping or being afraid of going down the slide.

One of my favorite books for story time is *Owl Babies* by Martin Waddell. Sarah, Percy, and Bill are three young owls who have always known safety and comfort in their tree with their mother. But one day she leaves, and doesn't immediately return. The two older owls try to rationalize her disappearance, but Bill simply calls out, on every page, "I want my mommy!" I soon learned that this book is serious stuff for young toddlers, so I alleviate some of their intense concern by having them loudly join in on Bill's repeated phrase. I have a small owl finger puppet that pops up from behind the book to give them the cue, and they eagerly join in. Their breaths are held when I read, "They closed their owl eyes and wished their owl mother would come." And there is a definite sigh of relief when Mommy Owl returns. "Soft and silent, she swooped through the trees to Sarah and Percy and Bill." Stories teach us that we all have fears, and that sometimes life can be scary. Most of the time, Mommy comes back, which is why we play peek-a-boo when children are new to the world, trying to understand all the comings and goings. When they are older, books such as *Owl Babies* or folktales of courage and wisdom help them find ways to be brave, climb the mountain, and slay the dragon.

Always select the best of the best. Read aloud books that are everlasting favorites (*The Baby Beebee Bird* by Diane Redfield Massie) or that will touch a parent's heart (*I Love You, Little One* by Nancy Tafuri). Read ones that allow for quiet reflection (*Time for Bed* by Mem Fox) or riotous laughter (*Is Everyone Ready for Fun?* by Jan Thomas). Read books that parents would not normally discover on their own (*What Did You Put in Your Pocket* by Beatrice Schenk de Regniers) as well as ones that are sure to become family favorites (*Pete the Cat: I Love My White Shoes* by Eric Litwin). And, of course, read books about topics that they love, such as trains (*Down by the Station* by Will Hillenbrand) or pets (*The Best Pet Ever* by Victoria Roberts) or food (*Cow Loves Cookies* by Karma Wilson). None of this is new or amazing; it's just a reminder that you have the power to bring powerful literature to children and motivate them to love, love, love books.

Caroline Blakemore and Barbara Weston Ramirez, in their book *Baby Read-Aloud Basics: Fun and Interactive Ways to Help Your Little One Discover the World of Words,* list "Ten Benefits of Reading Aloud to Your Baby from Day One," as well as offer examples for each benefit:

1. Read-alouds promote listening skills.
2. Read-alouds increase the number of vocabulary words babies hear.
3. Read-alouds develop attention span and memory.
4. Read-alouds help babies learn uncommon words.
5. Read-alouds help babies learn to understand the meanings of words.
6. Read-alouds help babies learn concepts about print.
7. Read-alouds help babies learn to get information from illustrations.
8. Read-alouds promote bonding and calmness for both baby and parent.
9. Read-alouds stimulate the imagination and all the senses.
10. Read-alouds instill the love of books and learning.

(Blakemore and Ramirez, 9–25.
Used with permission.)

Every one of those reasons is filled with love, and the possibilities of success at school, the ability to express thoughts and feelings, and the desire to know more.

WHAT CAN YOU DO?: AT HOME

A parent recently described to me about the delightful afternoon she spent with her three-year-old son watching dirt movers and other loud

---

Facts 'n Stats

Learning to read begins the first time an infant is held and read a story. How often this happens, or fails to happen, in the first five years of childhood turns out to be one of the best predictors of later reading.

Wolf, Maryanne. *Proust and the Squid: The Story and Science of the Reading Brain,* 20. New York: Harper, 2007.

construction vehicles. A house was being built across the street and the boy was fascinated by all the noise, commotion, and action. So they packed a lunch and enjoyed a picnic while they watched. She knitted, and he asked lots and lots of questions.

When I heard the account of their time together, I wished I had been there to recommend the perfect ending: a trip to the library for books about—you guessed it—construction. *Good Morning, Digger* by Anne Rockwell includes such enticing words as dump truck, cement mixer, and tall crane. Or *Construction Countdown* by K. C. Olson has 10 dump trucks, 9 earthmovers, 8 bulldozers, and so on. They could enhance their knowledge even more with *Extreme Excavators* by Blaine Wiseman, an information book full of details about all the various rigs that are used to move dirt and rock. And to help lull him to sleep at bedtime, she could read *Goodnight, Goodnight, Construction Site* by Sherri Duskey Rinker and Tom Linchtenheld.

One of the best changes to the publishing world in the past 20 years has been the addition of nonfiction books for the youngest of listeners. After all, they are the ones with all the questions. "How does a bird build a nest?" "Why do flies buzz?" "Where is the moon?" "How do they make that shovel go up and down?" There are many wonderful books at libraries and book stores to answer the questions. Yes, the answers might be found on the Internet, but which is more intimate and relaxing? Looking at a screen and clicking on multiple websites in hopes of finding the answer in words that the three-year-old can understand, or cuddling close together on a couch, oohing and aahing at the amazing illustrations in *Actual Size,* Steve Jenkins's book about the size of animals, or learning together about the ancestors of elephants in *Mammoths on the Move* by Lisa Wheeler?

Books also help children with their frustrations and other feelings. When my daughter was about four, I would take her to playgrounds and she would absolutely refuse to enjoy anything. Swings, slides, tunnels—it didn't matter, they all scared her and she wasn't even going to try. I demonstrated the joys of each one, offered for her to sit in my lap, but I had no luck. She was just too afraid.

Then we shared the book *Little Quack* by Lauren Thompson. Little Quack has four siblings: Widdle, Waddle, Piddle, and Puddle. They are all trying to find the courage to jump into the water and learn to swim with their mother. Mama Duck encourages each duckling with the recurring phrase, "Come, little ducklings. . . . Paddle on the water with me." One by one they each succeed—except Little Quack. He proceeds to look at the water, sniff the water, touch the water with a toe, and finally decides to swim. "Then— Splish! Splash! Sploosh! Splosh!—into the water he plunged." Not jumped, not fell, not dove. Plunged. A perfect word.

The next time we went to the playground we watched other children, younger than Jamie, having a gloriously good time on all the equipment. Not Jamie. So I tried the phrase, "Come, little duckling. Come paddle on the water with me." I'd like to tell you that she instantly climbed up the stairs and slid down the slide, but that isn't how easy life is. However, the phrase did make the day a bit more comfortable for us. We talked about fears, we remembered Little Quack, and we tried a touch of this and a dab of that. Eventually, there was a day when she went down the slide, loved it, and couldn't be stopped, just like she was with her first ride on a merry-go-round and her first steps into the ocean. She had to dip her toes in, bit by bit, until she was ready to paddle on the water.

Another favorite, I'm sorry to say, was about a mother who isn't always perfect. Yes, I have been known to raise my voice, to get mad, to say words I wish I hadn't. *When Mommy Was Mad* by Lynne Jonell is about two brothers who notice that "Something was wrong with Mommy." They don't know why she bangs things about and won't smile, but what they do know is, "Mommy looked prickly all over." It's Robbie who breaks the spell by "borking" her with his "prickles," bumping into her like an angry porcupine. "Borking" became a way for Jamie and I to giggle our way out of a bad day. We also shared *Harriet, You'll Drive Me Wild* by Mem Fox many times because it helped us both understand that we all have limits, and that sometimes feelings get out of whack, just like that, even for mothers.

Jenny Wagner wrote a book years ago called *John Brown, Rose and the Midnight Cat.* It is a very short story about an old woman, Rose, who has lived with John Brown, the old sheep dog, for many years. "We are all right, Rose and me," says John Brown. Then, into their lives comes the midnight cat, and John Brown will not have it! He refuses to look at the cat, tips over the milk dish, and makes Rose so unhappy with his jealousy and selfishness that the old woman won't get out of bed. This book can help children in so many situations, but without being didactic or condescending. It could be used as a starting point for conversation about the new stepfather, the new baby, or the new friend. But it also can be read as a lovely and heartwarming story that ends just right.

You know your child better than anyone. What is your child passionate about? Princesses? (*Not All Princesses Dress in Pink* by Jane Yolen and Heidi E. Y. Stemple) Bugs? (*Bugs Are Insects by Anne Rockwell*) Trucks? (*My Truck Is Stuck* by Kevin Lewis) Pirates? (*Shiver Me Letters: A Pirate ABC* by June Sobel) What is your child struggling with? Learning to share in the sandbox? (*Mine!* by Shutta Crum) Potty training? (*On Your Potty* by Virgina Miller) Jealousy over the new baby? (*Baby Baby Blah Blah Blah* by Jonathan Shipton) What makes your child laugh? The word "underpants"? (*Dinosaurs Love Underpants* by Claire Freedman) Silly monsters? (*If You're a Monster and You Know It* by Rebecca Emberley) Crazy animals? (*What Animals Really Like* by Fiona Robinson) What changes are coming that might worry you? A divorce? (*Oliver at the Window* by Elizabeth Shreeve) A new house? (*I Like Where I Am* by Jessica Harper) An illness? (*You Are the Best Medicine* by Julie Aigner-Clark) Where did you and your child wander recently? The museum where you saw a baby porcupine? (*How Do You Hug a Porcupine?* by Laurie Isop) The farmer's market where you sampled warm, summer peaches? (*Market Day* by Carol Fosket Cordsen) The beach where you poked purple sea anemones? (*Looking Closely along the Shore* by Frank Serafini) All of these topics, and oh, so many more, are addressed in children's books for ages zero to five. Ask the librarian for recommendations of the best. And when the child sees you are interested in learning more about porcupines and underpants, then he will want to explore and discover even, and ever, more. With you.

> "We read to children for all the same reasons we talk with children: to reassure, to entertain, to bond, to inform or explain, to arouse curiosity, to inspire. But in reading aloud, we also:
>
> - Condition the child's brain to associate reading with pleasure;
> - Create background knowledge;
> - Build vocabulary;
> - Provide a reading role model."
>
> From *The New Read Aloud Handbook* by Jim Trelease, copyright © 1979, 1982, 1985, 1989 by Jim Trelease. Used by permission of Viking Penguin, a division of Penguin Group (USA) Inc.

Books as Toys

Cloth books, bathtub books, pop-up books, touch-and-feel books. The publishing market is glutted with these presentations of interactive books. Are they worth it? Yes! Or at least, some of them are. My daughter's cloth book traveled everywhere with her when she was an infant so she could pull the tiger's tail, lift the car's hood, crinkle the bug's wings, and chew on everything. I still have the cloth book that was mine, *All by Himself* by Kay Clark. (Can you tell it was a hand-me-down from my older brother?) It had buttons to button, zippers to zip, and laces to tie, all done by "a manly little boy" in shorts, a button-down shirt, and undershorts that snap. Remember, this was the 1950s.

The very young child, or the child who has difficulty sitting and listening, or the child who loves to explore with his hands can be enchanted with the books that invite interaction through touching different textures or lifting flaps to discover surprises. When the child is older, and can control the ripping, try some of the amazing pop-up creations that are being published.

Books for All Reasons

When birthdays or holidays come, give books as gifts. If your daughter is owly and difficult, curl up with her and a silly book, such as *Grumpy Bird* by

---

HEATHER RECOMMENDS

12 Interactive Picture Books

Boynton, Sandra. *Fuzzy, Fuzzy, Fuzzy!: Touch, Skritch, and Tickle Book.* Textures and hilarious illustrations make this perfect for babies.

Carter, David A. *Peek in My Pocket.* Flaps and pop-ups reveal shapes, textures, and surprises.

Cimarusti, Marie Torres. *Peek-a-Moo!* Farm animals play peek-a-boo. Look also for *Peek-a-Zoo* and *Peek-a-Choo Choo.*

Denchfield, Nick. *Charlie the Chick.* A hilarious and short lift-the-flap book about an enormous chick who loves to eat.

Faulkner, Keith. *The Wide-Mouthed Frog: A Pop-Up Book.* A frog learns a lesson when he searches for the answer to what other animals like to eat.

Garrett, Ann, and Gene-Michael Higney. *What's for Dinner?* Rhyming text and lifting flaps reveal what animals like to eat.

Gillingham, Sara, and Lorena Siminovich. *In My Nest.* One in a series of cardboard books with cutouts that reveal a young animal made of cloth.

Kim, Sue. *How Does a Seed Grow?* Foldout pages make this explanation of how plants grow enticing to the young.

Rowe, Jeannette. *Whose Ears?* Lift the flap to figure out whose ears are peeking out.

Steer, Dugald. *Snappy Little Pets.* Bright and colorful pop-ups show all kinds of pets.

Taback, Simms. *Farm Animals.* Flaps open to reveal hidden animals.

Van Fleet, Matthew. *Tails.* All kinds of textures reveal all kinds of tails.

CRAZY CAKES

I have talked with my daughter, Jamie, about her adoption since July 31, 1998, fondly known as Gotcha Day, when her foster mother placed a chubby-cheeked infant—MY DAUGHTER!—in my arms in Hanoi, Vietnam. My long journey toward adoption was as painful and soul-searching as it is for many others, and when I finally became a parent, I wanted desperately to do everything just right. (I have since learned that all we can hope for is to do it well enough, loving enough, honestly enough.) So, along with all the favorites she wanted to hear over and over and over, I regularly read books about adoption. One of those was *I Love You Like Crazy Cakes* by Rose Lewis. This adoption story was the right book for the right child (and her mother) at the right time. "Read it again," three-year-old Jamie would say, and she would meticulously pore over the illustrations, noticing a tiny foot, a blanket embroidered with stars, red roses on a tea cup, a mother's tear. Over and over we read that story, and the title became a song I made up and sang to her as a lullaby before turning out the light. "I love you like crazy cakes, like crazy cakes, like crazy cakes. I love you like crazy cakes for you are my joy." But what I remember the most was the one night she looked up at me from her crib, those black eyes sparkling, and unexpectedly repeated another line from the story.

"I waited for you my whole life."

Jeremy Tankard. (But you both have to get up and do some serious jumping at the end.) When it's a rainy day, and plans to go to the pumpkin patch have to be cancelled, have a picnic on the living room floor, build a fort of blankets over chairs, and read your favorites that are comfort food, just like macaroni and cheese. Make your visits to the library or bookstore long and luxurious, not always squeezed in between other errands. Help your child find himself in a book, so that he knows books are lifelong treasures of discovery and joy.

BIBLIOGRAPHY

For Librarians, Teachers, and Parents

Blakemore, Caroline, and Barbara Weston Ramirez. *Baby Read-Aloud Basics: Fun and Interactive Ways to Help Your Little One Discover the World of Words*. New York: AMACOM, 2006.

Gopnik, Alison, Andrew N. Meltzoff, and Patricia K. Kuhl. *The Scientist in the Crib: Minds, Brains and How Children Learn*. New York: William Morrow & Co., 1999.

Johnston, Allyn, and Marla Frazee. "Why We're Still in Love with Picture Books (Even Though They're Supposed To Be Dead." *Horn Book Magazine,* May/June, 2011.

Trelease, Jim. *The New Read Aloud Handbook.* New York: Penguin Books, 2006.

Wolf, Maryanne. *Proust and the Squid: The Story and Science of the Reading Brain.* New York: Harper, 2007.

For Children

Aigner-Clark, Julie. *You Are the Best Medicine.* New York: Balzer & Bray, 2010.

Boynton, Sandra. *Fuzzy, Fuzzy, Fuzzy! Touch, Skritch, and Tickle Book.* New York: Little Simon, 2003.

Bruel, Nick. *Bad Kitty.* New Milford, CT: Roaring Book Press, 2005.

Carter, David. *Peek in My Pocket.* Orlando, FL: Harcourt, Inc., 2007.

Cimarusti, Marie Torres. *Peek-a-Moo!* New York: Dutton Children's Books, 1998.

Clark, Kay. *All By Himself.* Youngstown, OH: Plakie Product, 1950.

Cordsen, Carol Fosket. *Market Day.* New York: Dutton Children's Books, 2008.

Snuggling with your child and a book right from the beginning of the child's life helps with bonding, brain development, and all the early literacy skills a child needs to be ready to read. I'm reading aloud *Guess How Much I Love You* by Sam McBratney to six-month-old Jamie.

Crum, Shutta. *Mine!* New York: Knopf, 2011.

de Regniers, Beatrice Schenk. *What Did You Put in Your Pocket?* New York: HarperCollins, 2003.

Denchfield, Nick. *Charlie the Chick.* San Diego, CA: Harcourt, 2007.

Dewdney, Anna. *Llama Llama Mad at Mama.* New York: Viking, 2007.

Emberley, Rebecca. *If You're a Monster and You Know It.* New York: Orchard Books, 2010.

Faulkner, Keith. *The Wide-Mouthed Frog: A Pop-Up Book.* New York: Dial Books for Young Readers, 1996.

Fox, Mem. *Time for Bed.* San Diego, CA: Harcourt, Brace & Co., 1997.

Fox, Mem. *Harriet, You'll Drive Me Wild.* San Diego, CA: Harcourt Brace, 2000.

Freedman, Claire. *Dinosaurs Love Underpants.* New York: Aladdin, 2010.

Garrett, Ann, and Gene-Michael Higney. *What's for Dinner?* New York: Dutton Children's Books, 2000.

Gillingham, Sara, and Lorena Siminovich. *In My Nest.* San Francisco, CA: Chronicle Books, LLC, 2009.

Gorbachev, Valeri. *Chicken Chickens.* New York: North-South Books, 2001.

Harper, Jessica. *I Like Where I Am.* New York: Putnam's, 2004.

Hest, Amy. *Off to School, Baby Duck.* Cambridge, MA: Candlewick Press, 1999.

Hillenbrand, Will. *Down by the Station.* San Diego, CA: Harcourt Brace, 1999.

Isop, Laurie. *How Do You Hug a Porcupine?* New York: Simon & Schuster Books for Young Readers, 2011.

Jenkins, Steve. *Actual Size.* Boston, MA: Houghton Mifflin, 2004.

Jonell, Lynne. *When Mommy Was Mad.* New York: Putnam's, 2002.

Kim, Sue. *How Does a Seed Grow? A Book with Foldout Pages.* New York: Little Simon, 2010.

Lewis, Kevin. *My Truck Is Stuck.* New York: Hyperion Books for Children, 2002.

Lewis, Rose A. *I Love You Like Crazy Cakes.* Boston, MA: Little, Brown, 2000.

Litwin, Eric. *Pete the Cat: I Love My White Shoes.* New York: Harper, 2010.

Massie, Diane Redfield. *The Baby Beebee Bird.* New York: HarperCollins Publishers, 2000.

McBratney, Sam. *Guess How Much I Love You.* Cambridge, MA: Candlewick Press, 1995.

Miller, Virginia. *On Your Potty.* Cambridge, MA: Candlewick Press, 2000.

Olson, K. C. *Construction Countdown.* New York: Henry Holt, 2004.

Perl, Erica S. *Chicken Butt!* New York: Abrams Books for Young Readers, 2009.

Perlman, Janet. *The Delicious Bug.* New York: Kids Can Press, 2009.

Rinker, Sherri Duskey, and Tom Linchtenheld. *Goodnight, Goodnight, Construction Site.* San Francisco, CA: Chronicle Books, 2011.

Roberts, Victoria. *The Best Pet Ever.* Wilton, CT: Tiger Tales, 2010.

Robinson, Fiona. *What Animals Really Like: A New Song Composed & Conducted By Mr Herbert Timberteeth.* New York: Abrams Books for Young Readers, 2011.

Rockwell, Anne. *Good Morning, Digger.* New York: Viking, 2005

Rockwell, Anne. *Bugs Are Insects.* New York: HarperCollins, 2011. Toronto: Kids Can Press, 2008.

Rowe, Jeannette. *Whose Ears?* Boston, MA: Little, Brown, 1998.

Serafini, Frank. *Looking Closely along the Shore.* Toronto: Kids Can Press, 2008.

Shipton, Jonathan. *Baby Baby Blah Blah Blah.* New York: Holiday House, 2009.

Shreeve, Elizabeth. *Oliver at the Window.* Honesdale, PA: Front Street, 2009.

Sierra, Judy. *Wild about Books.* New York: Knopf, 2004.

Sobel, June. *Shiver Me Letters: A Pirate ABC.* Orlando, FL: Harcourt, 2006.

Steer, Dugald. *Snappy Little Pets.* San Diego, CA: Silver Dolphin Books, 2003.

Stein, David Ezra. *Pouch!* New York: G. P. Putnam's Sons, 2009.

Taback, Simms. *Simms Taback's Farm Animals.* Maplewood, NJ: Blue Apple Books, 2011.

Tafuri, Nancy. *I Love You, Little One.* New York: Scholastic Press, 1999.

Tankard, Jeremy. *Grumpy Bird.* New York: Scholastic Press, 2007.

Thomas, Jan. *Is Everyone Ready for Fun?* New York: Beach Lane Books, 2011.

Thompson, Lauren. *Little Quack.* New York: Simon & Schuster Books for Young Readers, 2003.

Van Fleet, Matthew. *Tails.* San Diego, CA: Silver Whistle, 2003.

Varley, Susan. *Badger's Parting Gift.* New York: Lothrop, Lee & Shepard Books, 1984.

Waddell, Martin. *Owl Babies.* Cambridge, MA: Candlewick Press, 1992.

Wagner, Jenny. *John Brown, Rose and the Midnight Cat.* Scarsdale, NY: Bradbury Press, 1977.

Walton, Rick. *One More Bunny: Adding from One to Ten.* New York: Lothrop, Lee & Shepard, 2000.

Wheeler, Lisa. *Mammoths on the Move.* Orlando, FL: Harcourt, 2006.

Wilson, Karma. *Cow Loves Cookies.* New York: Margaret K. McElderry Books, 2010.

Wiseman, Blaine. *Extreme Excavators.* New York: Weigl Publishers, 2011.
Yolen, Jane, and Heidi E. Y. Stemple. *Not All Princesses Dress in Pink.* New York: Simon & Schuster Books for Young Readers, 2010.

WEBLIOGRAPHY

http://www.reachoutandread.org/FileRepository/ReadingAloudtoChildren_ADC_July2008.pdf.

Chapter Two

WOW! WORDS!:
LEARNING LANGUAGE

Facts 'n Stats

Researchers say that the number of different words a baby hears each day is the single most important predictor of later intelligence, school success, and social competence, if those words come from one of baby's special people—mother, daddy, grandma, nanny—rather than from a box on the wall. Reading counts.

Straub, Susan, and K. J. Dell'Antonia. *Reading with Babies, Toddlers and Twos: A Guide to Choosing, Reading and Loving Books Together,* p. 3. Naperville, IL: Sourcebooks, 2006.

An acquaintance of mine lived in a Colorado town known for its abundance of snow at least six months out of the year. Simply put, she hated it. Hated the snow-packed roads that made driving difficult, hated the hours spent shoveling heavy snow, hated the fact that it seemed like everyone else celebrated the arrival of the first snowfall when all she longed for was the return of summer.

The first snowfall had arrived, and she was gazing mournfully out the window, grieving for the months ahead. Her two-year-old daughter climbed up on the chair beside her, and looked out to what was probably her first snowfall in memory. "Oh!" she whispered. "Ice cream!"

Suddenly, there was a paradigm shift. Her words changed the whole perspective for her mother, and the world was filled with white, delicious wonder. The power of words.

Young children's brains are often described as sponges, soaking up every word and every experience. Experts agree that toddlers are learning nine new words a day. Jim Trelease, author of the classic *The Read-Aloud Handbook,* states that children are introduced to three times more rare words in books than they will hear in daily conversation. He cites a study by Donald P. Hayes and Margaret G. Ahrens, entitled "Vocabulary Simplification for Children: A Special Case for 'Motherese,'" printed in the *Journal of Child Language,* Vol. 15, 1988, pp. 395–410. During this study, it was found that an adult uses only 9 rare words per 1,000 when talking to a three-year-old. But children's books will offer almost 31. Who uses the word "sumptuous" when talking to a young child? Possibly no one. But the book *Plumply Dumply Pumpkin* by Mary Serfozo describes Peter's search for "not a stumpy, grumpy pumpkin, but a sunny, sumptuous pumpkin." Through the context of the other words, as well as the illustrations, the child listener knows exactly what sumptuous means, and just might use it to describe his next encounter with a pumpkin.

Tony Baloney by Pam Munoz Ryan is the story of "a macaroni penguin." He has plenty of troubles with his big sister, who always makes him be the kitty, and the "Bothersome Babies" who are "so exasperating." Adorable Tony runs away to his "hidey-place" with Dandelion, a stuffed toy. The language is not only unusual, but also brings on unexpected chuckles. "After Tony Baloney has been in the hidey-space for maybe a year, or twenty...."

What do these experts mean by the word "rare?" Cynthia Dollins highlights the tale of *Stellaluna* by Janell Cannon in her book *The ABCs of Literacy: Preparing Our Children for Lifelong Learning.* She includes a table of the 22 words that mean "said" in that one book about a bat raised by birds. They range from "crooned" to "mused" to "stuttered," and they all

---

Facts 'n Stats

Books contain many words that children are unlikely to encounter frequently in spoken language. Children's books actually contain 50% more rare words than primetime television or even college students' conversations.

Duursma, E., M. Augustyn, and B. Zuckerman, "Reading Aloud to Children: The Evidence." http://www.reachoutandread.org/FileRepository/ReadingAloudtoChildren_ADC_July2008.pdf.

help grow a child's vocabulary, as well as make the story just that much more interesting. *Ten on the Sled* by Kim Norman does the same with a variety of words explaining how the animals fall off the sled, such as "spilled," "whirled," and "squeezed." *The Very Lazy Ladybug* by Isobel Finn offers unusual words that clearly describe how the animals move. The kangaroo "bounded," the tiger "padded," and the bear "ambled."

We all know how startling it can be when we hear a young child use grown-up words, reminding us that they are always learning, remembering, and later offering it back. When my daughter was three, she was pretending to read to her stuffed animals. She held the open book in her lap, looked up at her toy audience, and said, "It was a party, a brilliant party, but something was amiss."

It's important that children hear unusual words from others. It's also important that they learn what those words mean. It's best not to carefully select simple words you are sure the child already knows, but rather to carry on a normal conversation while being willing to explain. "Grandpa has bad asthma, which means he has trouble breathing sometimes." "I'm going to make guacamole. It's made from tomatoes and avocados. This is an avocado. It's a kind of fruit with a big seed in the middle, and soft, squishy, green insides that are delicious." "Today's story is about a pangolin. That is an animal with hard scales on most of his body, except for a furry stomach. They can roll up into a ball like this. Can you?"

When a child knows the word elephant or table, just based on hearing them in conversation or stories, it makes it so much easier when they are learning to read. Otherwise, think of all the ways you might think those two words could be pronounced if you had never heard them before. Ta-BLEE? Tab-LEH? E-LEP-hant? Ee-lee-p-HANT? Familiarity with the words allows the new reader to focus on the reading, rather than also

Facts 'n Stats

[R]esearch demonstrates that what determines academically successful children is the amount of language or talk that they hear per hour from adults in the first few years of life. The study (Drs. Betty Hart and Todd Risley, *Meaningful Differences in the Everyday Lives of American Children*) also shows that the number of words babies hear each day is the single most important predictor of future intelligence, school success, and social skills.

Blakemore, Caroline J., and Barbara Weston Ramirez. *Baby Read-Aloud Basics: Fun and Interactive Ways to Help Your Little One Discover the World of Words*, p. 11. New York: AMACOM Books, 2006.

trying to figure out what the reading is about. When a young child is read aloud *Opposnakes* by Salina Yoon, she has the opportunity to not only hear, but also see the meanings of the words "straight" and "tangled" by looking at the hilarious antics of the snakes in costumes. Or for an older child, *Thesaurus Rex* by Laya Steinberg introduces homonyms through a day in the life of a very active and adorable dinosaur. "Thesaurus Rex drinks his milk: Sip. Sup. Swallow. Swill. Whoops! He's had a messy spill."

One of Jamie's favorite books when she was three and four was *Picture Dictionary* by Jennifer Boudart, Brian Conway, and Lisa Harkrader. It is a thick children's first dictionary, and every word has a descriptive photograph. She pored over this book every day, learning new words as well as revisiting favorites. I love remembering the contagious giggles that happened every time she purposely turned to the page with the word "boy." For some reason, the photo of a five-year-old boy, wearing a yellow sweatshirt and jeans, with his arm extended toward the sky, was absolutely THE MOST HILARIOUS thing Jamie had ever seen and she would laugh and laugh and laugh.

Another read-it-again book was *Bad Kitty* by Nick Bruel. This is the first in a series about a cat who has serious attitude issues and hilarious facial expressions. Jamie laughed at Bad Kitty sticking out her tongue at jalapenos, and choking at rhubarb. What I loved was that the story introduced Jamie to words and foods not normally found in our pantry or refrigerator, such as parsnips and asparagus. Not only that, but it's also an alphabet book, so the child is learning the organization of the ABC's and how to connect words by their beginning sounds. Not only that, but it's also hilarious, with ridiculous objects brought home from the grocery store for "Good Kitty," such as Hippo Hamburgers and Fried Flies. In other words (pun intended), there's a lot going on in this book to make it worthy of repeated reading aloud, laughing at the pictures and story, while learning new words that could come in handy when you want to introduce your child to the joys of broccoli.

WHAT CAN YOU DO?: AT THE PRESCHOOL

Play the Word of the Day game. Hang the word from the ceiling, and design activities that promote that word, and others associated with that word, all day. For instance, let's say the word is "carrot." How about serving carrot muffins or carrot juice? Have a simple discussion about nutrition, introducing fruits and vegetables. Craft Time could be having the children draw Mr. and Ms. Carrot, dressing them up for the annual Vegetable Ball. Sing "10 Crunchy Carrots," along with Charlotte Diamond on her CD, *10 Carrot Diamond*. Play "Guess the Food" game, with a bag from which you give hints about other nutritious foods, and when they guess it correctly, out it comes. End it with baby carrots for everyone to enjoy (assuming these children are old enough to chew a carrot). And, of course, make sure that story time focuses on food, with at least one story that features the Word of the Day, such as *Lunch* by Denise Fleming. Mouse has an undying hunger as he eats his way through "tasty orange carrots," and ends with "juicy pink watermelon, crunchy black seeds, and all." And if you're wondering how to track down all these kinds of resources—music, stories, crafts, recipes—just ask your public librarian.

Play 25 Words. You name a category, such as "animals with fur." Then the children have to identify 25 in less than 3 minutes. As they get older, the categories get more difficult, such as "mammals" or "colors." It's easy to come up with 10 colors, but it really challenges their vocabulary to list 25.

Read books that feature unusual language. *Listen to the Rain* by Bill Martin Jr. is a beautiful and creative story about an approaching rain storm. "Listen to the rain/the whisper of the rain, the slow soft sprinkle,/the drip-drop tinkle,/the first wet whisper of the rain." Before reading the story, guide the children through making the sounds of the rain. Begin with rubbing thumbs and two fingers together. Next, everyone quietly rubs palms together. Follow that with gently tapping thighs, then increasing to a heavier slap, then adding drumming feet. Lead them through the diminishing storm, by removing each of the sounds, one by one, until all that is left is rubbing thumb and fingers, and then, nothing. Now read the story, with another adult guiding the children through the sounds that accompany what is being said since your hands will be busy with the book. Make sure your voice also reflects the intensity of the storm, beginning gently, progressing to loud and strong, and finally, quietly ending with "the dripping, dripping, dropping,/the slowly, slowly stopping/the fresh/wet/silent/after-time/of rain." I have read this many times with children and parents, and it is always very effective and moving.

Have an "I'm a Word" costume party. Children dress up to portray an unusual word, such as "mighty" (a heavily padded superhero with plenty of muscles) or "tangled" (lots of ribbons and yarn).

If you are reading aloud a story with many unusual words that are essential to the story, consider explaining what they mean before beginning the read-aloud rather than having to stop multiple times. But if it's only one or two, simply describe the meaning at the moment the word is first mentioned. And sometimes, such as "sunny, sumptuous pumpkin," it won't be necessary at all.

WHAT CAN YOU DO?: AT THE LIBRARY

Librarians have the envious role of being surrounded by books that introduce new and unusual words, and then being able to fit them in to story time. Here are some favorites, with ideas for enhancing the experience.

Wombat. Now there's a word that doesn't show up in daily language in the United States. But there are absolutely wonderful books about this waddling creature that looks like a cross between a teddy bear and a giant marmot. Have a "Down Under" story time. For preschoolers, begin with *Wombat Stew* by Marcia Vaughan, which introduces not only a wombat, but also other unusual Australian creatures such as the dingo, the emu, and the blue-tongued lizard. There's even a song for everyone to join in on. All ages enjoy *Sometimes I Like to Curl up in a Ball* by Vicki Churchill, in which an adorable wombat explains his many feelings. Be sure to encourage your listeners to make all the silly faces. Next read *Diary of a Wombat* by Jackie French, in which the wombat's exciting day is described, "Monday. Morning: Slept. Afternoon: Slept. Evening: Ate grass. Scratched. Night: Ate grass. Slept." For an action rhyme, try this one to the tune of "Are You Sleeping":

Cuddly koala, cuddly koala, *(give yourself a hug)*
Possum, too. Possum, too. *(put your head between your legs,*
    upside down)
Waddling waddling wombat, waddling waddling wombat, *(waddle)*
Hopping kangaroo, hopping kangaroo. *(hop)*

A simpler song for toddlers, or for bouncing babies on laps, is "Kangaroo Joe," which you can find at http://www.kididdles.com/lyrics/k011.html.

Finally, to reinforce retention of the words, have a coloring sheet of some of the Australian animals, with the words below the pictures. Or, cut out the pictures, glue to craft sticks, write the names on the sticks, and do a puppet show.

HEATHER RECOMMENDS

17 Books with Unusual Words for Library Story Time

Becker, Bonny. *A Visitor for Bear.* The clever story has a somewhat British tone when the "small, gray and bright-eyed" mischievous mouse asks, "Perhaps we could have just a spot of tea?"
Blackaby, Susan. *Brownie Groundhog and the February Fox.* Unexpected words such as "shimmied," "fluff of snow," and "grousing" tell the story of a cautious friendship between two animals.

Browne, Anthony. *Little Beauty.* A huge gorilla's best friend is a tiny kitten.

Cumberbatch, Judy. *Can You Hear the Sea?* A young girl in West Africa listens for the ocean in a conch shell, but only hears the "flip-flapping" of clothes, the "swish-swishing" of banana trees, and the sizzling of plantains.

Dewdney, Anna. *Roly Poly Pangolin.* Roly Poly is afraid of new things.

Fox, Mem. *Hello, Baby!* "Are you a lion with dust on its paws?/Perhaps you're a hippo with yawning jaws."

Fox, Mem. *Wilfrid Gordon Macdonald Partridge.* The boy with four names is determined to find out what a memory is when Miss Nancy, his friend at the old people's home, loses hers.

Hadithi, Mwenye. *Crafty Chameleon.* A chameleon must use his wits to escape from leopard and crocodile.

Hillenbrand, Will. *Fiddle-I-Fee.* The traditional folk song features Hillenbrand's delightful illustrations and silly words such as "dub-ub" and "hum sum."

Johnston, Tony. *Cat, What Is That?* This is an incredibly imaginative collection of descriptions of what is a cat. "It is the Thief/beside the cream./Beside the fire/it is the Dream."

Johnston, Tony. *The Iguana Brothers.* Dom and Tom pretend they are dinosaurs and learn to be friends.

Johnston, Tony. *My Abuelita.* A Mexican boy describes his grandmother, who has very special work as a storyteller. "Then, with words as wild as blossoms blooming, as round as dimes, she begins."

Ketteman, Helen. *Armadilly Chili.* A tarantula, mockingbird, and horned toad don't want to help Armadillo make the chili, but they sure want to eat it.

Montgomery, Tamara. *When the Cassowary Pooped: A Tale of New Guinea.* This bird spreads color everywhere through the seeds he drops.

Newbery, Linda. *Posy.* Describes the charming tabby kitten with such delightful language as "whiskers wiper,/crayon swiper."

Rayner, Catherine. *Ernest, the Moose Who Doesn't Fit.* The author tells a hilarious tale of a moose who is "determined" to fit into the book. She uses such clever phrases as "shimmy, shift, and shuffle" and "squidge, squodge, and squeeze."

Stutson, Caroline. *By the Light of the Halloween Moon.* This is a masterpiece of unusual and brilliant words, such as "A bat! A bungling bouncy breezy bat" and "A girl! A small bright slip of a smiling girl."

WHEEZLES AND SNEEZLES

One day I came home to a miserable four-year-old daughter. "I have the wheezles and sneezles," she croaked. I knew exactly how she felt, thanks to A. A. Milne's endearing poem "Sneezles" in *The World of Christopher Robin*.

Christopher Robin

Had wheezles

And sneezles,

They bundled him

Into

His bed.

They gave him what goes

With a cold in the nose,

And some more for a cold

In the head.

Jamie loved many of the poems in this collection, especially "The King's Breakfast," which I read almost every day for many weeks. The poem remains alive in our home, and we often say, while reaching for the butter, "I do like a little bit of butter to my bread."

Her favorite, though, was "Pinkle Purr," a bittersweet story of a young kitten and his relationship with his mother. The words perfectly describe how a child begins his life thinking mother is perfect because "all that he learned he learned from her."

Later, Pinkle Purr grows up, and becomes too busy to bother with his mother.

The poem ends with Tattoo, now a grandmother, playing with Pinkle Purr's kittens, and Pinkle Purr watching his mother fondly. " 'Dear Little Tat,' says Pinkle Purr."

A. A. Milne gave us many wonderful hours of poems and stories (he is the author of *Winnie the Pooh,* after all) with memorable words, such as wheezles and sneezles, that are never forgotten.

Another variation would be to read books about a variety of animals with strange names and habitats, such as cassowary, pangolin, and hippopotamus.

There are so many books with truly rare words that will stretch a child's knowledge. As a librarian, you can introduce these at story time, and the

Facts 'n Stats

Parents and family have a profound influence upon children, not only for their vocabulary, but also for quality and quantity of literary experiences they provide. Oral language development is so important. It can be predicted at age 3 if a child will have problems with reading in elementary school.

Nevills, Pamela, and Patricia Wolfe. *Building the Reading Brain PreK-3.* 2nd ed., p. 45. Thousand Oaks, CA: Corwin Press, 2009.

parent can then follow up with repeated exposure to the title, and discussion about the words.

WHAT CAN YOU DO?: AT HOME

After a trip to the zoo or museum, or just to fill up a rainy day, gather up all your child's stuffed animals. Read aloud to everyone *Polar Bear, Polar Bear, What Did You Hear?* by Bill Martin Jr. Then make up your own story, using the variety of animals before you. The important thing is to make a game out of thinking up words that describes the sound the animal makes. For instance:

I went to the zoo.
What did you see?
I saw a leopard snarling at me.

Howling, screeching, warbling, chuckling—the more creative or unusual the words are that you choose, the more the child will remember. You could also do this with the movements of the animals—lolloping, zigzagging, lollygagging, barreling.

Make a paper body doll with your child. Each of you lies down on a sheet of butcher paper, and the other traces around the body. Cut two and paste together, with paper stuffing between the two layers so it looks more real. Color or decorate. Then you set them around the house in surprising places, with a new word in their hands. Suddenly, your child calls from the bathroom, "Mom! My body doll is in the bathtub. What's the word?" "The word is 'bathtub,'" you reply. Then you can play "Take It Apart" (in the "What Can You Do?: At the Preschool" section of Chapter Five), or talk about the individual sounds in the word (b-a-th-t-u-b), or make up silly songs with bathtub in them ("Oh, where, oh, where, can my bathtub be?"), or figure out other words that rhyme (back rub, hand scrub). Later on, your child discovers your body doll in the garden, with the word "flower" in her hands, and you make a game of naming all the different kinds of flowers you can remember, or all the words that rhyme with flower. Or, you plant flowers!

Some quiet evening, when the moon is full, read aloud *Otter Moon*. Tudor Humphries's lyrical language and elegant illustrations tell the tale of

Facts 'n Stats

There is one prekindergarten skill that matters above all others, because it is the prime predictor of school success or failure: the child's vocabulary upon entering school. Yes, the child goes to school to learn new words, but the words he or she already knows determine how much of what the teacher says will be understood. And since most instruction for the first four years of school is oral, the child who has the largest vocabulary will understand the most, while the child with the smallest vocabulary will grasp the least.

From *The New Read-Aloud Handbook* by Jim Trelease, copyright © 1979, 1982, 1985, 1989 by Jim Trelease. Used by permission of Viking Penguin, a division of Penguin Group (USA) Inc.

HEATHER RECOMMENDS

16 Books with Unusual Words for Story Time at Home

Bartoletti, Susan Campbell. *Naamah and the Ark at Night*. Water "swirls," animals "prowl," and Naamah sings "for stars to thrill the night" in this lullaby about Noah and the ark.

Doyle, Malachy. *Horse*. Glorious illustrations and unusual words such as "thundering," "muzzle," and "paddock" fill this story of a mare, her foal, and a girl who loves them both.

Elffers, Joost, and Curious Pictures. *Do You Love Me?* For the very youngest of listeners, unusual creatures receive reassurance from their parents, with unexpected words such as "ever near," "nestle," and "snuzzle."

Gaiman, Neil. *Blueberry Girl*. The Newbery award-winning author offers a poetic tribute to a baby growing into a woman, calling on the "ladies of light and ladies of darkness and ladies of never-you-mind" to help her along her way.

Jenkins, Steve, and Robin Page. *What Do You Do with a Tail Like This?* Water color and cut paper collage combine for fascinating illustrations in this guessing book about animals and their parts.

Let's-Read-and-Find-out Science series. Stage 1 of this series is just right for children who have many questions about nature and weather. Titles include *From Tadpole to Frog, How Animals Babies Stay Safe, Where Do Chicks Come From,* and more.

Mora, Pat. *Delicious Hullabaloo/Pachanga deliciosa.* Lizards and armadillos prepare an unusual feast in this bilingual story.

Muth, Jon J. *Zen Shorts.* A wise panda named Stillwater teaches three children about generosity, luck, and forgiveness through storytelling.

Root, Phyllis. *Big Momma Makes the World.* Big Momma is busy with a baby on her hip and laundry waiting to be washed, but she still has time to make the world.

Scanlon, Elizabeth Garton. *All the World.* Everything is glorious in the rhyme, from the captivating illustrations to the words that describe the wonders of the world.

Slater, Dashka. *Baby Shoes.* Baby's shoes start out a "fine-looking" white, but soon they're "dizzy-spinning," "fruit-kicking," "splish-splashing," and "rainbow-romping."

Sockabasin, Allen. *Thanks to the Animals.* A young child falls out of a sled and is warmed and comforted by animals in this tale from the Passamaquoddy. Unusual animals such as weasel, mink, and muskrat are in the story.

Stutson, Caroline. *Cat's Night Out.* Rhythm, rhyme, and poetic language combine in this story of cats dancing through the night, doing the rumba, line-dance, the fox-trot, and more.

Williams, Karen Lynn. *A Beach Tail.* Gloriously illustrated by Floyd Cooper, this gentle and rhythmic story tells of an African American boy and his explorations on the beach. Like the returning tide, Williams repeats phrases such as "Swish-swoosh" and "But Gregory did not go in the water, and he did not leave Sandy."

Winter, Jeanette. *Wangari's Trees of Peace: A True Story from Africa.* With elegant and powerful words such as "Word travels, like wind rustling through leaves," Winter tells the story of one woman who made a difference in Kenya by planting trees.

Ziefert, Harriet. *Bunny's Lessons.* A stuffed animal explains what words he's learned from his boy.

one otter's courage when the King of the River demands he bring him a fish on a silver dish. "In the land of the otters, while we all slept, Flibbertigibbet lay in his secret place, watching the freckly moon rise over the wood." I can't help but read this story with a hushed voice. The Heron "dressed in his suit of gray," the King of the River "brewing like a storm," and visual images such as "bats flying low over the water, swallowing moths" cast a spell of mystery and beauty. Later, when the moon is overhead, go on a full moon drive. My daughter and I have a longstanding tradition of doing these drives each month. We hop in the car and drive to an open meadow, where the moon glows so bright and clear that you can drive without headlights. We turn off the car, climb on the hood, and sing all the songs we can think of that have the word "moon" in them. "I See the Moon," "The Moonman," "Moon River," "Skiddamarink." It's magical.

In the book *What's Going on in There? How the Brain and Mind Develop in the First Five Years of Life,* author Lise Eliot stresses the importance of having a conversation *about* the book you are reading with the child, as well as reading the text. This is called *dialogic reading,* and involves encouraging your child to make comments, respond to questions, and elaborate on what is seen in the illustrations. Eliot states that dialogic reading "has been reported to accelerate two-year-old's language development by as much as nine months" (p. 390). Drs. Kathy Hirsh-Pasek and Roberta Michnick Golinkoff, co-authors of *Einstein Never Used Flash Cards: How Our Children REALLY Learn—And Why They Need to Play More and Memorize Less,* emphasize that just reading aloud is not enough to ensure success in learning to read. Instead, talk about what you see, encourage discussion about alternate endings, or relate the story to your child's experiences or feelings.

When you have a book with illustrations that are rich with imagination, or packed with things to discover everywhere, take time to talk about what is happening, where the plot is going, why the characters feel the way they do, and so on. Ask open-ended questions that will lead to discussion. Rather than, "Can you find the dog?", ask "Why do you think the dog is running away?" Rather than, "Who will catch the mouse?", ask "What do you think might happen next?" The conversation leads to comprehension, increased vocabulary, and discoveries you probably never imagined. Let the child lead the discussion, and if he wants to talk only about the ant that is sitting on the corner of the leaf, then let that be the discovery of the day. Dialogic reading is especially useful with reluctant readers or listeners. Although listening to text, or trying to sound it out themselves, might be unappealing, they can often be enticed to spend time with nonfiction books about the subject that fascinates them the most.

HEATHER RECOMMENDS

19 Books for Picture Book Conversation (Dialogic Reading)

Armstrong, Jennifer. *Once Upon a Banana.* A monkey and his banana peel cause a lot of trouble.

Askew, Amanda. *Mighty Machines: Diggers.* One in a series about machines with big, bold pictures, easy text, and labels of parts.

Biggs, Brian. *Everything Goes on Land.* Trains, cars, buses, taxis, a bird with a hat, and much more to talk about and discover.

Curtis, Jamie Lee. *Today I Feel Silly & Other MOODS That Make My Day.* A young girl explores her world and her feelings.

Donovan, Jane Monroe. *Small Medium & Large.* A young girl finds a real cat, dog, and horse under her Christmas tree.

Dylan, Bob. *Man Gave Names to All the Animals.* Jim Arnosky's lush illustrations depict animals from around the world.

Eye Know series by Dorling Kindersley Publishing, Inc. Nonfiction books with an abundance of photographs about favorite topics such as dinosaurs and reptiles.

Faller, Regis. *Polo: The Runaway Book.* The dog Polo loves his book, but loses it to a strange creature.

Jay, Alison. *Welcome to the Zoo.* Look carefully for all the surprises and curiosities at the zoo.

Neubecker, Robert. *Wow! School.* Illustrations are overflowing with all that can be found and done at school.

Pinkney, Jerry. *The Lion and the Mouse.* Without any text, Pinkney's powerful illustrations clearly tell the Aesop's fable of two animals who help each other in times of trouble.

Pinkney, Jerry. *Twinkle, Twinkle, Little Star.* A chipmunk follows a dandelion puff and discovers stars are everywhere.

Rathman, Peggy. *10 Minutes till Bedtime.* A young boy and hundreds of hamsters prepare for bed.

Slate, Joseph. *Miss Bindergarten Gets Ready for Kindergarten.* All 26 children and the teacher are getting ready for school to begin.

Spier, Peter. *Peter Spier's Rain.* Discover all the ways to enjoy a rainstorm.

Staake, Bob. *Look! A Book!: A Zany Seek and Find Adventure.* Rhymes and die-cut holes reveal all kinds of pictures and action.

Thomson, Bill. *Chalk.* Three children discover their chalk drawings come to life.

Tolman, Marije, and Ronald Tolman. *The Tree House.* What seems like a simple wordless book about two polar bears is really a clever tale of imagination and discovery.

Weitzman, Jacqueline Preiss, and Robin Preiss Glasser. *You Can't Take a Balloon into the Metropolitan Museum.* There is chaos amid the paintings when a little girl brings in a balloon.

Another important addition to the vocabulary your child needs to know are those words that describe feelings. Young children have a hard time explaining their feelings. They just know they're unhappy so they cry or fuss or have a meltdown. Books can help them name more specifically what is going on inside their hearts. "I'm jealous because he got a new toy truck." "It makes me mad when I can't stay up and watch TV with you." "I feel lonesome when I have to play by myself." "I'm too shy to talk to my teacher." Or, sometimes the feelings are devastatingly serious. "I'm angry at the man who touched me." Hearing books about a variety of feelings can help children not only give a name to their emotion, but also figure out what can be done to feel better.

HEATHER RECOMMENDS

13 Books about Feelings

Boynton, Sandra. *Happy Hippo, Angry Duck.* Like all of Boynton's stories, this cardboard book is simple, clever, and hilarious, as animals demonstrate feelings.

Cleary, Daniel. *Stop Bugging Me!* A dog wants privacy, but his friends just don't understand why.

Cowell, Cressida. *What Shall We Do with the Boo-Hoo Baby?* A barnyard of animals try many activities to stop the baby's crying, when all he wanted was a nap.

Ellwand, David. *The Big Book of Beautiful Babies.* Black and white photographs show emotions and babies with rhymes such as "Baby hands, baby feet, baby messy, and baby neat."

Emberly, Rebecca, and Ed Emberly. *If You're a Monster and You Know It*. Everyone can growl and stomp their way to happiness.

Freyman, Saxton. *How Are You Peeling?* Fruits and vegetables express emotions such as being bored, shy, bold, and more. You will want to explore this book over and over again, discovering a smiling mushroom, a grumpy orange, an insecure onion.

Havill, Juanita. *Jamaica and Brianna*. An African American girl and an Asian American girl work their way through feelings of jealousy about their boots.

Hest, Amy. *In the Rain with Baby Duck*. Baby Duck's grandfather is the only one who can help her find happiness on a rainy day.

Smee, Nicola. *Funny Face*. A toddler goes through a wide range of emotions when his ball is taken by a bear.

Tankard, Jeremy. *Grumpy Bird*. A bird's friends help him get rid of his grumpy mood.

Walsh, Barbara. *Sammy in the Sky*. Sammy is a beloved dog who will never be forgotten.

Woodson, Jacqueline. *Pecan Pie Baby*. An African American girl is not happy about the "ding-dang" baby that's coming soon.

Yum, Hyewon. *Twins' Blanket*. Twin Asian girls have always shared everything but are becoming more independent.

DO NOT FEAR OR FORGET THE POEM

Poetry is the language of the heart. Good poetry features perfect words, chosen carefully, so that no other word would do at that specific place in that particular phrase. Bad poetry is sing-songy, dripping with sentiment, and obvious rhymes. Avoid those. Choose poetry that will give your child a chance to hear how powerful words can be.

So where to begin? There are thousands of poetry books in libraries and bookstores. Ask for recommendations from library staff. Select ones that have a theme you know will appeal, such as dinosaurs, sports, or animals. Make a tradition out of reading a poem about food at dinner time, or a poem about the night before sleeping. Just do not fear or forget the poem; it will take you to another place, an unusual place of magic and giggles and sighs and, when it finds the right person, exclamations of "Yes, that's just how I feel!"

HEATHER RECOMMENDS

A Dozen Poetry Books for the Young

Alonzo, Sandra. *Gallop-O-Gallop.* Horse lovers will relish these poems that cover everything from birth of a foal to bucking broncos.

Elliott, David. *In the Wild.* Not only are the poems brilliant in their brevity, but the woodcut illustrations are also magnificent.

Florian, Douglas. *Bow Wow Meow Meow: It's Rhyming Cats and Dogs.* Florian's poems and illustrations are amazingly clever, whether it's this collection about cats and dogs, or any of his others, such as *Comets, Stars, the Moon and Mars: Space Poems and Paintings,* or *Dinothesaurus: Prehistoric Poems and Paintings.*

Foster, John, comp. *My First Oxford Book of Poems.* Poems both classic and contemporary, and colorful, whimsical illustrations, fill the pages.

Hopkins, Lee Bennett, selector. *Yummy! Eating Through a Day.* Oranges, ketchup, and macaroni and cheese are just a few of the topics of these poems guaranteed to appeal to children.

Mitton, Tony. *Gnash, Gnaw, Dinosaur!: Prehistoric Poems with Lift-the-flap Surprises!* This is sure to capture the attention of those who think they don't like poetry.

Morris, Jackie, comp. *The Barefoot Book of Classic Poems.* An anthology that expands the mind and stirs the imagination with lavish illustrations and poems that have lasted through the years.

Paschen, Elise, ed. *Poetry Speaks to Children.* A collection of children's favorites with brightly colorful illustrations and a CD of the poets reading their poems to enhance the fun.

Prelutsky, Jack, selector. *Read-Aloud Rhymes for the Very Young.* Marc Brown's illustrations and short poems are just right for brief moments of poetry.

Rosen, Michael, selector. *Poems for the Very Young.* Bob Graham's winsome illustrations add much humor to short poems from around the world about everything from getting dressed to losing grandmother in the sea.

Sidman, Joyce. *Dark Emperor and Other Poems of the Night.* Sidman's brilliant choice of words made this a Newbery Honor Award winner, and her illustrations for *Song of the Water Boatman & Other Pond Poems* received the Caldecott Honor Award.

Simon, Francesca. *Toddler Time.* These poems are all about the world of the toddler, and are sure to amuse them.

ONCE UPON A TIME IS IMPORTANT TIME

Cinderella's grandmother never said, "Bippity boppity boo." The dwarves who took care of Snow White did not have cutesy names, and the wicked stepmother danced to her death with red-hot slippers on her feet. How many children even know that Rapunzel's name came from the herb that her mother demanded be plucked from the witch's garden, so she could eat it during her pregnancy? These are the components of the original folk tales. They are stories of greed, jealousy, heartache, bravery, wisdom, courage, and revenge. With those feelings come actions that are not sugar-coated with bluebirds warbling a cheery tune, or dopey and chubby dwarves who whistle while they work. Instead, the folktales of long ago are rich with life lessons and men and women who face challenges beyond anything most of us will ever have to endure. For those who do face extreme fear or loss or sadness in their early years, hearing the real stories can be a great comfort, providing a source of inner strength and understanding. You know your child best, and what she can handle comfortably, without nightmares or serious misunderstandings. But I encourage you to consider enhancing your child's experience with these stories, and introduce them to the versions that have been told and retold for hundreds of years. They offer powerful language, certainly not found in versions based on movies. And children must know the traditional folk tales before they can understand the many fractured fairy tales they'll hear in school, or be able to comprehend references such as "Are you trying to sell me the Emperor's New Clothes" or "Be sure to leave a Hansel and Gretel trail so you can come home again."

Here's just a sampling of the memorable language you'll find in well-written adaptations.

"And envy and pride, like weeds, kept growing higher and higher in her heart, so that day and night she had no peace." (From *Snow-White and the Seven Dwarfs: A Tale from the Brothers Grimm*, translated by Randall Jarrell.)

"They came with valiant dreams and hearts full of fire, but the thorns, like angry hands, held them fast and the young men remained caught in them and could not free themselves, and so they died a terrible death." (From *The Sleeping Beauty*, retold and illustrated by Trina Schart Hyman.)

"Far away out at sea, the water is as blue as the petals of the most beautiful cornflower and as clear as the purest glass, but it is very deep, deeper than any anchor chain will reach." (From *The Little Mermaid* by

Hans Christian Andersen, translated by Anthea Bell, with pictures by Lisbeth Zwerger.)

"But I didn't need a pea to tell me she is a real princess. I could see it in the gentleness of her eyes, hear it in the softness of her voice, and feel it in the kindness of her heart." (From *The Princess and the Pea* by Hans Christian Andersen, retold by John Cech, and illustrated by Bernhard Oberdieck.)

My daughter is now a young teen. She has always been a cautious child. She does not read about vampires and she would never enter a haunted house. But since she was no more than three she has always loved the folktales, wanting to hear over and over again the versions lavishly illustrated by Trina Schart Hyman. She is not afraid of the violent endings, nor is she bored by the elaborate challenges the heroines must face. I have always wondered if she finds in folktales the courage she sometimes needs to face a life that began, as an adopted child, with overwhelming disappointment and loss.

MORE WORD GAMES AND ACTIVITIES

Create a Creature

A favorite book at story time is *Call Me Gorgeous* by Giles Milton. The story introduces an animal that is a cornucopia of other animals, such as a toucan's beak and a dalmatian's spots. At the end, they all come together to create one "reined-piggy-porcu-croco-touca-flami-roos-dalma-chameleo-bat-frog. But…you can call me Gorgeous!" What a great activity on a gloomy day to do with your child! Create your own "Gorgeous" by choosing the animal parts, drawing them or gluing together magazine pictures, and then giving it a fabulous one-of-a-kind name.

Aiken Drum

Another game I often play with children is based on the folk song "Aiken Drum." The children sing the chorus, while you lead them toward creating Aiken Drum, the man on the moon, to be made up of whatever category you select. Here's how it works:

First Verse:

There was a man lived on the moon, on the moon, on the moon.
There was a man lived on the moon and his name was
  Aiken Drum.

Chorus:

And he played upon the ladle, the ladle, the ladle,
He played upon the ladle, and his name was Aiken Drum.

Now you decide what words you want to focus on. Food? Then children offer names of foods, and you place them where it makes sense. "His nose was made of a radish, a radish, a radish. His nose was made of a radish, and his name was Aiken Drum." His head could be a watermelon, his ears are apricots, and so on. Or you could tell them to give you names of animals. "His teeth were made of elephant tusks…His feet were made of gorilla paws." Or how about forms of transportation? "His eyes were made of police car lights…His nose was made of a fire truck horn." One of the librarians at Deschutes Public Library created a felt board version of the song, but the main character was Flip Flap Jack. All his parts were breakfast foods, and the chorus was a bit different:

And he danced upon the table, the table, the table,
He danced upon the table and his name was Flip Flap Jack.

Young children will use the vocabulary they heard from you when they pretend to read aloud, as well as in conversation. Jamie practices her words and reads aloud to Dipsy.

It's important to take time with a book, pointing out the illustrations, allowing the child to ask questions, and having a conversation that relates the book to your child's experiences. Jamie's Uncle Rod was always wonderful about introducing new words to his niece.

His eyes are blueberries, his ears are orange slices, his legs are bacon strips, his arms are bananas, and everyone's favorite is his belly button—a raspberry.

Long ago I loved a book called *When the Sky Is Like Lace* by Elinor Lander Horwitz. Sadly, it is now out of print. But I remember clearly the magical, mystical words that described a "bimulous" night when the grass is like gooseberry jam and there are "plum-purple shadows." I remember singing otters, and children dancing, and something about spaghetti. Most of all I remember the spell that the words cast, creating an evening in which anything is possible. That's what unusual words can do, open young minds to amazing possibilities, and allow them to speak with glorious wisdom.

BIBLIOGRAPHY

For Librarians, Teachers, and Parents

Blakemore, Caroline J., and Barbara Weston Ramirez. *Baby Read-Aloud Basics: Fun and Interactive Ways to Help Your Little One Discover the World of Words.* New York: AMACOM Books, 2006.

Dollins, Cynthia. *The ABC's of Literacy: Preparing Our Children for Lifelong Learning.* Nashville, TN: Cumberland House, 2008.

Eliot, Lise. *What's Going on in There? How the Brain and Mind Develop in the First Five Years of Life.* New York: Bantam Books, 1999.

Hirsh-Pasek, Kathy, and Roberta Michnick Golinkoff. *Einstein Never Used Flash Cards: How Our Children REALLY Learn—And Why They Need to Play More and Memorize Less.* Emmaus, PA: St. Martin's Press, 2003.

Nevills, Pamela, and Patricia Wolfe. *Building the Reading Brain PreK-3.* 2nd ed. Thousand Oaks, CA: Corwin Press, 2009.

Straub, Susan, and K. J. Dell'Antonia. *Reading with Babies, Toddlers and Twos: A Guide to Choosing, Reading and Loving Books Together.* Naperville, IL: Sourcebooks, 2006

Trelease, Jim. *The New Read Aloud Handbook.* New York: Penguin Books, 2006.

For Children

Alonzo, Sandra. *Gallop-O-Gallop.* New York: Dial Books for Young Readers, 2007.

Andersen, Hans Christian. *The Little Mermaid.* New York: Minedition/ Penguin, 2005.

Andersen, Hans Christian. *The Princess and the Pea,* retold by John Cech. New York: Sterling, 2007.

Armstrong, Jennifer. *Once Upon a Banana.* New York: Simon and Schuster Books for Young Readers, 2006.

Askew, Amanda. *Mighty Machines: Diggers.* Irvine, CA: QEB Publishing, 2010.

Bartoletti, Susan Campbell. *Naamah and the Ark at Night.* Somerville, MA: Candlewick Press, 2011.

Becker, Bonny. *A Visitor for Bear.* Cambridge, MA: Candlewick Press, 2008.

Biggs, Brian. *Everything Goes on Land.* New York: Balzer + Bray, 2011.

Blackaby, Susan. *Brownie Groundhog and the February Fox.* New York: Sterling, 2011.

Boudart, Jennifer, Brian Conway, and Lisa Harkrader. *Picture Dictionary: Over 1,000 Words, Photographs and Definitions.* Lincolnwood, IL: Publications International, 1999.

Boynton, Sandra. *Happy Hippo, Angry Duck.* New York: Little Simon, 2011.

Browne, Anthony. *Little Beauty.* Somerville, MA: Candlewick Press, 2008.

Bruel, Nick. *Bad Kitty.* New Milford, CT: Roaring Book Press, 2005.

Cannon, Janell. *Stellaluna.* San Diego, CA: Harcourt Brace Jovanovich, 1993.

Churchill, Vicki. *Sometimes I Like to Curl Up in a Ball.* New York: Sterling Publishers, 2001,

Cleary, Daniel. *Stop Bugging Me: But That's What Friends Are For.* Maplewood, NJ: Blue Apple Books, 2010.

Cowell, Cressida. *What Shall We Do with the Boo-Hoo Baby?* New York: Scholastic Press, 2000.

Cumberbatch, Judy. *Can You Hear the Sea?* New York: Bloomsbury Children's Books, 2006.

Curtis, Jamie Lee. *Today I Feel Silly & Other MOODS That Make My Day.* New York: HarperCollins Publishers, 1998.

Dewdney, Anna. *Roly Poly Pangolin.* New York: Viking, 2010.

Donovan, Jane Monroe. *Small Medium & Large.* Ann Arbor, MI: Sleeping Bear Press, 2010.

Doyle, Malachy. *Horse.* New York: Margaret K. McElderry Books, 2008.

Dylan, Bob. *Man Gave Names to All the Animals.* New York: Sterling, 2010.

Elffers, Joost, and Curious Pictures. *Do You Love Me?* New York: Bowen Press, 2009.

Elliott, David. *In the Wild.* Somerville, MA: Candlewick Press, 2010.

Ellwand, David. *The Big Book of Beautiful Babies.* New York: Dutton Children's Books, 1995.

Emberly, Rebecca, and Ed Emberly. *If You're a Monster and You Know It.* New York: Orchard Books, 2010.

Faller, Regis. *Polo: The Runaway Book.* New Milfor, CT: Roaring Book Press, 2006.

Finn, Isobel. *The Very Lazy Ladybug.* Wilton, CT: Tiger Tales, 2001.

Fleming, Denise. *Lunch.* New York: Henry Holt and Co., 1992.

Florian, Douglas. *Bow Wow Meow Meow: It's Rhyming Cats and Dogs.* San Diego, CA: Harcourt, 2003.

Florian, Douglas. *Comets, Stars, the Moon and Mars: Space Poems and Paintings.* Orlando, FL: Harcourt, 2007.

Florian, Douglas. *Dinothesaurus: Prehistoric Poems and Paintings.* New York: Beach Lane Books, 2009.

Foster, John, comp. *My First Oxford Book of Poems.* Oxford: Oxford University Press, 2000.

Fox, Mem. *Wilfrid Gordon Macdonald Partridge.* Brooklyn, NY: Kane/Miller Book Publishers, 1985.

Fox, Mem. *Hello, Baby!* New York: Beach Lane Books, 2009.

Fraser, Mary Anne. *How Animal Babies Stay Safe: Let's Read and Find Out Science.* New York: HarperCollins Publishers, 2002.

French, Jackie. *Diary of a Wombat.* New York: Clarion Books, 2003.

Freyman, Saxton. *How Are You Peeling?: Foods with Moods.* New York: Arthur A. Levine Books, 1999.

Gaiman, Neil. *Blueberry Girl.* New York: HarperCollins Publishers, 2008.

Grimm, Jakob and Wilhelm Grimm. *Snow White and the Seven Dwarfs: A Tale from the Brothers Grimm,* translated by Randall Jarrell. New York: Farrar, Straus and Giroux, 1972.

Grimm, Jakob and Wilhelm Grimm. *The Sleeping Beauty,* retold by Trina Schart Hyman. Boston, MA: Little, Brown and Company, 1977.

Havill, Juanita. *Jamaica and Brianna.* Boston, MA: Houghton Mifflin, 1993.

Hest, Amy. *In the Rain with Baby Duck.* Cambridge, MA: Candlewick Press, 1995.

Hillenbrand, Will. *Fiddle-I-Fee.* San Diego, CA: Harcourt, Inc., 2002.

Hopkins, Lee Bennett, selector. *Yummy! Eating Through a Day: Poems.* New York: Simon and Schuster Books for Young Readers, 2000.

Horwitz, Elinor Lander. *When the Sky Is Like Lace.* Philadelphia, PA: Lippincott, Williams & Wilkins, 1987.

Humphries, Tudor. *Otter Moon.* New York: Sterling Publishing Co., 2009.

Jay, Alison. *Welcome to the Zoo.* New York: Dial Books for Young Readers, 2008.

Jenkins, Steve, and Robin Page. *What Do You Do with a Tail Like This?* Boston, MA: Houghton Mifflin, 2003.

Johnston, Tony. *The Iguana Brothers, a Tale of Two Lizards.* New York: Blue Sky Press, 1995.

Johnston, Tony. *Cat, What Is That?* New York: HarperCollins Publishers, 2001.

Johnston, Tony. *My Abuelita.* Orlando, FL: Harcourt, Inc., 2009.

Ketteman, Helen. *Armadilly Chili.* Morton Grove, IL: Albert Whitman & Co., 2004.

Martin, Bill, Jr. *Listen to the Rain.* New York: Henry Holt, 1988.

Martin, Bill, Jr. *Polar Bear, Polar Bear, What Did You Hear?* New York: Henry Holt, 1997.

Milne, A. A. *The World of Christopher Robin.* New York: E. P. Dutton & Company, Inc., 1958.

Milton, Giles. *Call Me Gorgeous.* New York: Boxer Books, 2009.

Mitton, Tony. *Gnash, Gnaw, Dinosaur!: Prehistoric Poems with Lift-the-Flap Surprises!* New York: Kingfisher, 2009.

Montgomery, Tamara. *When the Cassowary Pooped: A Tale of New Guinea.* Honolulu, HI: Calabash Books, 2009.

Mora, Pat. *Delicious Hullabaloo/Pachanga deliciosa.* Houston, TX: Pinata Books, 1998.

Morris, Jackie, comp. *The Barefoot Book of Classic Poems.* Cambridge, MA: Barefoot Books, 2006.

Muth, Jon J. *Zen Shorts.* New York: Scholastic Press, 2005.

Mwenye Hadithi. *Crafty Chameleon.* London: Hodder Children's Books, 2004.

Neubecker, Robert. *Wow! School.* New York: Hyperion Books for Children, 2007.

Newbery, Linda. *Posy.* New York: Atheneum Books for Young Readers, 2009.

Norman, Kimberly. *Ten on the Sled.* New York: Sterling, 2010.

Paschen, Elise, ed. *Poetry Speaks to Children.* Naperville, IL: Sourcebooks, 2005.

Pfeffer, Wendy. *From Tadpole to Frog: Let's Read and Find Out Science.* New York: HarperCollins Publishers, 1994.

Pinkney, Jerry. *The Lion and the Mouse.* New York: Little, Brown Books for Young Readers, 2009.

Pinkney, Jerry. *Twinkle, Twinkle, Little Star.* New York: Little, Brown and Company, 2011.

Prelutsky, Jack, selector. *Read-Aloud Rhymes for the Very Young.* New York: A. Knopf, 1986.

Rathman, Peggy. *10 Minutes till Bedtime.* New York: G. P. Putnam's Sons, 1998.

Rayner, Catherine. *Ernest, the Moose Who Doesn't Fit.* New York: Farrar Straus Giroux, 2010.

Root, Phyllis. *Big Momma Makes the World.* Cambridge, MA: Candlewick Press, 2003.

Rosen, Michael, selector. *Poems for the Very Young.* New York: Kingfisher Books, 1993.

Ryan, Pam Munoz. *Tony Baloney.* New York: Scholastic Press, 2011.

Scanlon, Elizabeth Garton. *All the World.* New York: Beach Lane Books, 2009.

Serfozo, Mary. *The Plumply Dumply Pumpkin.* New York: Margaret K. McElderry Books, 2001.

Sidman, Joyce. *Song of the Water Boatman & Other Pond Poems.* Boston, MA: Houghton Mifflin, 2005.

Sidman, Joyce. *Dark Emperor and Other Poems of the Night.* Boston, MA: Houghton Mifflin Harcourt, 2010.

Simon, Francesca. *Toddler Time.* New York: Orchard Books, 2000.

Sklansky, Amy E. *Where Do Chicks Come From: Let's Read and Find Out Science.* New York: HarperCollins Publishers, 2005.

Slate, Joseph. *Miss Bindergarten Gets Ready for Kindergarten.* New York: Dutton Children's Books, 1996.

Slater, Dashka. *Baby Shoes.* New York: Bloomsbury Children's Books, 2006.

Smee, Nicola. *Funny Face.* New York: Bloomsbury Children's Books, 2006.

Sockabasin, Allen. *Thanks to the Animals.* Gardiner, ME: Tilbury House, 2005.

Spier, Peter. *Peter Spier's Rain*. Garden City, NY: Doubleday, 1982.

Staake, Bob. *Look! A Book!: A Zany Seek and Find Adventure*. New York: Little, Brown, 2011.

Steinberg, Laya. *Thesaurus Rex*. Cambridge, MA: Barefoot Books, 2003.

Stutson, Caroline. *By the Light of the Halloween Moon*. Tarrytown, NY: Marshall Cavendish, 2009.

Stutson, Caroline. *Cat's Night Out*. New York: Simon and Schuster Books for Young Readers, 2010.

Tankard, Jeremy. *Grumpy Bird*. New York: Scholastic Press, 2007.

Thomson, Bill. *Chalk*. New York: Marshall Cavendish Children, 2010.

Tolman, Marije, and Ronald Tolman. *The Tree House*. Honesdale, PA: 8 Lemniscaat, 2010.

Walsh, Barbara. *Sammy in the Sky*. Somerville, MA: Candlewick Press, 2011.

Weitzman, Jacqueline Preiss, and Robin Preiss Glasser. *You Can't Take a Balloon into the Metropolitan Museum*. New York: Dial Books for Young Readers, 1998.

Williams, Karen Lynn. *A Beach Tail*. Honesdale, PA: Boyds Mills Press, 2010.

Winter, Jeanette. *Wangari's Trees of Peace: A True Story from Africa*. Orlando, FL: Harcourt, 2008.

Woodson, Jacqueline. *Pecan Pie Baby*. New York: G. P. Putnam's Sons, 2010.

Yoon, Salina. *Opposnakes*. New York: Little Simon, 2009.

Yum, Hyewon. *Twins' Blanket*. New York: Farrar Straus Giroux, 2011.

Ziefert, Harriet. *Bunny's Lessons*. Maplewood, NJ: Blue Apple Books, 2011.

WEBLIOGRAPHY

http://www.kididdles.com/lyrics/k011.html

http://www.reachoutandread.org/FileRepository/ReadingAloudto Children_ADC_July2008.pdf

DISCOGRAPHY

Diamond, Charlotte. *10 Carrot Diamond*. Vancouver, BC: Hug Bug Records, 1985.

Chapter Three

PRINT HAS PURPOSE

Why read? What's in it for the child? Children need proof that reading is a worthwhile activity before they'll join in. Luckily, literacy is an easy sell. Just snuggle up with a good book and release the wondrous ideas so magically held in print for a child. After all, the goal of reading is not to sound out words but to unlock meaning.... Reading aloud is one of the best ways to connect kids to the rich rewards of reading.

Hauser, Jill Frankel. *Wow! I'm Reading: Fun Activities to Make Reading Happen,* pp. 11–12. Charlotte, VT: Williamson Publishing Company, 2000.

Lily and Jack are two siblings I adore. Their mother has raised them on books, and it is always a treat to see them at the library because they love, love, love books, and they always leave with a bag full. Plus the mother allows them to wander and discover on their own, instead of hustling them in and out in five minutes.

Lily learned to read by the time she was four. Soon she was printing, and by the time she started kindergarten, she was amazingly adept at writing messages. That Christmas she wrote a letter to Santa Claus, and her mother later told me what it said:

Dear Santa,

How are you? I hope you are fine. Did you have a good year? I hope you are staying warm up there in the North Pole.

For Christmas I would like a zipper so I can keep my brother's mouth shut.

Love, Lily

Obviously, Lily understood clearly that print has a purpose!

In order for a child to be ready to read, she needs to understand about print. She needs to know that print is everywhere, that it means something, and that what it sounds like and means in the story this time will be the same meaning and sound the next time. She also needs to know how a book works, that we read the text, not the pictures, and that in English books, the text reads from left to right. She needs to know how to hold a book, and where the story begins and ends.

All of that is easily learned just by handling books, pointing out words in books, and gently guiding the child to hold a book correctly so that the story can begin and end. When the child is an infant, place a cloth book that crinkles and shines with him in his stroller. When the child is one, let him explore a cardboard book that has fuzzy or scratchy textures. When the child is two, give him a book about worms because he likes to pick them up in your garden. When he's three, and he's asking questions that all seem to begin with the word "Why?," give him a book with answers and let him turn the pages to find the topic he wants to discuss. Encourage your child to touch, turn, point at, and even taste his books. That's what will make him feel comfortable with, and fond of, print.

Comprehension is based on experience. If someone has shared a book about cats with that child, she will already have a sense of what words and letters are all about. If she loved the book, she'll begin to understand the payoff for making the effort to read the word cat. And if reading cat successfully jogs her memory to recall one of life's rich experiences, reading becomes super fun and meaningful! Someday she'll have the power to make sense of the print around her, print that contains a wonderful world of stories and fantastic facts about her favorite furry friend!

Hauser, Jill Frankel. *Wow! I'm Reading: Fun Activities to Make Reading Happen*, p. 9. Charlotte, VT: Williamson Publishing Company, 2000.

WHAT CAN YOU DO?: AT THE PRESCHOOL

All day long point out print. Print is on tee shirts, signs, food boxes, and, of course, books. It's all around the classroom, labeling the calendar, the weather board, the cubbies for the children's belongings. At every opportunity, comment about the print, ask the child what it means, point out certain letters that might be extra important to the child ("Look! Farm begins with the letter F, just like your name, Frank."), and show them that print has importance in their lives. When you go for a walk with the children, and you come to a stop sign, explain, "That sign says something. S-T-O-P. Stop. So that's what we're going to do at this corner. Stop." When you're choosing the word of the day, make sure they see you print it out. "Today's word is orange. This is how it is written. O-R-A-N-G-E. That says orange. Can anyone see the word orange someplace in the room? Yes, that's right. The word orange is on the pumpkin."

One of my daughter's favorite places to play was the Working Wonders Museum in Bend, Oregon. Sadly, it is now gone, but for many years it was a great source of creative fun for children. It was all about imagination, play, dressing up, and creating. One of the activities was delivering mail. There were laminated postcards with simple messages on them. Children would pick up a mail pouch, and open the mailbox at the space that was about being a veterinarian, or at the make-believe grocery store, or the pretend carpentry shop. They'd drop off and pick up mail, and they thought it was great fun. You could do a similar activity, with the child dictating what you are to write on the card, and placing boxes around the classroom for pick up and delivery.

Read (or tell) a story that is very familiar, such as *Goldilocks and the Three Bears*. Then ask the children to tell it back to you, while you print out the words in big letters on butcher paper. Then let them draw the pictures to match the words. This helps them to connect the fact that a story is made of words that can be printed into a book.

Facts 'n Stats

What children need to know about print and its relevance to reading can be summed up in four basic principles: (1) Words are read, pictures are viewed; (2) words appear and are read in English from left to right across the page; (3) letters placed next to each other form words; and (4) letters each have a large and small version and can be printed in various forms.

Nevills, Pamela. *Building the Reading Brain PreK-3*, p. 68. Thousand Oaks, CA: Corwin Press, 2009.

It might seem like overkill, all this explanation. But learning the purpose and design of print has to be learned, just like learning colors, the ABC's, and how to share.

WHAT CAN YOU DO?: AT THE LIBRARY

As with preschool, mention print and its meaning, whenever possible. "Your tee shirt says, 'I'm the big brother.' I'm so glad you brought your little sister to story time today and helped her with the song."

If you are reading a story that has repetitive words, point them out. *Mama Cat Has Three Kittens* by Denise Fleming has the repeating phrase "Boris naps." Each time you come to it, point out the words so children make the connection between the sounds coming from your mouth, and the print on the page.

Use the oversized paperback big books so the print is very clear. *Where Is the Green Sheep* by Mem Fox is a perfect choice because the repeating phrase "Where is the green sheep?" appears all on its own on a white background. You can easily point to the words as you read them, helping them to understand the connection.

Play a game with children holding up letters to form a word. Make it a simple word so you can have fun with it. For instance, after singing "Bingo," five children stand up front, each with a letter, B-I-N-G-O. Arrange them so it doesn't make sense. "That word is BOING. Is that the dog's name? Let's try again." Rearrange them so it's sillier. "That word spells GONIB. Is that the dog's name?" And so on, until you get to the right spelling.

Use the felt board to show print. Put Velcro on the backs of large paper letters, and put them on the board to highlight an important word from the story you're about to read. For instance, *Jump!* by Scott Fischer has that word throughout the story. Put the word JUMP on your felt board, or print it out on a white board, and invite your audience to say it with you whenever it appears in the story. When you are singing "Bingo" with the children, write the letters on a white board so they clearly understand what they are saying. And think of other words that fit the song, such as "There was a farmer had a snake, and Hissy was his name-oh. H-I-S-S-Y."

WHAT CAN YOU DO?: AT HOME

Drs. Kathy Hirsh-Pasek and Roberta Michnick Golinkoff, coauthors of *Einstein Never Used Flash Cards: How Our Children REALLY Learn—And Why They Need to Play More and Memorize Less,* describe a study done by Professor Linda Lavine of Cortland State University in New York, designed to determine when children know what is or is not writing. Professor

Lavine discovered one of the factors that plays a crucial role in helping children to recognize print is environment. "If they are in environments rich in print, they uncover the features of writing a lot sooner than if they are not. If they are read to and are exposed to written materials, they figure out many things about books, letters, and writing before they even come to school" (p. 114).

In other words, you and your home make the difference. Is there a grocery list on the refrigerator? Is a calendar hanging in the child's room? Do you put up on the kitchen cupboard your child's first scribbling attempts at writing her name? Do you point out repeated words in a picture book? Do you mention an interesting article in the magazine you're reading while he's having a snack? Whatever you can do to point out print, to emphasize that it is useful and interesting, will motivate your child to learn more.

When your child is very young, make him a photo album. Buy a small one he can hold. On the left page, insert a photo of a person or object that means a great deal to the child, such as a picture of Daddy, or a favorite toy. On the right side, insert a paper with the identifying word written in big, block letters. Read the photo album to your child. "Look, there's a picture of Sammy, your squirrel toy. And here is the word Sammy. S-A-M-M-Y. Sammy. What's on the next page?" The child says, "That's Nana." You say, "That's right, that's Nana. And there is the word N-A-N-A." Make sure the child has easy access to this album. It could be in his crib, the car, your diaper bag, or on the lowest bookshelf, so that the child can quickly grab it and read it all on his own.

When your child is a bit older, make a book together. Read a simple book that has a definite pattern, with plenty of repetition. *The Feel Good Book* by Todd Parr is one of my favorites. After reading it aloud, make your own feel good book, with your child identifying what makes her feel good and drawing the pictures, while you print out the words. If your child says, "Ice cream makes me feel good," then she draws a picture of a bowl of ice cream, and you write out those exact words beneath the picture. After the child has created 10–12 pictures with you writing the accompanying print, the child designs the cover, and you add the title and author "My Feel Good Book, by Wendy." Punch three holes on the left side of all the pages, poke through brads or tie with yarn, and Presto! You have a book. By the way, they make wonderful gifts for grandparents.

Before you go to the grocery store, have your child print out three things you need to buy. The words probably won't make sense, so you'll need to remember what they mean. When you get to the store, you point to the paper and say, "You wrote peanut butter, so we need to find it. I think it might be in this row with the jams. Do you see peanut butter? Yes, that's right. See, right here on the label it says, 'Peanut Butter,' just like you wrote

---

HEATHER RECOMMENDS

Nine Books to Help Write a Book

Charlip, Remy. *Fortunately.* What you think is fortunate might really
be a problem.

Cooper, Floyd. *Cumbayah.* Multicultural children depict the inspiring words of this popular song; you and your child can think of
more verses and illustrate their meaning.

Cuyler, Margery. *That's Good, That's Bad.* Everything good might be
a little bit bad.

Gill, Jim. *May There Always Be Sunshine.* What do you think is
important?

Martin, Bill, Jr. *Brown Bear, Brown Bear, What Did You See?* A classic
story that combines colors, animals, and simple text.

Parr, Todd. *It's Okay to Be Different.* From color to shape, everyone
is special.

Peek, Merle. *Mary Wore Her Red Dress.* You can choose colors, cloth-
ing, or any other characteristic about friends and family.

Walter, Virginia. *Hi, Pizza Man!* Animals bring the pizza, but your
child can add more.

Williams, Sue. *I Went Walking.* A young girl notices animals. This
is especially good if you just took a walk around the neighborhood, or at the park, and you can record in the book what
you saw.

---

on our grocery list." "Now we're looking for apples. Do you see the apples?
Yes, there they are. Can you find the word 'Apples' on the sign? See, it's right
here. Apples, just like you wrote on our grocery list. How many shall we
buy today?"

Have your child help you plan out dinner. He can write the menu. You
can read aloud the recipe on the box of risotto. Create dinner invitations;
you print the words and he decorates. Fold index cards in half and make
place cards for the table. It's all about helping him understand that print
has a purpose.

Read *Reading to Peanut* by Leda Schubert. This joyful book is all about
a child printing words on sticky notes, and the dog who finds them
and chews them up. You'll find plenty of ideas for activities to do with your
own child, such as labeling the garden, making up songs, making signs,
and creating a treat for the family pet.

Mudkin by Stephen Gammell is a brilliant story that shows just how much can be understood, even when the print is a mess of mud. When the rain stops, a young girl befriends a mud creature who wants to make her the queen of mud. The two of them have a gloriously squishy good time until the rain returns. What makes this book perfect for learning about print is that the Mudkin's words are just smears and globs, much like a toddler's would be. And yet you know exactly what the Mudkin is saying. Share this creative gem with your child, and then, some muddy day, go outside and write with mud. Or finger paint. Or pudding. Or whatever seems right for your fingers.

Another favorite of mine for encouraging print and writing is *Love, Mouserella* by David Ezra Stein. Mouserella is writing to her grandmother who has recently left. "I mouse you!" she says several times. The book is a combination of photographs, hand-printed messages from grandchild to grandmother, and pictures drawn by Mouserella to illustrate her day. After reading this with your child, help her create her own letter to grandmother, using all the various techniques. (But you might not want to include a package of ketchup when you mail it!)

Finally, make sure your child has plenty of opportunities to handle books. Point out the title page, and where the story begins. If the child brings you a book that is upside down, make a few comments to explain what's wrong. "Oh, I love this book! But it's upside down. Let's see if we can fix it so I can read it. Can you turn it around so the cover looks right? Very good! Now the bird isn't standing on her head and I can read the words right side up from the beginning."

All of this information is soaking into the child's spongelike brain, helping him to understand all about print and books. He'll be ready to read, and ready for kindergarten, in no time.

I want to share with you a story about my daughter and her grandmother, and how they used the power of print to create a world of magic and love. When Jamie was about three, my mother purchased a rose vine for our backyard. It is artificial, and features deep pink roses climbing up a small wrought iron fence. Each spring the rose arbor is brought out of storage and placed somewhere in the backyard. One afternoon Mara (the

Learning to read is an almost miraculous story filled with many developmental processes that come together to give the child entry into the teeming underlife of a word usable by the child.

Wolf, Maryanne. *Proust and the Squid: The Story and Science of the Reading Brain*, p. 112. New York: Harper, 2007.

grandchildren's name for my mother) and Jamie were sitting on the front porch of Mara's house, talking about fairies. A fairy named Rosamunde, who lived in the rose arbor, was created during their discussion. Day after day they talked about Rosamunde's life—how she takes baths (in the bird bath), how she travels (by dandelion puff), where she sleeps (inside a rose), and where she goes when the cold winds blow and the rose arbor is put away (to Florida, to visit her friend Drucinda). While Rosamunde was enjoying her warm months down south, Mara would send letters to Jamie through the regular mail, full of questions for Jamie to answer as well as details about her days with Drucinda. This game went on for years, and when Jamie was old enough, she wrote back to Rosamunde. "Dear Rosamunde. You may come live in my fairy house. The house is ready for you. You can get here by dandelion puff." "Dear Rosamunde, I still believe in fairies! I really like having somebody to write to. In Peter Pan a fairie died because people didn't believe. I will put the rose arbor up when it gets warmer. Love, Jamie. P.S. You are my best friend."

When Jamie began to question why Rosamunde's writing looked like Mara's writing, Rosamunde wrote back a careful explanation that has never been forgotten by my daughter:

"I understand that you are puzzling about how I get your letters and why Mara writes the letters I send to you. Well, there's a lot of magic and a lot of love involved, Jamie, and those are two things that are hard to describe and hard to put into words.

"It all started several years ago when you were very young. In the beginning it was a sort of make believe game, like you and Mara love to play together. The more you talked about me, the more I became real to you. Once you gave me my name, I suddenly began to feel your love and I knew I was going to belong to you and Mara. I was SO happy to be your very own fairy. When one believes in magic—magic happens. You and Mara believe, and I am the magic fairy your love created.

"Now, think about it—how could a little fairy like me hold a great big pencil and write you a letter. Impossible—right? So Mara and I had to work some of that magic again. I send my thoughts to Mara so she could write the letters for me. That's why you noticed my letters looked like Mara's handwriting.

"Like I said, it would all be something hard to understand if one didn't believe in magic and love and fairies. Luckily you and I and Mara do. I think your Mom does, too. I heard once that she used to blow dandelion fairies into the air. In fact, I met one once—her name was 'Fluff' and she was dressed in the prettiest white lacey dress. Ask your Mom about her."

This could easily be called an early literacy activity—writing letters back and forth. But it was more than that. Jamie, now 13, still remembers fondly the excitement she felt when a letter arrived from Rosamunde. This spring when I put out the rose arbor she asked again about Rosamunde, wondering if she will come to visit. And all the letters are carefully kept, treasures to be read aloud as the years go by.

Later, letters back and forth to Santa Claus became a game for one December day. Mara was taking care of Jamie while I was at work, and all day long hilarious letters were left in conspicuous places around the house. Jamie was Santa, with a wife named Avery. Her imagination knew no bounds. "Dear Bonnie (my mother's real name), My house is far away! I can't anser your ansers. I'm very sorry! I would like something for my wife. She is starving! Yes! I have a son! Santa." "Dear Bonnie, Come qick!! My wife is very sick!!! We have no dockter! I don't know what she has!! I'M VERY WORRIED! Please come qick! Santa."

Each letter received a response from Bonnie (Mara), written secretly but found easily. There was a long series of questions and responses about what Santa would like for Christmas. Slippers? "My wife, Mrs. Claws, gave me some slippers. I don't need lots of gifts!" Cookies? "I don't want any cookies! I get full all the time!" "Bonnie, I think I want a tool box for Christmas. Mabe. Got to go! Bye! Love, Santa."

It is easier for a child to learn to read if she is already familiar with how a book works and why print is important. Lily is discovering that her book is upside down.

As a child begins to understand about books, encourage her to read it on her own, remembering as much of the story as she can and freely making up the rest. Jamie explored *Is That You, Winter?* by Stephen Gammell over and over and over and over...

These letters were written when Jamie was in elementary school, but the foundation was laid when she was no more than three. She knew that the letters she received were made of printed words. Those letters told stories, or asked questions. The letters sent love and laughter back and forth, from generation to generation. And, later, she was able to write her own letters, creating a unique world from her own imagination.

I mean, who knew that Santa's wife is named Avery and that they have a son?

BIBLIOGRAPHY

For Librarians, Teachers, and Parents

Hauser, Jill Frankel. *Wow! I'm Reading: Fun Activities to Make Reading Happen.* Charlotte, VT: Williamson Publishing Company, 2000.

Hirsh-Pasek, Kathy, and Roberta Michnick Golinkoff. *Einstein Never Used Flash Cards: How Our Children REALLY Learn—And Why They Need to Play More and Memorize Less.* Emmaus, PA: Rodale, 2003.

Nevills, Pamela. *Building the Reading Brain PreK-3.* Thousand Oaks, CA: Corwin Press, 2009.

Wolf, Maryanne. *Proust and the Squid: The Story and Science of the Reading Brain.* New York: Harper, 2007.

For Children

Charlip, Remy. *Fortunately.* New York: Aladdin Books, 1993.

Cooper, Floyd. *Cumbayah.* New York: Morrow Junior Books, 1998.

Cuyler, Margery. *That's Good, That's Bad.* New York: Henry Holt, 1991.

Fleming, Denise. *Mama Cat Has Three Kittens.* New York: Henry Holt, 1998.

Fox, Mem. *Where Is the Green Sheep?* Boston, MA: Sandpiper, 2010.

Gammell, Stephen. *Is That You, Winter?* San Diego, CA: Silver Whistle/ Harcourt Brace & Company, 1997.

Gammell, Stephen. *Mudkin.* Minneapolis, MN: Carolrhoda Books, 2011.

Gill, Jim. *May There Always Be Sunshine: A Traditional Song.* Oak Park, IL: Jim Gill Books, 2001.

Martin, Bill, Jr. *Brown Bear, Brown Bear, What Do You See?* New York: Henry Holt and Company, 2007.

Parr, Todd. *It's Okay to Be Different.* New York: Little Brown, 2001.

Parr, Todd. *The Feel Good Book.* Boston, MA: Little, Brown, 2002.

Peek, Merle. *Mary Wore Her Red Dress.* New York: Clarion Books, 1985.

Schubert, Leda. *Reading to Peanut.* New York: Holiday House, 2011.

Stein, David Ezra. *Love, Mouserella.* New York: Nancy Paulsen Books, 2011.

Walter, Virginia. *Hi, Pizza Man!* New York: Orchard Books, 1995.

Williams, Sue. *I Went Walking.* San Diego, CA: Harcourt Brace Jovanovich, 1990.

Chapter Four

BOOBOOSHOTS AND
OTHER STORIES OF STORIES

When a story is told from the heart, it is true communication, natural and straightforward. It becomes living language in which words are intrinsically bound up with spirit and are more than themselves. A story told is a reciprocal event, a poem created in midair.

Simms, Laura. "'Words in Our Hearts': The Experience of the Story." Reprinted from the June 1983 issue of *Horn Book Magazine,* p. 344. By permission of The Horn Book, Inc., www.hbook.com.

Between the ages of four and seven, my daughter had several episodes of croup. They always seem to occur in the darkest hours of the night, when sleep for the parent is deep and comfortable. Suddenly you are awakened by what can only be described as the barking cough of a seal. "What is a seal doing in my house?" you wonder with absolute clarity. Then you drift off to sleep again, only to be awakened moments later by another bark. That's when you realize it's not a seal (duh!), it's your child!

The first time it happened I was terrified. Jamie had trouble breathing, she was scared, I was scared, and no one did much sleeping for the rest of the night. The next day the doctor explained about croup. "Did she sound like a seal?" "YES! How did you know?" Had he been in my house? Surely I was the first mother to experience such a terrifying sound. But, of course,

I was just one of many. He recommended two methods for alleviating the barks. Either take her outside into the cool, night air, or take her into the bathroom and create steam for her to breathe in.

The next time it occurred I did both, wanting to double the chance of relaxing and comforting my daughter. OK, and me. When we got into the bathroom, I turned on the shower full blast and scalding hot, letting the steam billow out from behind the patchwork quilt shower curtain. We sat on the floor, Jamie in my lap, and I began to tell a silly story based on the traditional folktale of The Three Little Pigs. It had only a glancing resemblance to the original, and the pigs had plenty of attitude and escapades. I frequently asked for Jamie's input on the story, beginning with the names of these porcine troublemakers. She named them Tony, Bologna, and Boobooshots.

I have absolutely no idea where those names came from. Tony was Italian and sassy, Bologna was over-the-top dramatic (think Miss Piggy), and Boobooshots was the true hero, with a house made of stones and bricks and heavy logs. The wolf was just downright stupid. The story wound its way through the steam and into our hearts. Jamie was able to relax and have fun, even though she felt miserable. Every time she required a steam bath in the years that followed, she always asked for a retelling of Tony, Bologna, and Boobooshots, the three little pigs who saved the day. And many nights.

One of the early literacy skills identified as being important for a child getting ready to read is the ability to tell stories, to put actions in sequence, describe things, and explain events. Young children need to understand that a story has a beginning, a middle, and an end. If they are able to tell about the trip they took to the pet store with their preschool, or make up a story about a dinosaur who likes to blow bubbles, or create their own version of a fairy tale, then understanding how a book works, and learning how to read, will make a great deal more sense to them.

WHAT CAN YOU DO?: AT THE PRESCHOOL

Teachers in a classroom have a great advantage over librarians in the public library because the children remain with them after the story reading is done. This gives them the opportunity to have dramatic play, to keep a story alive by involving the children in acting it out in a variety of ways. Let's look at one example, using *Hattie and the Fox* by Mem Fox.

This is the story of a somewhat silly, but very observant, hen, who notices first a nose, then eyes, then ears, then a tail, in the bushes. Each time she sees the portion of the animal she hasn't yet identified (but your very smart preschoolers will have no trouble figuring out it is a fox), she announces it to the rest of the farm animals. They respond with complete boredom, and their response is always the same, from the pig's "Well, well," to the horse's "Who cares?" I always make the cow's comment of "What next?" very long and slow, as if they have all heard similar gossip a hundred times before from Hattie. But when the hen clearly identifies the culprit as a fox all the animals go into ridiculous panic, leaping into the air, calling out new phrases, and displaying total chaos. It is the cow who surprisingly saves everyone by calling out "Moo" so loudly that the fox is frightened and runs away. And I take a deep breath and make that "Moo" very long indeed, which greatly impresses the listeners.

The story is perfect for preschoolers to act out because it is deceptively simple, very repetitive, has parts for seven characters, plus a narrator, and allows for everyone to go crazy at the end, yelling and flapping and jumping, which they love.

Another way to encourage telling is with crafts. By playing with paper bag or craft stick puppets, or with masks or headbands, they are remembering the tale. Here are two craft ideas that I have seen lead to further discussion about and comprehension of the story:

- Read *Here Are My Hands* by Bill Martin Jr. and John Archambault. With the help of adults, on the first day have everyone trace around their hands, and cut out as many as there are children in the classroom. On the next day, read *These Hands* by Hope Lynne Price. Have everyone decorate their paper hands with glitter, stickers, markers, and so on. While they're drying, read and act out *Clap Your Hands* by Lorinda Bryan Cauley. The next day distribute the hands, so that each child ends up with one of his or her own hands, and one of everyone else. Now glue them together into the shape of a wreath. End the weeklong exercise with reading a multicultural book such as *Hands Can* by Cheryl Willis Hudson or *I Call My Hand Gentle* by Amanda Haan.

- Read *Jamberry* by Bruce Degen. Then make "No-Cook Smashberry Jamberry Jam," from *Oppenheim Toy Portfolio's Read It! Play It! With Babies and Toddlers: Building Literacy through Reading and Play* by Joanne and Stephanie Oppenheim. The recipe on page 101 is perfect for mashing the berries while reciting the rhyme, "One berry/Two berry/Pick me a blueberry." The next day read *The Giant Jam Sandwich* by John Vernon Lord, which tells how the people of Itching Down figured out how to get rid of four million wasps. Spread bread with the Smashberry Jam and, while munching, sit in a circle and have everyone help retell the story.

Any form of creative play—puppets, stuffed animals, dress up—helps to build knowledge about story, as well as imagination and vocabulary. Without those, this world would never have known *Cat in the Hat, Madeline,* or *Winnie the Pooh,* and I would not want a world like that, would you?

WHAT CAN YOU DO?: AT THE LIBRARY

At the very least, invite your story time listeners to participate in the various phrases that repeat in *Hattie and the Fox*. I use very distinctive voices for each of the characters, making sure that the sheep's voice vibrates, the pig's voice is deep and husky, the cow's is low and long. Before each of Hattie's "Goodness gracious me," I cluck like a chicken. Even toddlers can do that!

After reading the story yourself, have the children color templates of each of the characters, and glue them onto craft sticks. Then read the story again, so they can hold up the appropriate animal and join in on the comment. Of course, they all get to run around during the chaos, but make sure you have told them ahead of time the signal you will use to end the chaos. Yes, indeed, there must be an end!

POTS AND PANS

I worked for many years at a library in Littleton, Colorado. I loved my job, and I had been there enough years that children who came to story time were now grown up and bringing their own children to story time. But the time came when it was necessary to move on to another job, the one I now have in Bend, Oregon, as youth services manager. I knew that my last day at the Bemis Public Library was going to be tough, especially since I was doing preschool story time. How would I keep from being overly emotional about saying good-bye? I decided that noise and play were the solutions. I read silly stories that featured plenty of sounds everyone could participate on. The last story was *Pots and Pans* by Patricia Hubbell, a rhythmic tale that begins, "Pots and pans, pots and pans. Baby's in the kitchen with the pots and pans. GRAB those lids. CLANG those pans! Baby's in the kitchen with the pots and pans." After I finished reading the story, I opened a box that was filled with— POTS AND PANS! Everybody got something to bang together and we paraded through the library, repeating the opening phrase and having a smashingly, obnoxiously noisy good time in the library. I mean, what could they do, fire me?

WHAT CAN YOU DO?: AT HOME

Assuming you have read *Hattie and the Fox* several times to your child, try telling it without the book some rainy afternoon. If you are comfortable, act it out with your child, each of you playing several parts. Or gather up stuffed animals and use them to act out the parts. Don't worry. A penguin can pretend to be a chicken, and a bear can be a cow. It's all about teaching your child, through dramatic play, that stories begin at the beginning, then there's action in the middle, and it comes to a satisfying conclusion at the end. Allow for creativity along the way, so that the child feels free to add a dance, or another character. You're not being filmed or graded. You're bonding with your child in a very memorable way, and teaching them narrative skills, which will help grow a reader who loves to create her own stories, a necessary talent for academic achievement.

One of Jamie's favorite cardboard books was Sandra Boynton's *Barnyard Dance.* (I love everything and anything by Boynton; her books are hilarious!) "Bow to the horse./Bow to the cow./Twirl with the pig if you know how." A perfect story to act out together! But wait, there's more. Did you realize it fits the tune of "Skip to My Lou?" So you can sing, if you please. But wait, there's more. Combine this with a reading of *Mama Don't Allow* by Thacher Hurd, which can also be sung. Now make simple musical instruments, like beans between two taped paper plates, or an empty tin can (that has been safely taped all around the ages) being banged by a spoon, or a scoop of Cheerios in a sippy cup to shake. "Mama don't allow no music playin' around here. Mama don't allow no music playin' around here. We don't care what Mama don't allow. We're gonna play it anyhow. Mama don't allow no music playin' around here." But wait, there's more. Get Jim Gill's CD, *Jim Gill Sings the Sneezing Song and Other Contagious Tunes,* and play "The Silly Dance Contest." All you have to do is dance as silly as you please, but "stop when I say freeze." What a memorable way to spend a snowy day together.

Another narrative skills activity with your child is to ask him for a possible ending to a new story, or a different ending to a familiar story. When you are close to the end of a story, pause, and ask, "What do you think is going to happen?" Let the child's imagination soar. Now finish reading the story and compare endings.

Children love to hear about their birthday, or "Gotcha Day," the day when they were adopted. On your child's special day, make a wide paper headband, and divide it into four parts. Each part represents something special that happened on that day. Your child draws a picture, and you print the words. For my daughter, the first box might be "I was brought to the orphanage," with a picture of her in her foster mother's arms. Second square might be "There were lots of babies." Next square, "Mommy held me and cried." Then, "I fell asleep." Then you decorate as you wish, and the child wears the headband to her birthday dinner and gets to tell the story to everyone.

Try making up stories with your child. It's not as hard as you think. The adult begins with an opening line such as "Once upon a time there was a—," and then you pause. The child finishes the sentence. The adult agrees, with enthusiasm, "Yes, there was a dinosaur!" The adult continues with the beginning of the next sentence, such as, "This dinosaur had a problem because he was—." "Scared!" says the child. "Yes, he was very scared," says the adult, "because he thought he had lost his—." And so on. The only rules are that the adult should guide the child away from violence or disrespect, and make sure that the story doesn't keep repeating itself with the same ingredients that are favorites for the child. For instance, the dinosaur lost his trucks, so he got in a truck, and the truck ran into another truck, and the dinosaur got out and got in another truck... You get the picture.

A favorite pastime of my daughter's when we were eating at a particular Mexican restaurant was to put the people around us into a story. The restaurant was above the road, with windows looking out on the cars as they drove by. A stop light was close by, which meant the cars sometimes stopped and waited. We gazed into the cars and made up stories about where the people were going, what they were escaping, who was in trouble, and what they were saying. "That's Doris and Filbert Egglebottom. They live inside an egg. They were just about to have dinner when they discovered their house was cracked! So now they are going…"

Another form of family storytelling is to make up stories in which the main character is your child. My grandfather used to tell stories at bedtime to his two daughters about three bears named Jimmy, Jammy, and Jummy. Jimmy and Jummy were very good bears, but Jammy was always in a jam. It didn't occur to my mother until she was much older that whatever adventure/problem/jam Jammy was in strongly resembled something that had happened recently to either herself or her sister. It was a great opportunity for Pop to weave teachable moments and life lessons into stories.

If your child is having trouble making friends at school, find a quiet moment during the day to make up a story about your own special character (Chelsea the Chipmunk? Rufus the Rabbit?) who has a similar problem, and offer suggestions for solutions. Chelsea helps someone go down the slide at the playground, or Rufus has a pool party. Keep this character real and honest so that the child can easily identify with what you're teaching, but be sure to add plenty of humor and adventure so that the story isn't didactic or tedious.

Pam Schiller's book, *Creating Readers: Over 1000 Games, Activities, Tongue Twisters, Fingerplays, Songs, and Stories to Get Children Excited about Reading,* lists "A Dozen Ways to Tell a Story." Topics include Puppets (nine different kinds), Reenactment, Shadow Stories, Flannel Board, Magnetic Stories, Storytelling without Props of Any Kind, Using Props, and Walk-On Story. The latter is particularly clever, and involves using butcher paper on which you draw "pictures and symbols of key elements and actions in the story," as well as footprints that lead from one symbol to the next, and then the child(ren) walk through the story, either telling it themselves or following your narration.

Finally, give a new twist to the art of telling a story by going backward through the day. Albert Lamb cleverly does this in his book *Tell Me the Day Backwards.* As Mama Bear tucks Timmy Bear into bed, he asks her to play by rewinding the day through storytelling. He begins with brushing his teeth, then she remembers watching the sunset together. Back and forth they tell the story of the day, ending at the beginning with the long winter sleep they finished last night. This would be an excellent way to recreate the special memories of the day, while enhancing the narrative and vocabulary skills of your child.

THE MOUSE AND HIS CAT

One day I was driving somewhere (aren't we always driving somewhere?), with my then three-year-old daughter in her car seat. I was trying to keep her awake until we got home so she would take her nap and I could accomplish the 38 chores that needed accomplishing. So, together, we were making up a story.

"Once upon a time there was a—," I began.

"Mouse," says Jamie.

"And what is the mouse wearing?" I ask.

"A red hat."

"And what is the mouse doing?"

"Walking his cat."

Walking his cat!!! "What color cat?"

"Pink."

"And where are they going on this walk?"

"To the ocean!"

"And they are going to the ocean because—"

"To visit the starfish."

I don't remember all the details of this story, but what I do remember was her surprising creativity, and the pride she took in coming up with the ideas, and in making me giggle or gasp when I heard what she said. To this day, I have a very clear image in my mind of a mouse walking his pink cat along the beach while ocean breezes blow away his plumed and red hat.

IN THE CLASSROOM OR AT THE LIBRARY:
FELT BOARD STORIES

Many story presenters use felt board pictures to tell a story. Here are some questions to ask yourself before putting in the time to create or purchase the pieces. Do the pictures placed on a felt board make the story more interesting, or should I just use the book? Are the felt pieces big enough for everyone to see? Am I familiar enough with the story so I can tell it smoothly? (Of course, you can have a cheat sheet with you!) Will I use this over and over so it's worth the time to create the pictures? Since I can't move the felt board from side to side, will everyone still be able to see? If your answers indicate that transforming the story from book to felt board would be worthwhile, then go for it!

Using felt board pieces is a simple way to bridge between reading the story, and telling the story. If you want to use specific illustrations from a book such as *Dog's Colorful Day* by Emma Dodd or *It Looked Like Spilt Milk* by Charles Shaw, there are several methods for creating them:

Make a photocopy of the illustration, cut it out, pin it onto felt, then cut out the felt. Add decorations, as you wish. (I highly recommend fabric art paint!)

Or, use an overhead projector or visual presenter to trace the illustrations onto felt.

Or, make color photocopies of the illustrations, cut those out, and glue them onto tag board with Velcro on the back to make it stick to the felt board.

Or, draw your own adaptations of the illustrations.

Or, there are many resources for prepared collections of felt board figures from a story. Here are just a few, but you'll find plenty more on the Internet and at craft fairs:

http://www.feltboardstories.com/home

http://www.funfeltstories.com/

http://www.theteacherexpress.com/indexstorytellingsets.html

www.constructiveplaythings.com

All of these can be used to accompany reading a book, or telling the story on its own. After the reading or telling, allow the children to use the felt board pieces, acting out what they remember. Make sure the book is nearby for them to refer to, and help them out if they ask for details. Best of all, just let them create and play.

Facts 'n Stats

Several studies find that the ability to tell stories is directly related to the ability to learn how to read. The fancy name for what goes on in storytelling is "decontextualized" language. That is, when you tell a good story, you set up the listener with all of the structure and language he needs to interpret what you are saying. The listener should be able to follow the story and "get it."

Hirsh-Pasek, Kathy, and Roberta Michnick Golinkoff. *Einstein Never Used Flash Cards: How Our Children REALLY Learn—and Why They Need to Play More and Memorize Less,* p. 104. Emmaus, PA: Rodale, 2003.

THE ART OF STORYTELLING

For as storytellers we are concerned not alone with amusement, or with education, or with distraction; nor is it enough to give pleasure. We are concerned with letting a single stream of light pass through us as through one facet of the gem or prism that there may be revealed some aspect of the spirit, some beauty and truth that lies hidden within the world and humankind.

Sawyer, Ruth. *The Way of the Storyteller,* p. 107. New York: Viking Press, 1970. Used with permission.

I have given you ideas about telling stories using literature or imagination to create tales that are intended for that moment or that child. But there is also *storytelling,* an ancient art that combines personal talent, practice, and a great deal of heart to create a unique performance of a story. A storyteller researches the history and many versions of a folktale in order to compose her own unique interpretation. Or a storyteller brings into being an original tale, employing his own personal experiences and artistry. Listening to a master storyteller can be a powerful and intimate sharing of dreams, hope, reflection, understanding, and awakening.

For the purpose of this book, the storytelling described here will be a style that is less time-consuming and more appropriate for the busy teacher or librarian. If you wish to become a professional storyteller, there is much more involved—extensive research, hours of practice, a desire to experience in order to understand, willingness to travel, ability to collect, adapt or create stories, and listening to other storytellers. But for you who are simply interested in occasionally telling a story in the classroom or library, or entertaining a family audience, here are basic steps toward telling a tale that is right for you, and in a way that is appropriate for that audience at that moment in time.

First, find the story. The best place to start is in folklore, which is 398.2 at the library, a Dewey Decimal number emblazoned on every storyteller's heart. These are the stories that have been told and retold for hundreds of years, now finally written into a book. Find one that is simple, repetitive, and age appropriate for the very young listener. Learning a story that is repetitious, or builds like links in a chain, is the easiest way to begin as a storyteller.

Read as many versions as you can find, then put them away to let the story dance around in your head. Favorite bits and pieces of the different retellings will settle into your memory, waiting for you to select them for your own creation.

HEATHER RECOMMENDS

More Than 14 Folktales That Are Easy to Learn

Brett, Jan. *The Mitten.* How many animals can fit inside the mitten before it bursts?

Farris, Pamela J. *Young Mouse and Elephant: An East African Folktale.* Mouse is sure that he is the strongest animal on the savannah.

Galdone, Paul. *The Amazing Pig.* Invite the children to join in on the king's refrain, "I believe you," as a wise man tricks the ruler so he can marry the princess.

Galdone, Paul. *Henny Penny.* Everyone needs to know this folktale of the foolish chicken, turkey, goose, and duck who are out-tricked by a fox.

Harper, Wilhelmina. *The Gunniwolf.* A little girl outwits the gunni-wolf with a song.

Hogrogian, Nonny. *One Fine Day.* A fox must help others to get back his tail.

Kimmel, Eric. *The Gingerbread Man.* Children love this story, and the chance to join in on his chant, "Run, run as fast as you can. You can't catch me, I'm the gingerbread man."

Kimmel, Eric. *The Old Woman and Her Pig.* An old woman must get help from others in order to get home.

MacDonald, Margaret Read. *Go to Sleep, Gecko!: A Balinese Folktale.* Gecko must learn that all the world is connected, even the fireflies that keep him awake.

MacDonald, Margaret Read. *The Storyteller's Start Up Book: Finding, Learning, Performing and Using Folktales*. Excellent tips on becoming a storyteller, as well as a collection of easy-to-learn stories.

McDermott, Gerald. *Zomo the Rabbit*. This West African folktale tells of the trickster rabbit who wants wisdom.

Paye, Won-Ldy, and Margaret H. Lippert. *Mrs. Chicken and the Hungry Crocodile*. Are chicken and crocodile really sisters?

So, Meilo. *Gobble, Gobble, Slip, Slop: A Tale of a Very Greedy Cat*. A cat eats 500 cakes, a farmer, an elephant, and more, but it's two crabs who catch him in the end.

Tolstoy, Aleksey K. *The Gigantic Turnip*. A family and many animals pull and pull to get the turnip out of the ground.

Zemach, Margot. *It Could Always Be Worse* (good as a flannel board, too). A man thinks his house is too noisy but learns that it could be much worse.

Second, figure out what kind of a learner you are. Saroj Ghoting, in her book *Early Literacy Storytimes @ Your Library,* cites eight main kinds of learners, adapted from Thomas Armstrong's *In Their Own Way: Discovering and Encouraging Your Child's Multiple Intelligences.* The most prevalent are spatial, linguistic, or kinesthetic. For the purpose of learning a story, I equate these to being visual, auditory, or tactile.

Visual. This means you need to see in order to remember. For these kinds of learners, you prepare for a test by reading a text many times. For storytelling, you'll need a copy of the book or story. Read over the first page or paragraph, then set it aside and retell in your own words. Then read page two or paragraph two, set it aside, and retell the first and the second part in your own words. Repeat again and again, taking the story apart into smaller parts, adding one part but always repeating all the parts before. By the time you've gotten through the entire story, you'll have the majority already learned.

Auditory. This means you learn quickest by hearing. Do you record lectures by professors? Do you love to listen to recorded books? After you've seen a movie, can you recite dialogue word for word? If these habits describe you then you need to record the story. Listen to it over and over. And over and over. And over and over and over and over. As you listen, you're also thinking about what you can do with the story. Different voices? A repetitive song that invites audience participation? Then listen to smaller portions, and retell in your own words. After you've gotten through the entire story several times, put away the recording and begin developing your own version.

Tactile. This means you have to handle what you want to learn. You like to take apart, construct, diagram, chart, rebuild. Tactile storytellers need to write out the story themselves, allowing the words to travel from fingertip to heart. Or they might draw a diagram that explains each of the story parts and how they intertwine, leading to new discoveries and adventures.

Third, practice, practice, practice. Tell the story to your cat. Tell the story in your car, driving to work. Tell the story before falling asleep (it's a great way to focus the brain, and you'll rarely get to the end of the story before drifting off). Tell the story until you can tell it effortlessly and without worry. Now you're ready for an audience.

Do not memorize every word. Storytelling means using your own words, not memorizing the words of others. If you memorize, you are stealing the very personal invention and achievement of someone else. You are also not allowing your own talents and insights to add life to the story.

There's another reason for not memorizing. Have you ever tried to remember the words in the middle of a song? You have to go backward and recite from the beginning in order to find the missing ones. That will be true with a memorized story as well. Storytellers are often interrupted, by a noisy toddler, a recess bell, a slamming door. You need to be able to pick right back up where you left off, rather than struggle to find the exact words. "Now, where were we before the fire alarm went off? Oh, yes, the 3rd billy goat, the biggest billy goat, the smartest billy goat, was just about to walk across that rickety rackety bridge." And off you go again, bringing them along to your place of wonder.

Fourth, don't worry. Mistakes will happen and your mind will blip. But this is a *telling*, not an audition. Allow yourself to breathe, pause, even casually apologize for forgetting something. You might find that something new will be born, adding more punch. What you don't want is to be focused on perfection, especially the first few times you tell the story. Relax and enjoy the gift you are giving to your listeners.

Tips for a better telling:

1. Remember eye contact. You don't have to constantly stare into the eyes of your audience, but you don't want to be looking up at the ceiling or down at the floor. Skim across, occasionally looking into someone's eyes at an important moment in the story. He will remember!

2. Be consistent. If you have a squeaky voice for the mouse, and a big booming voice for the elephant, those voices need to be the same throughout the story, never fading away or getting mismatched. Did I mention the importance of practice?

3. Avoid props. When you begin as a storyteller, it's important to focus on the story, not a basket full of stuffed animals that need to be pulled out at just the right time, or costume pieces that have to be taken on and off throughout the telling. If you're using felt board pieces during your story, just make sure they're in order and easily picked up so you're not flustered or distracted. Need I remind you? Practice!

4. Always tell your listeners where the story came from, but preferably at the end of the telling. Otherwise, if you say, before you begin telling, "I'm going to tell you the story of 'Sody Sallyraytus,'" two things are liable to happen. The first is that several of the children

IT'S MY STORYTELLER!

Years ago I was coming home to Colorado after performing at a conference somewhere else. I was tired, it was late, and I just wanted to get home to sleep in my own bed without the necessity of earplugs. The airport was not the present lovely, light-filled Denver International Airport, but rather dark and dismal Stapleton Airport. I journeyed down into the bowels, where luggage arrived. Sometimes. But not tonight. So now I was tired and irritated. I filled out the forms, heard all the platitudes from the airlines employee, and turned to leave, minus luggage.

Suddenly, from across the United luggage area, I heard a young girl yell out, at the top of her vocal ability, "IT'S MY STORYTELLER!!!!" The six-year-old came running toward me, threw her arms around my legs, and said, "Remember me? You told me that story!" Of course I did not remember her. She was just one of hundreds at her school. But I was honored by her obvious joy at discovering me again in her life. I asked her to remind me what the story was, and then we had a conversation about the squirrel that ran away from the bear in Sody Sallyraytus. Her parents wandered over, somewhat amazed by their daughter's enthusiasm. I thanked them all, and left the airport completely rejuvenated with the bond that had passed between storyteller and story listener. I did not remember her face in the crowd at school, but I will always remember what she called me at the airport. Not "a" storyteller, or "the" storyteller, but "MY" storyteller. That's how powerful, and rewarding, storytelling can be.

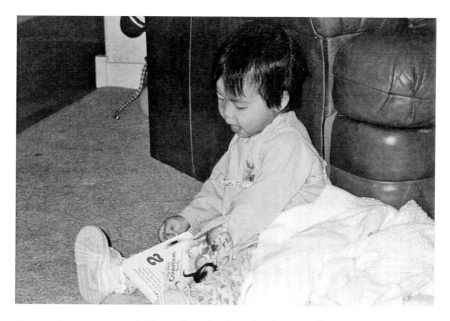

Encouraging your young child to tell stories about her day, or make up stories about what they see in books, will help them be more comfortable when they begin sounding out words because they are prepared for how it all might come together to tell a tale. Jamie is too young to be actually reading, but she is having great fun creating a story about the animals in her book.

will get incredibly excited, and will yell out, "I have that book!" "I already know that story!" "That book is silly. I like the part when…" The second reason is that those who are familiar with the book might be inclined to challenge you if you have dared to make any changes to what they believe is the one and only version of the truth. "That's not what the bear did!' "I don't remember that song!" "No, no, no! The squirrel never said that." And when you show the book at the end of your telling do be prepared that someone might say, "Will you read it to us?"

BIBLIOGRAPHY

For Librarians, Teachers, and Parents

Ghoting, Saroj. *Early Literacy Storytimes @ Your Library: Partnering with Caregivers for Success.* Chicago, IL: American Library Association, 2006.

Hirsh-Pasek, Kathy, and Roberta Michnick Golinkoff. *Einstein Never Used Flash Cards: How Our Children REALLY Learn—And*

Why They Need to Play More and Memorize Less. Emmaus, PA: Rodale, 2003.

MacDonald, Margaret Read. *The Storyteller's Start-Up Book: Finding, Learning, Performing and Using Folktales.* Little Rock, AR: August House, 1993.

Oppenheim, Joanne, and Stephanie Oppenheim. *Oppenheim Toy Portfolio's Read It! Play It! With Babies and Toddlers: Building Literacy through Reading and Play.* New York: Oppenheim Toy Portfolio, 2006.

Sawyer, Ruth. *The Way of the Storyteller.* New York: Viking Press, 1970.

Schiller, Pam. *Creating Readers: Over 1000 Games, Activities, Tongue Twisters, Fingerplays, Songs, and Stories to Get Children Excited about Reading.* Beltsville, MD: Gryphon House, 2001.

Simms, Laura. "Words in Our Hearts: The Experience of the Story." *The Horn Book Magazine,* June 1983, 344–49.

For Children

Bemelmans, Ludwig. *Madeline.* New York: Viking Press, 1967.

Boynton, Sandra. *Barnyard Dance.* New York: Workman Pub., 1993.

Brett, Jan. *The Mitten: A Ukranian Folktale.* New York: Putnam, 1989.

Cauley, Lorinda Bryan. *Clap Your Hands.* New York: Putnam, 1992.

Chase, Richard. "Sody Sallyraytus." In *Grandfather Tales: American-English Folk Tales.* Boston, MA: Houghton Mifflin, 1976.

Degen, Bruce. *Jamberry.* New York: Harper & Row, 1983.

Farris, Pamela J. *Young Mouse and Elephant: An East African Folktale.* Boston, MA: Houghton Mifflin, 1996.

Fox, Mem. *Hattie and the Fox.* New York: Bradbury Press, 1986.

Galdone, Paul. *Henny Penny.* New York: Ticknor & Fields, 1968.

Haan, Amanda. *I Call My Hand Gentle.* New York: Viking, 2003.

Harper, Wilhelmina. *The Gunniwolf.* New York: Dutton Children's Books, 2003.

Hogrogian, Nonny. *One Fine Day.* New York: Macmillan, 1971.

Hubbell, Patricia. *Pots and Pans.* New York: HarperFestival, 1998.

Hudson, Cheryl Willis. *Hands Can.* Cambridge, MA: Candlewick Press, 2003.

Hurd, Thacher. *Mama Don't Allow: Starring Miles and the Swamp Band.* New York: Harper & Row, 1984.

Kimmel, Eric. *The Old Woman and Her Pig.* New York: Holiday House, 1992.

Kimmel, Eric. *The Gingerbread Man.* New York: Holiday House, 1993.

Lamb, Albert. *Tell Me the Day Backwards.* Somerville, MA: Candlewick Press, 2011.

MacDonald, Margaret Read. *Go to Sleep, Gecko!: A Balinese Folktale.* Little Rock, AR: August House LittleFolk, 2006.

Martin, Bill, Jr., and John Archambault. *Here Are My Hands.* New York: Henry Holt and Co., 1998.

McDermott, Gerald. *Zomo the Rabbit.* San Diego, CA: Harcourt Brace Jovanovich, 1992.

Milne, A. A. *Winnie the Pooh.* New York: Dutton, 1926.

Paye, Won-Ldy, and Margaret H. Lippert. *Mrs. Chicken and the Hungry Crocodile.* New York: Henry Holt, 2003.

Price, Hope Lynne. *These Hands.* New York: Hyperion Books for Children/ Jump At the Sun, 1999.

Seuss, Dr. *Cat in the Hat.* New York: Random House, 1957.

Shaw, Charles. *It Looked Like Spilt Milk.* New York: Harper, 1947.

So, Meilo. *Gobble, Gobble, Slip, Slop: A Tale of a Very Greedy Cat.* New York: Alfred A. Knopf, 2004.

Tolstoy, Aleksey K. *The Gigantic Turnip.* Brooklyn, NY: Barefoot Books, 1999.

Zemach, Margot. *It Could Always Be Worse: A Yiddish Folktale.* New York: Farrar, Straus and Giroux, 1976.

DISCOGRAPHY

Gill, Jim. *Jim Gill Sings the Sneezing Song and Other Contagious Tunes.* Chicago, IL: Jim Gill Music, 1993.

Chapter Five

SING A SONG,
RHYME A RHYME

When Jamie was four, one of her favorite books was *What Did You Put in Your Pocket?* by Beatrice Schenk de Regniers. I read that book to her over and over. And over. And again. And again. She chimed in on the repeating silly words, "Slushy glushy pudding. Nicy icy water. Fluppy gluppy potatoes." Whenever anyone reached into a pocket, we would chant the rhythmic phrase, "What did you put in your pocket? What did you put in your pocket? Your pockety pockety pocket. Early Monday morning."

We explored Michael Grejniec's outrageous illustrations that are bright, chaotic, and very child-friendly. One day Jamie said, "I'm going to read *What Did You Put in Your Pocket?* by myself."

"Great!" I replied, delighted she wanted to try, and quite sure it would be the usual accomplishment of getting some words in the right place and making up the rest. So I puttered about in the kitchen, and Jamie sat on her Jamie-sized wooden rocking chair, and she read the book. Perfectly. From beginning to end. Every word in the right place, every page turned at the correct spot, and even with some of the silly intonations I would use. She was reading!!!!!

Of course, what she was actually doing was repeating what she had memorized. I knew that. But I also knew that repeating was a beginning to reading, and that she had correctly noticed where each word was placed on the pages, and how the words flowed, and where the next phrase began, and more. She knew that the words written meant the words spoken, and that together it made a story.

Being first a mother, and second a librarian, I went crazy with delirious delight. I cheered and I hugged. I asked her to read it again. I called her grandmother. I cheered some more. I let Jamie know that what she had done was wonderful, clever, and important. I also made sure that that book was under the Christmas tree months later so we would always remember and celebrate "the first book Jamie read all by herself."

There are many reasons why *What Did You Put in Your Pocket?* was Jamie's first book. It's quirky, imaginative, and different. Some of the words are made up, such as "fluppy" and "gluppy," which just adds to the fun, much like Dr. Seuss's books. But most of all, it uses rhythm, repetition, and rhyme, which makes it memorable. Those characteristics also make it easier for the child to predict what comes next, so that sounding out new words is just that much easier.

At home, or in the preschool or library, children can be introduced to the important concept of phonological awareness through singing and rhym-

Facts 'n Stats

The following are the basic definitions and terms for the "Language of Literacy," used in reading instruction.

Phoneme

A phoneme is the smallest part of spoken language that makes a difference in the meaning of words. English has about 41 phonemes. A few words, such as a or oh, have only one phoneme. Most words, however, have more than one phoneme: The word if has two phonemes (/i/ /f/); check has three phonemes (/ch/ /e/ /k/); and stop has four phonemes (/s/ /t/ /o/ /p/). Sometimes one phoneme is represented by more than one letter.

Grapheme

A grapheme is the smallest part of written language that represents a phoneme in the spelling of a word. A grapheme may be just one letter, such as b, d, f, p, s; or several letters, such as ch, sh, th, -ck, ea, -igh.

Phonics

Phonics is the understanding that there is a predictable relationship between phonemes (the sounds of spoken language) and graphemes (the letters and spellings that represent those sounds in written language).

Phonemic Awareness

Phonemic awareness is the ability to hear, identify, and manipulate the individual sounds—phonemes—in spoken words.

Phonological Awareness

Phonological awareness is a broad term that includes phonemic awareness. In addition to phonemes, phonological awareness activities can involve work with rhymes, words, syllables, and onsets and rimes.

Syllable

A syllable is a word part that contains a vowel or, in spoken language, a vowel sound (e-vent; news-pa-per; ver-y).

Onset and rime

Onsets and rimes are parts of spoken language that are smaller than syllables but larger than phonemes. An onset is the initial consonant(s) sound of a syllable (the onset of bag is b-; of swim, sw-). A rime is the part of a syllable that contains the vowel and all that follows it (the rime of bag is -ag; of swim, -im).

(*Put Reading First—The Research Building Blocks for Teaching Children to Read.* Eunice Kennedy Shriver National Institute of Child Health and Human Development (NICHD), NIH, DHHS; http://www.nichd.nih.gov/publications/pubs/PRF-teachers-k-3.cfm. Used with permission.)

ing. This means they begin to hear the chunks that make up words, and can manipulate the beginnings or endings of words to create new words. Eventually, through reading instruction, they will be taught phonemic awareness, which means being able to hear individual sounds in words, as well as rhyming, and making new words. It is the auditory skill of getting ready to learn to read, leading to the visual skill of identifying letters, which is phonics, which leads to the skill of actually reading and writing.

I have had conversations with parents about what they should be doing to encourage their children to learn to read. I tell them, "Experts believe that the most important activities are to read, sing and rhyme with them." "Oh, I already do that," they reply. "But what should I be doing to teach them reading?" They are hoping for a recommendation of a packaged program, a video game, a drill that will guarantee their children will read early and be ahead of others when they enter kindergarten.

Instead, I assure them they are doing exactly what they should be doing. "Leave the formal teaching to the teachers. Right now, having fun with words, making books appealing, and playing with your child are what makes the difference. That's what improves brain development and bonding, as well as helps them to truly love reading. So read, rhyme, and sing. That's all."

Do I change their vision of their role? Not always. High-achieving parents, anxious to excel at being a parent, want more. But it is the play that children crave, as well as the intimacy of reading aloud to them. If a parent gives them reading, rhyming, and romping, and encourages outrageous experimentation with words, then the desire and ability to read will come naturally for those who are blessed with all that it takes for the brain to figure out this amazing process called "reading."

WHAT CAN YOU DO?: AT THE PRESCHOOL

Songs and rhymes should be a part of every child's day at a preschool. For one thing, singing a song catches a child's attention. I remember being so impressed at hearing my daughter's preschool teacher quietly sing, "Clean up! Clean up! Everybody, everywhere. Clean up, clean up. Everybody do your share." There were no complaints or grumblings; they just joined in, picking up toys, putting away crayons, singing all the while. Similarly, at story time, I often sing a simple rhyme, "Monkey one. *(point to myself)* Monkey two. *(point to child)* Monkey see. *(circle fingers around eyes)* Monkey do!" Then I run, or jump, or wiggle, and they do the same. *Sotto voce,* I tell the parents, "This is a great rhyme to use to encourage your child to eat their peas."

Besides catching their attention, songs also take apart words into their smaller parts, thus teaching syllables and phonics without focused effort. When a child sings, "Twinkle, Twinkle Little Star," they are hearing how a word is made of chunks. "Twin-kle twin-kle lit-tle star." Later on they'll learn how to put chunks together to make words. "Pea-nut." "Di-no-saur." They're also hearing words that sound alike. Star and are. High and sky. Later on they will learn about changing the first letters in order to make rhyming words, and sounding out words to determine which one is different from the others. Dog, log, and pig. All of this leads to reading.

HEATHER RECOMMENDS

10 Games to Teach Phonological Awareness

1. Read *Rhyming Dust Bunnies* by Jan Thomas. (You might have to explain first what a dust bunny is!) Then take some of the words

that the dust bunnies rhyme, and see what others your listeners can figure out. If you have large foam letters, you could hold them up, one at a time, and see if they could become the beginning of a word. And if the word doesn't make sense, have fun with imagining what it might be. For instance, you're rhyming with the last two letters of "og." They've come up with bog and dog and fog, and you've had the opportunity to explain what they are. But now you hold up a G. Gog? Is that a word? No. But, if it was, what would it be? A monster! What does it look like? Big and round and purple. Let's all make a gog. So everyone gets to draw or sculpt or create a gog. And, goodness gracious, what about its sister, Pog? And their pet, Rog? And don't forget their last name, Wog. Of course, you end this activity by making up a short story about Gog Wog and Pog Wog, who lost their dog Rog on their way to the bog to see their friend—wait for it—FROG! Hopefully, by now, everyone is having a rollicking good time.

2. Play "I Spy," highlighting either rhymes or letter sounds. "I spy something that rhymes with jar." (star)

3. Use nursery rhymes, and get creative with them. For instance:

> Higglety Pigglety Pop! *(jump)*
> The dog has eaten the mop.
> The pig's in a hurry, the cat's in a flurry, *(run in place)*
> Higglety Pigglety Pop! *(jump and clap)*

After they've had fun with this one, change the "Pop" to "Clap" and see what they can think of to rhyme with it. The dog has eaten the map? The dog likes to rap? Change "hurry" to "The pig wants to jump," and maybe they'll think of "The cat likes to bump." Gradually, you'll make up an entirely different rhyme, with actions that they choose to match. And if the words are nonsense words, that doesn't really matter. It makes it just that much more creative when they decide "The pig likes to snort." *(everyone snorts)* "The cat likes to zort." *(everyone wiggles)*

4. Play a recording of "The Name Game." Play it just for fun, for several days, maybe during snack time or before story time. After they've become familiar with its pattern, choose a name of someone in class for learning the name game. Here are the basic rules:

    i.   Exclaim the name once.
   ii.   Then say the name twice.
  iii.   Say "bo."

iv.   Then say the name with a B at the beginning.

v.   Say bonana fanna fo.

vi.   Say the name again with an F at the beginning.

vii.   Say fee fy mo.

viii.   Say the name again with an M at the beginning.
Here's what it would sound like with the name
Heather:
Heather!
Heather, Heather bo Beather
Bonana fanna fo Feather
Fee fy Mo Meather,
Heather!

If the name begins with "B" or "F" or "M," just drop the first letters and say the name twice without the first letter. For instance, if
the name is Michael:

Michael!
Ichael, Ichael, bo Bichael
Bonana fanna fo Fichael
Fee fy Mo Michael,
Michael!

It is amazing how quickly older preschoolers will catch on
to this and fill your day with repetitions and alterations of the
song.

5. A simpler variation of playing with names is to clap the syllables,
with the following nursery rhyme:

Heckedy Peckedy Bumble Bee
What is your name, please tell me.
(point to child and she says her name, Melody)
Me-lo-dy. *(clap with each syllable)*
Me-lo-dy. *(slap thighs with each syllable)*
Me-lo-dy. *(whisper)*
MELODY! (throw arms up high, and shout out the name)

6. Play a game of taking words apart. First, write the word "airplane"
on two index cards, with "air" on one and "plane" on the other.
Hold them up as one word, and ask the children, "If I have the
word 'airplane,' and I take away the part that says 'air,' what is left?"

As you ask this, you remove the card with "air" on it, and hide it behind your back. Continue with other two-syllable words that easily come apart, such as hotdog and pinecone. Progress to more complicated versions, where the words come apart into pieces that don't make sense on their own, such as chee-tah and pen-guin. Remove the last part sometimes and the first part sometimes. Then you can move on to three-syllable words. Remember to keep it a game, and celebrate with lots of enthusiasm when they get the idea.

7. Jill Frankel Hauser, in her wonderful book of ideas, *WOW! I'm Reading!: Fun Activities to Make Reading Happen*, recommends using the tune of "Oh, Do You Know the Muffin Man?," and making up rhyming jingles (p. 33). For instance, "Oh, have you seen a fox in a box/A fox in a box/A fox in a box/Oh, have you seen a fox in a box/Quite a sight to see!"

8. Jackie Silberg's *Reading Games* has many great ideas for playing with rhymes. "Food Rhymes" is about making up a simple sentence about eating, leaving the last rhyming word open for the child to figure out. For instance, "Eat some cheese, and pat your _____." "Eat some bread and scratch your _____." "Eat a tomato then mash a _____."

9. Silberg's game "Sit Down Rhymes" has the children walking in a circle as you chant words that rhyme. When you say one that doesn't rhyme, they all sit down. You don't need to have every word be different; you can repeat the same words throughout the list. "Cat, rat, sat, cat, bat, mat, fat, cat, dog." Did everyone sit down?

10. Use the tune to "Mary Had a Little Lamb" and play, "What's the color?" Put up large circles of specific colors so the children have some idea of what they're trying to connect. Then sing, "What's the color that rhymes with head, rhymes with head, rhymes with head? If you're wearing that color today, please stand and jump." Everyone who is wearing red stands and jumps. Then move on to "What's the color that rhymes with shoe...rhymes with fellow...," and so on.

Finally, be sure to read aloud plenty of books that rhyme, or that are based on popular songs.

HEATHER RECOMMENDS

13 Rhyming Books to Read Aloud in the Preschool

Beaumont, Karen. *No Sleep for the Sheep!* The poor sheep just wants to sleep but the other farm animals make too much noise.

Down by the Bay, illustrated by Robert Collier-Morales. This is like the "song that never ends," because once children learn the pattern they can make up verses of their own forever. "Did you ever see a moose sipping orange juice … a baboon hopping to the moon … a bee chasing a flea … "

Fischer, Scott. *Jump!* Each animal, from frog to whale, has a brief rhyme, followed by the word "Jump," in this cumulative tale that invites participation not only with the rhymes, but also with the action of jumping.

Fox, Mem. *The Magic Hat.* "The magic hat, the magic hat/It moved like this, it moved like that." There is so much rhythm you just have to move, and children will enjoy guessing the rhyming word that describes what magic the hat is able to perform.

Hoberman, Mary Ann. *Bill Grogan's Goat.* This is one in a series of traditional songs illustrated by Nadine Bernard Westcott, with new verses just right for exploring. Others include *The Eensy Weensy Spider, The Lady with the Alligator Purse, Miss Mary Mack,* and *There Once Was a Man Name Michael Finnegan.*

London, Jonathan. *I'm a Truck Driver.* All kinds of trucks and their sounds are introduced in rhyme.

Martin, Bill, Jr., and Michael Sampson. *Kitty Cat, Kitty Cat, Are You Going to Sleep?* A kitten has ideas other than going to sleep.

McCall, Francis, and Patricia Keeler. *A Huge Hog Is a Big Pig.* Children figure out what rhyming words combine, such as "A wet hound is a … soggy doggy."

Morales, Melita. *Jam and Honey.* A girl and a bee learn they can each get what they want without hurting the other.

Pinkney, Jerry. *Three Little Kittens.* There's plenty of action in this version of the naughty kittens and their search for their mittens.

Riley, Linnea. *Mouse Mess.* The mouse is about the house, looking for food. "Crunch-crunch, he wants a cracker. Munch-munch, a cookie snacker."

Walton, Rick. *Bunny School: A Learning Fun-for-All.* One in a series about bunnies, this time they're learning what to expect at the preschool.

Williams, Suzanne. *Ten Naughty Little Monkeys.* The author makes this familiar rhyme even more fun with added verses and a twist at the end.

WHAT CAN YOU DO?: AT THE LIBRARY

Singing and rhyming at story time sets the tone for interactive fun. Songs invite the children to participate, and give them the message that making noise, being silly, and allowing yourself to be creative through movement and vocabulary, are all OK at story time. Songs help get the children up and moving, as well as settle them down to be ready to listen for the next story. Librarians can also add phonological games as part of story time, role modeling for parents how important they are, as well as simple and fun.

"Rags" is a popular traditional song you can find on many recordings. I use it if I'm doing a story time about dogs, pets, the letter R or Z, eating, silly or rhyming stories, or love. In other words, I use it a lot. The tune is the same one for "Three Little Fishies," which you'll find at http://kids.niehs. nih.gov/games/songs/childrens/fishiesmid.htm.

I have a dog and his name is Rags.
He eats so much that his tummy sags. *(stick out tummy)*
His ears flip flop *(hands beside ears, flopping up and down)* and his
    tail wig wags, *(wiggle bottom)*
And when he walks, he goes zig zag. *(cross arms in front of you,
    one on top of the other, then move them back and forth)*
He goes flip flop, *(hands beside ears, flopping up and down)* wig
    wag, *(wiggle bottom)* zig zag, *(cross arms in front of you, one on
    top of the other, then move them back and forth)*
He goes flip flop, wig wag, zig zag.
He goes flip flop, wig wag, zig zag.
I love Rags, and he loves me. *(hug yourself)* Woof!

Another one that is ever so much fun is "Bounce Upon My Knees." Here's a sample verse:

I had a little mouse who never would eat his cheese.
All he ever wanted to do was bounce upon my knees.
Bounce upon my knees, bounce upon my knees,
All he ever wanted to do was bounce upon my knees.

Every time you sing the word "bounce," the children get to jump, or, for the very young, get gently bounced on the care provider's lap. The song continues with as many rhymes or verses you need:

I had a little elephant who never would say please...
I had a little dog who never would scratch his fleas...
I had a little monkey who never would climb trees...
I had a little horse who never would eat his peas...

I pull out one of the aforementioned animals from a large gunny sack, place it on my knees, and bounce, bounce, bounce!

I Had a Little Mouse

Traditional/Unknown

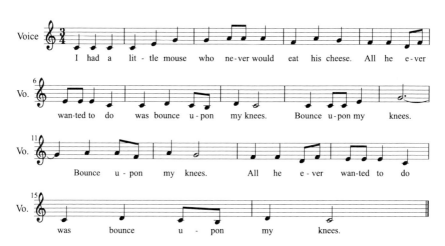

In *Beyond Bedtime Stories: A Parent's Guide to Promoting Reading, Writing, and Other Literacy Skills from Birth to 5,* authors V. Susan Bennett-Armistad, Nell K. Duke, and Annie M. Moses suggest taking a familiar song and adding new letters. Their example is making the chorus of "E-I-E-I-O" in "Old MacDonald Had a Farm" become "Le-Li-Le-Li-Lo." A similar idea would be to try singing "If You're Bappy and You Know It, Bap Your Hands...Bomp Your Feet...Shout Booray!" This also works as a game for Letter of the Day, or as an example of teaching about beginning or ending sounds. "Row, row, row your boat, gently down the stream. But if you see a crocodile, you must surely scream!" Or, "Drive, drive, drive your plane, way up in the sky. But if you see a flying pig, be sure to say, 'Bye, bye!'"

HOWDY DO AND SEE YA SOON

Sometimes I begin and end story time with a series of pictures, encouraging the children to guess the rhyming words. I hold up a picture of a kangaroo, and say, "Howdy do—," then pause until they call out, "kangaroo!" Here's the whole set:

> Howdy do, kangaroo.
> Lookin' fine, porcupine.
> Hello, hello, buffalo.
> Just say hi, pesky fly.
> Glad to see ya, spotted cheetah.
> Stay awhile, crocodile.
> Stick around, basset hound.
> Let's begin, penguin.
> No more rhyme, it's story time!

We close story time with another set:

> See you later, alligator.
> Wave goodbye, butterfly.
> Give a hug, ladybug.
> Blow a kiss, jellyfish.
> See ya soon, raccoon.
> Take care, polar bear.
> Out the door, dinosaur.
> Come again, dolphin.
> No more rhyme, till next story time!

Include nursery rhymes with the babies and toddlers. You're modeling for the parent how important and relevant nursery rhymes are, as well as teaching phonological awareness to the children. A very helpful series is the *Mother Goose Rhyme Time* books by Kimberly K. Faurot, published by Upstart Books. Activities for each of the six early literacy skills are featured under the themes of animals, people, and night. For instance, in the volume about Animals, you'll find the rhyme "Hickory Dickory Dock." Faurot then offers different ways to use the rhyme with babies vs. older children. There are activities such as rhyming, acting out the story, recognition of the letter "H," and craft ideas and patterns.

HEATHER RECOMMENDS

18 Rhyming and Rhythm Books for Story Time Success

Andrews, Sylvia. *Dancing in My Bones.* Each verse invites a different action from the listeners. You can use the tune to "Put Your
Finger in the Air," and everyone will jive along with verses such
as: "I've got bouncing in my knees, in my knees./I've got bouncing in my knees, in my knees./I've got hip-hopping, tip-topping,/
Be-bopping, no-stopping/Bouncing in my knees, in my knees."

Baker, Keith. *Potato Joe.* The potatoes are adorable and the rhyme is
catchy. A great one for children to predict the rhyme.

Cabrera, Jane. *Old Mother Hubbard.* The author tells the nursery
rhyme tale of a dog, a bare cupboard, and so much more.

Durango, Julia. *Cha-Cha Chimps.* These mischievous monkeys are
all about dancing. Listeners get to join in on monkey sounds,
"ee-ee-oo-oo-ah-ah-ah!"

Green, Alison. *The Fox in the Dark.* Animals try to escape from the
fox in the dark in this excellent example of rhyme and rhythm,
plus a repeating phrase that stands out because it doesn't rhyme:
"Then…Rat-a-tat-tat!/Who's that at the door?/'It's me!' squeaks a
voice,/'Is there room for one more?/I don't need much space,/And
my paws are so sore,/I've just run from a fox in the dark.'"

Hillenbrand, Will. *Down by the Station.* A young girl is on her way
to the zoo, picking up baby animals along the way. It's a cumulative rhyme that allows for everyone to join in on, "Puff, puff,/Toot,
toot,/Thrump, thrump,/Peep, peep,/Grump, grump,/Mew, mew,/
Flip, flop,/Bump, bump,/Off we go!"

Ho, Minfong. *Peek! A Thai Hide and Seek.* A father and daughter play
hide and seek in Thailand.

MacDonald, Margaret Read. *Old Woman and Her Pig.* This Appalachian folktale is all about a stubborn pig and a wise woman, and
has a catchy rhyming song for everyone to enjoy.

Norman, Kimberly. *Ten on the Sled.* This is a hilarious romp in the
snow with animals falling off the sled and being engulfed by a
giant snowball. Read it to the tune of "There Were Ten in the Bed."

There are many versions of the old folk song "Over in the Meadow,"
and they can all be sung. The oversized edition of *Over in the
Meadow* by Louise Voce is perfect for large crowds. Try *Over in
the Arctic Where the Cold Winds Blow* or *Over in the Jungle: A*

> *Rainforest Rhyme* by Marianne Berkes. Anna Wilson and Alison Bartlett take children to the savannah in *Over in the Grassland,* and Rebecca Dickinson's *Over in the Hollow* is a fun song for Halloween. *Over in the Garden* by Jennifer Ward features everyone's favorite—bugs!
>
> Sierra, Judy. *Zoozical.* The zoo animals decide to entertain themselves with song and dance during the cold winter.
>
> Weston, Tamson. *Hey, Pancakes!* Three children celebrate the joys of delicious pancakes.
>
> Wilson, Karma. *A Frog in the Bog.* After you've repeated "A small, green frog/on a half-sunk log/in the middle of the bog" at least twice, then pause at the end of each line and let them guess the ending word. I like to sing "And the frog grows a little bit bigger," each time, in a bass voice, inviting them to croak along.

WHAT CAN YOU DO?: AT HOME

There are a bazillion ways to bring songs and rhymes into your child's life. You only need to do those that are fun and comfortable for you. And here's a tip: Children truly do not care if you have a perfectly pitched and glorious voice. They just want to hear you sing along. My father was the stereotype of "Little Johnny One Note," but he always sang along on Christmas carols and at church. I loved hearing his deep voice join in with Mom and my brother, but, trust me, it wasn't a pretty sound. But it was family.

Begin with nursery rhymes. They are rhythmic, silly, and easily remembered. They often make no sense whatsoever, but that doesn't matter. Children love the easy, rocking rhythm, and you'll love how quickly they remember the words on their own. As Susan Straub says in her book *Reading with Babies, Toddlers and Twos: A Guide to Choosing, Reading and Lov-*

> It is now clear that lack of phonological awareness is one of the causes of reading failure. We also know that children who have this knowledge are better readers. While we're not quite sure how this realization begins to dawn in children, we know from much research how to help children become phonologically aware. Basically, it's child's play! You can't explain the concept in a way that will make sense to a preschooler, but you can sure play games that illustrate the concept.
>
> Hirsh-Pasek, Kathy, and Roberta Michnick Golinkoff. *Einstein Never Used Flash Cards: How Our Children REALLY Learn—and Why They Need to Play More and Memorize Less,* p. 108. Emmaus, PA: Rodale, 2003.

ing Books Together, "Because nursery rhymes are so compelling, they can be a wonderfully effective form of shared connection." Make sure you have a collection of nursery rhymes in your home library, such as *My Very First Mother Goose* by Rosemary Wells or *Sylvia Long's Mother Goose.* Check out the library's collection of Annie Kubler's multicultural cardboard series, including *Pat-a-Cake* and *I'm a Dingle Dangle Scarecrow.* Moira Kemp's series of individual rhymes feature large illustrations of adorable animals. My daughter's favorites were the small cardboard collection by Heather Collins because they fit just right in her tiny hands.

Remember that nursery rhymes include more than Mother Goose; you'll find nursery rhymes in almost all cultures. *Pio Peep! Traditional Spanish Nursery Rhymes* selected by Alma Flor Ada and F. Isabel Campoy, *Songs from the Garden of Eden: Jewish Lullabies and Nursery Rhymes* collected by Nathalie Soussana, *Skip across the Ocean: Nursery Rhymes from Around the World* collected by Floella Benjamin, and *Hula Lullaby* by Erin Eitter Kono are just a few examples.

When you're trapped in the car, maybe on a long road trip, take a familiar song and put verses to it about the family. Here's a song all about my family, to the tune of "Farmer in the Dell":

The McNeil's are all here,
The McNeil's like to cheer, Hooray!
Heigh-ho the derry-oh,
The McNeil's are all here.
Heather likes to write,
She writes with all her might,
Heigh-ho, the derry-oh,
Heather likes to write.

Mara likes to read…Jamie likes to sing…Uncle Rod likes to invent…Aunt Jan likes to shop…Cousin Ryan likes to scuba…Cousin Dana likes to fish…Cousin Chris likes to knit…Cousin Amelia likes to dance…Cousin Robert likes to explore.… You can add in grandparents, cousins, even the pets to keep this going for a really long time!

Here's a little song I made up for simple fun in the car, or when waiting in line, or while fixing dinner. It's sung to the tune of "Frere Jacques." Start out by asking your child for a word that you are going to insert into the song. They need to be simple words to begin with. Pretend your child gives you "cat":

We are rhyming, we are rhyming,
Cat, sat, rat. Bat, hat, mat.
Take a simple, short word,

Then we'll make another word,
Cat, sat, rat. Bat, hat, mat.

Once your child becomes familiar with this game, try harder words, such as zebra: "Zebra, tebra, webra." Of course, the last two are not really words at all. They're just for fun, and you can while away the hours making up a story about Tebra the Zebra who always wanted to be a webra. What's a webra? A horse with polka dots!

Try making up very simple poems and have the child finish them. For instance, "When I eat pepper/I always sneeze./So I don't put pepper/On my green round _____." "I am your Daddy/I live in this house./I love to eat cheese/Just like a _____." This is a great game for filling time in the car, since it requires listening as well as phonological awareness.

Jill Frankel Hauser describes the "Clap, Clap, Pat" game in her book *Wow! I'm Reading! Fun Activities to Make Reading Happen.* First, practice with your child the pattern of clapping hands twice, then patting knees once. Then the adult says a rhyming word on the "Pat." The child will go next, saying a word that rhymes. For instance, "Clap, clap, (*pat*) dish." The child follows with "Clap, clap, (*pat*) fish."

If you would like even more ideas, read *All Together Singing in the Kitchen: Creative Ways to Make & Listen to Music as a Family* by Nerissa and Katryna Nields. You'll find tips on everything musical, from making

---

HEATHER RECOMMENDS

16 Books for Rhyming Fun at Home

Alborough, Jez. *Where's My Teddy?* This is a case of hilarious mistaken identity, when a boy and a bear mix up their teddy bears.

Anderson, Peggy Perry. *Chuck's Truck.* Huck the horse, and Luck the duck, and the chicken that goes "cluck" all ride with Chuck in the truck.

Bloom, Suzanne. *Bus for Us.* On the first day of school a girl asks Gus which vehicle is the "bus for us."

Bunting, Eve. *Flower Garden.* A girl makes a window garden for someone special.

Chaconas, Dori. *Don't Slam the Door!* A girl warns everyone that if they slam the door it will begin a chain reaction of chaos.

Dylan, Bob. *Man Gave Names to All the Animals.* Jim Arnosky's lush illustrations of more than 170 animals perfectly interpret this catchy song by one of the great folk song collectors of all time.

George, Kristine O'Connell. *Up!* A toddler and her father play together.

Geringer, Laura. *Boom Boom Go Away!* A gnome in his home, an elf on the shelf, a knight beside the light, plus wonderful sounds such as bong, ding, and boom, make this a rhyming, rollicking, and noisy story for participation—but not just before bed.

Heider, Frederich H., and Carl Kress. *There's a Train Out for Dreamland.* Jane and Brooke Dyer's illustrations make this simple song about the train "that rides on a peppermint rail" and is run "by a chocolate brown bear" a perfect lullaby story.

Johnston, Tony. *Sticky People.* It's fun to be sticky people with lots of sticky fun. "Sticky people love the mud, such/Goopy-oopy-ooze./They scoop it, flop it into mud cakes/With their little shoes!"

Lewin, Betsy. *Where Is Tippy Toes?* An adorable orange cat explores the world during the day, but nobody knows where he goes at night.

Mitton, Tony. *A Very Curious Bear.* A young bear is filled with questions about the world, and his parent has all the right answers.

O'Hair, Margaret. *My Kitten.* By predicting the rhymes and looking at the illustrations, young children will be reading this text about a rascally kitten in no time.

Pym, Tasha. *Have You Ever Seen a Sneep?* Made-up words such as sneep and floon could lead to you and your child making up your own books about imaginary creatures.

Sloat, Teri. *This Is the House That Was Tidy & Neat.* With a title like that, I'm sure you can think of many opportunities to share this cumulative tale of active children and their pets.

Walton, Rick. *The Bear Came Over to My House.* Not only is the bear adorable, but it's great fun to guess the rhyme on the next page.

up songs about the family, to adapting songs for lullabies or holidays, to playing games that use songs. Plus, there's directions for making home-made musical instruments, chords for popular traditional folk songs, and a CD of the Nields performing many of the songs mentioned in the book.

Finally, don't forget about lullabies. Lullabies are meant to be soothing, gentle encouragement for a child to prepare for sleep. The rocking rhythm, the quiet words, and the soft melody combine to relax both parent and child. If you're not comfortable singing, then select some of the wonderful recordings available at libraries to play for your child. Or read aloud a rhyming lullaby story, such as *Time for Bed* by Mem Fox, *Hush: A Thai Lullaby* by Minfong Ho, or *All the Pretty Little Horses: A Traditional Lullaby,*

Nursery rhymes are the perfect way to begin having fun with rhyming words and demonstrating how words can change. Jamie especially loved the ones by Heather Collins because they fit in her hands just right.

illustrated by Linda Saport. You'll send your child off to dreamland, while still encouraging literacy through rhythm and rhyme.

Like most parents, I was always uncomfortable with the traditional lullaby of the child in a cradle that falls from the tree. The idea is to have your child in your lap, and you gently drop her between your knees, then lift her to your chest for a loving hug. But I rewrote the words when Jamie came into my life, and I still sing it to her before turning out the light:

Rock-a-bye, Jamie, in my arms.
I will keep you safe from harm.
I will hold you close to my heart,
And love you forever, right from the start.

I hope you can use this lullaby with your own sweet miracle.

BIBLIOGRAPHY

For Librarians, Teachers, and Parents

Bennett-Armistad, V. Susan, Nell K. Duke, and Annie M. Moses. *Beyond Bedtime Stories: A Parent's Guide to Promoting Reading, Writing, and Other Literacy Skills from Birth to 5.* New York: Scholastic, 2007.

Hauser, Jill. *Wow! I'm Reading!: Fun Activities to Make Reading Happen.* Charlotte, VT: Williamson Publishing Co., 2000.

Hirsh-Pasek, Kathy, and Roberta Michnick Golinkoff. *Einstein Never Used Flash Cards: How Our Children REALLY Learn—and Why They Need to Play More and Memorize Less.* Emmaus, PA: Rodale, 2003.

Nields, Nerissa, and Katryna Nields. *All Together Singing in the Kitchen: Creative Ways to Make & Listen to Music as a Family.* Boston, MA: Trumpeter, 2011.

Straub, Susan. *Reading with Babies, Toddlers and Twos: A Guide to Choosing, Reading and Loving Books Together.* Naperville, IL: Sourcebooks, 2006.

For Children

Ada, Alma Flor, and F. Isabel Campoy. *Pio Peep! Traditional Spanish Nursery Rhymes.* New York: HarperCollins, 2003.

Alborough, Jez. *Where's My Teddy?* Cambridge, MA: Candlewick Press, 1992.

Anderson, Peggy Perry. *Chuck's Truck.* Boston, MA: Houghton Mifflin, 2006.

Andrews, Sylvia. *Dancing in My Bones.* New York: HarperFestival, 2001.

Baker, Keith. *Potato Joe.* Orlando, FL: Harcourt, 2008.

Beaumont, Karen. *No Sleep for the Sheep.* Boston, MA: Houghton Mifflin Harcourt, 2011.

Benjamin, Floella. *Skip across the Ocean: Nursery Rhymes from Around the World.* New York: Orchard Books, 1995.

Berkes, Marianne. *Over in the Jungle: A Rainforest Rhyme.* Nevada City, CA: Dawn Publications, 2007.

Berkes, Marianne. *Over in the Arctic Where the Cold Winds Blow.* Nevada City, CA: Dawn Publications, 2008.

Bloom, Suzanne. *Bus for Us.* Honesdale, PA: Boyds Mills Press, 2001.

Bunting, Eve. *Flower Garden.* San Diego, CA: Harcourt Brace Jovanavich, 1994.

Cabrera, Jane. *Old Mother Hubbard.* New York: Holiday House, 2008.

Chaconas, Dori. *Don't Slam the Door!* Somerville, MA: Candlewick Press, 2010.

Collins, Heather. *Eensy Weensy Spider.* New York: Kids Can Press, 1997.

Collins, Heather. *Hickory Dickory Dock.* New York: Kids Can Press, 1997.

Collins, Heather. *One, Two, Buckle My Shoe.* New York: Kids Can Press, 1997.

Collins, Heather. *Rock-a-Bye, Baby.* New York: Kids Can Press, 2000.

Collins, Heather. *Row, Row, Row Your Boat.* New York: Kids Can Press, 2000.

Collins, Heather. *Twinkle, Twinkle, Little Star.* New York: Kids Can Press, 2000.

Collins, Heather. *Hey, Diddle Diddle.* New York: Kids Can Press, 2003.

Collins, Heather. *Jack and Jill.* New York: Kids Can Press, 2003.

Collins, Heather. *Little Miss Muffet.* New York: Kids Can Press, 2003.

Collins, Heather. *Pat-a-Cake.* New York: Kids Can Press, 2003.

De Regniers, Beatrice Schenk. *What Did You Put in Your Pocket?* New York: HarperCollins, 2003.

Dickinson, Rebecca. *Over in the Hollow.* San Francisco, CA: Chronicle Books, 2009.

Down by the Bay. Columbus, OH: School Specialty Pub., 2007.

Durango, Julia. *Cha-cha Chimps.* New York: Simon & Schuster Books for Young Readers, 2006.

Dylan, Bob. *Man Gave Names to All the Animals.* New York: Sterling, 2010.

Faurot, Kimberly K. *Mother Goose Rhyme Time Animals.* Madison, WI: Highsmith, Inc., 2006.

Faurot, Kimberly K. *Mother Goose Rhyme Time Night.* Madison, WI: Highsmith Inc., 2006.

Faurot, Kimberly K. *Mother Goose Rhyme Time People.* Madison, WI: Highsmith, Inc., 2006.

Fischer, Scott. *Jump!* New York: Simon & Schuster Books for Young Readers, 2010.

Fox, Mem. *Time for Bed.* San Diego, CA: Harcourt Brace, 1993.

Fox, Mem. *The Magic Hat.* San Diego, CA: Harcourt, 2002.

George, Kristine O'Connell. *Up!* New York: Clarion Books, 2005.

Geringer, Laura. *Boom Boom Go Away!* New York: Atheneum Books for Young Readers, 2010.

Green, Alison. *The Fox in the Dark.* Wilton, CT: Tiger Tales, 2010.

Heider, Frederick H., and Carl Kress. *There's a Train Out for Dreamland.* New York: Harper, 2010.

Hillenbrand, Will. *Down by the Station.* San Diego, CA: Harcourt Brace, 1999.

Ho, Minfong. *Hush! A Thai Lullaby.* New York: Orchard Books, 1996.

Ho, Minfong. *Peek! A Thai Hide and Seek.* Cambridge, MA: Candlewick Press, 2004.

Hoberman, Mary Ann. *Miss Mary Mack.* Boston, MA: Little, Brown, 1998.

Hoberman, Mary Ann. *The Eensy Weensy Spider*. Boston, MA: Little, Brown, 2000.

Hoberman, Mary Ann. *There Once Was a Man Named Michael Finnegan*. Boston, MA: Little, Brown, 2001.

Hoberman, Mary Ann. *Bill Grogan's Goat*. Boston, MA: Little, Brown, 2002.

Hoberman, Mary Ann. *The Lady with the Alligator Purse*. New York: Little, Brown, 2003.

Johnston, Tony. *Sticky People*. New York: HarperCollins, 2006.

Kemp, Moira. *Baa, Baa Black Sheep*. Mankato, MN: Child's World, 2010.

Kemp, Moira. *Hey, Diddle Diddle*. Mankato, MN: Child's World, 2010.

Kemp, Moira. *Hickory Dickory Dock*. Mankato, MN: Child's World, 2010.

Kemp, Moira. *This Little Piggy*. Mankato, MN: Child's World, 2010.

Kono, Erin Eitter. *Hula Lullaby*. New York: Little, Brown, 2005.

Kubler, Annie. *I'm a Dingle-Dangle Scarecrow*. Auburn, ME: Child's Play, 2003.

Kubler, Annie. *Pat-a-Cake*. Swindon: Child's Play, 2010.

Lewin, Betsy. *Where Is Tippy Toes?* New York: Atheneum Books for Young Readers, 2010.

London, Jonathan. *I'm a Truck Driver*. New York: Henry Holt, 2010.

Long, Sylvia. *Sylvia Long's Mother Goose*. San Francisco, CA: Chronicle Books, 1999.

MacDonald, Margaret Read. *Old Woman and Her Pig: An Appalachian Folktale*. New York: HarperCollins, 2007.

Martin, Bill, Jr., and Michael Sampson. *Kitty Cat, Kitty Cat, Are You Going to Sleep?* Tarrytown, NY: Marshall Cavendish Children's, 2011.

McCall, Francis, and Patricia Keeler. *A Huge Hog Is a Big Pig*. New York: Greenwillow Books, 2002.

Mitton, Tony. *A Very Curious Bear*. New York: Random House Children's Books, 2009.

Morales, Melita. *Jam and Honey*. Berkeley, CA: Tricycle Press, 2011.

Norman, Kimberly. *Ten on the Sled*. New York: Sterling, 2010.

O'Hair, Margaret. *My Kitten*. Tarrytown, NY: Marshall Cavendish Children's, 2011.

Pinkney, Jerry. *Three Little Kittens*. New York: Dial Books for Young Readers, 2010.

Pym, Tasha. *Have You Ever Seen a Sneep?* New York: Farrar, Straus and Giroux, 2009.

Riley, Linnea. *Mouse Mess*. New York: Blue Sky Press, 1997.

Saport, Linda. *All the Pretty Little Horses: A Traditional Lullaby*. New York: Clarion Books, 1999.

Sierra, Judy. *Zoozical*. New York: Alfred A. Knopf, 2011.

Silberg, Jackie. *Reading Games*. Beltsville, MD: Gryphon House, 2005.

Sloat, Teri. *This Is the House That Was Tidy & Neat.* New York: Henry Holt, 2005.

Soussana, Nathalie. *Songs from the Garden of Eden: Jewish Lullabies and Nursery Rhymes.* Montreal: Secret Mountain, 2009.

Thomas, Jan. *Rhyming Dust Bunnies.* New York: Beach Lane Books, 2009.

Voce, Louise. *Over in the Meadow: A Counting Rhyme.* Cambridge, MA: Candlewick Press, 2000.

Walton, Rick. *The Bear Came Over to My House.* New York: Putnam, 2001.

Walton, Rick. *Bunny School: A Learning Fun-for-All.* New York: HarperCollins, 2005.

Ward, Jennifer. *Over in the Garden.* Flagstaff, AZ: Rising Moon, 2002.

Wells, Rosemary. *My Very First Mother Goose.* Cambridge, MA: Candlewick Press, 1996.

Weston, Tamson. *Hey, Pancakes!* San Diego, CA: Harcourt, 2003.

Williams, Suzanne. *Ten Naughty Little Monkeys.* New York: HarperCollins, 2007.

Wilson, Anna, and Alison Bartlett. *Over in the Grasslands.* Boston, MA: Little, Brown and Company, 1999.

Wilson, Karma. *A Frog in the Bog.* New York: Margaret K. McElderry Books, 2003.

WEBLIOGRAPHY

http://kids.niehs.nih.gov/games/songs/childrens/fishiesmid.htm
http://www.nichd.nih.gov/publications/pubs/PRF-teachers-k-3.cfm

Chapter Six

B IS BUH AND OTHER ALPHABET DISCOVERIES

A fellow librarian was telling the story of *The Three Billy Goats Gruff* to a room full of preschoolers at the library. Several of the children already knew the story, and were eagerly chiming in when she asked for participation. "The first billy goat came to the bridge and started across, eager to eat the luscious green grass on the other side. Her little hooves went—." She paused, waiting to see if anyone knew the traditional, "Trip! Trap! Trip! Trap!"

"I know! I know!" called out a listener. "T—T—T—Trick or treat!"

Who knows? Maybe that approach would have worked much better with the troll.

Almost every young child knows "The Alphabet Song." "Sing your ABC's," says the proud parent, and the child sings it loud and clear, all the while wondering if an Elemenohpee can be found at a pet store, and if a Wieunzee is something that goes really fast.

In order to be ready to learn to read, a child needs to know that B sounds like "buh." He needs to know that each letter has its own distinct sound, and sometimes more than one sound. Recognizing letters, playing with letters, and being able to write letters will make learning to read much easier. A child can then sound out the mysterious new word "octopus" by adding the sounds that he has become familiar with through books and games.

Letter knowledge is best developed after a toddler has become familiar with books, has a vocabulary that allows for conversation and questions, and is aware that print is everywhere and that it has meaning. He should already be playing with words through rhyming and singing. When all those skills are in place, playing games with letters, introducing letter sounds, and identifying letters in words will be "as easy as A B C."

WHAT CAN YOU DO?: AT THE PRESCHOOL, AT THE LIBRARY, AND AT HOME

This skill is best taught through games and creative activities that encourage play while learning, rather than drills with flash cards or rote memorizing. Rather than dividing out preschool, home, and the library, I'm combining all of the locations where the child can be introduced to letters because most of these strategies can be done anywhere. You would simply adapt it to fit the design of your day or the focus at your location.

Alphabet Books

Alphabet books abound. From endangered animals to methods of transportation, from terrifying dinosaurs to adorable kittens, you can find an alphabet book about almost anything. They range from simple to abstract, and often feature glorious art at the expense of a text that has absolutely nothing to do with what a young child is ready to understand, enjoy, or process. Beware and be wary of alphabet books.

That said, definitely introduce the alphabet through books, using careful selection by considering the interest and age of the child. For the infant, 0–18 months, simple is best. Avoid books that feature words not related to the primary sound of the letter, such as "cheetah" for the letter "c." Select ones that feature capital letters, or both capital and lower case. Illustrations should be clear of clutter, so the child can easily focus on familiar object(s) that relate to the sound. And remember, it's very likely that these will end up in the child's mouth so cloth, board, and puffy books are best.

HEATHER RECOMMENDS

10 Simple Alphabet Books for Baby

Baby's First Library ABC. Very simple, bold illustrations for each letter.

Carle, Eric. *Eric Carle's ABC.* One item per letter, plus flaps to lift.

Cousins, Lucy. *Maisy's ABC.* Everyone's favorite mouse leads baby through the alphabet.

Eastman, P. D. *The Alphabet Book.* Zany illustrations add fun to the alphabet.

Katz, Susan B. *ABC, Baby Me.* Multicultural parents and children depict many ways to express love.

Munari, Bruno. *Bruno Munari's ABC.* A blue butterfly, an ant on an apple, and more, in bright, simple illustrations.

Pechter, Lesley Wynne. *Alligator Bear Crab: A Baby's ABC.* Each animal is cuter than the next.

Priddy, Roger. *B Is for Bear.* A touch and feel book, with wonderful photographs of babies and toddlers.

Priddy, Roger. *Happy Baby ABC.* A soft touch book with bold photographs.

Van Fleet, Matthew. *Alphabet.* Textures, tabs, and more than 100 animals and plants.

By the time the child is a toddler, you can select books that feature a story along with the alphabet, showing how much fun letters can be as they dance across the pages.

HEATHER RECOMMENDS

Seven Alphabet Books for Toddlers

Andreae, Giles. *K Is for Kissing a Cool Kangaroo.* A riotous romp of animals and objects, from an aardvark, an armadillo, an antelope, and an anteater trying to pluck an apple from a tree to a sleepy zebra mother tucked around her child, who, in turn, is tucked around her stuffed zebra toy. All of the books illustrated by Guy Parker-Rees, such as this one, are limitless journeys of discovery, with surprises hidden everywhere in the pictures.

Aylesworth, Jim. *Little Bitty Mousie.* A mouse explores the house, plus there's a repeating verse, "Tip-tip tippy tippy/Went her little mousie toes./Sniff-sniff sniffy sniffy went her little mousie nose."

Baker, Keith. *LMNO Peas.* Tiny peas demonstrate the alphabet in a multitude of ways, from acrobats to zoologists.

Basher, Simon. *ABC Kids.* Uses abundant alliteration to enhance vocabulary, as well as teach the letters: "Franklin frightens fiendish fish," and "Queenie questions quivering quails."

Brown, Margaret Wise. *Sleepy ABC.* Karen Katz's multicultural illustrations and gentle words prepare a child for sleep: "K is for Kissing your mother goodnight/L is for Listening when they turn out

the light/M is for Mother who tucks you in tight/N is for the dark
and starry Night."

Howland, Naomi. *ABC Drive: A Car Trip Alphabet.* Sounds and
sights a child can see from his car seat.

Rose, Deborah Lee. *Into the A, B, Sea.* Not only are the collage illustrations by Steve Jenkins extremely colorful and clever, but the
text stretches a child's knowledge: "where **I**nsects prance and **J**el-
lies dance/where **K**elp forests sway and **L**eopard sharks prey."

Preschool children are ready for even more creativity and thought within
the concepts of the alphabet book so stories can be more complex.

HEATHER RECOMMENDS

Nine Alphabet Books for Preschool

Aylesworth, Jim. *Old Black Fly.* A disgusting, yet somehow still adorable, fly licks up **F**rosting, **n**ibbles on the **N**oodles, and **s**niffs the
Salami. Stephen Gammell's illustrations are hilarious, plus there is
the bonus of a reoccurring phrase that invites participation, "Shoo
fly! Shoo fly! Shoo!"

Bottner, Barbara. *An Annoying ABC.* A chain reaction of bad behavior in a multicultural classroom leads to plenty of action.

Doyle, Charlotte. *The Bouncing, Dancing, Galloping ABC.* Active
children do a variety of motions, from climbing to quacking.

Murray, Alison. *Apple Pie ABC.* Rare words such as "ogle" and "quietly
determined" make this an excellent alphabet and vocabulary book.

Pearle, Ida. *A Child's Day: An Alphabet of Play.* A day filled with creative activities that have nothing to do with technology or electric-
ity. The book is very simple, but can lead to many ideas for child
and parent to share together, such as **M**ixing batter or **R**iding an
imaginary zebra.

Rankin, Laura. *The Handmade Alphabet.* Teaches the American Sign
Language alphabet, so a hand in the pose of the letter A is also
holding asparagus, and the hand demonstrating P is dipping its
fingers into paint.

Sobel, June. *B Is for Bulldozer: A Construction ABC*. Perfect for anyone who enjoys all the machinery required to build an amusement park.

Werner, Sharon, and Sarah Forss. *Alphabeasties and Other Amazing Types*. Animals made of different fonts and types of the letters, plus pictures of various objects illustrated the same way, make this a fascinating book to explore.

Zuckerman, Andrew. *Creature ABC*. Deceptively simple alphabet book that has more than you expect to discover and discuss. The photographs of animals are absolutely breathtaking, from a close-up of an elephant's foot to the majesty of a wolf gazing into the distance. And just when you think you have figured out the pattern Zuckerman throws in a switch. For instance, you get to the letter I and there are ants crawling across the page. Huh? Turn the page, and you discover the word "insect" with photographs of bee, grasshopper, beetle, and ant on the double spread, which is a great way to begin a conversation with a child about all the many kinds of insects that decorate our world.

A LITERACY-RICH DAY: 26 WAYS TO CELEBRATE THE ALPHABET

Choose the letter of the day. If you're at home, begin this game with the first letter of your child's first name. If this is at preschool, choose whatever letter you want to feature all day. If you're at the library, select one or two of the following activities to enhance story time. Have a magnet letter for the refrigerator, or a giant foam letter for school or library, so everyone knows what is being celebrated.

Let's pretend the child's name is **B**ethany, or that you are honoring the **b**irthdays of the month at your preschool. Here are 26 ways you could play "Letter of the Day" with B:

1. Start the day with **b**ananas at **b**reakfast. Then have fun with the crazy rhyme "Go Bananas." You'll find it (and many other songs) at www.kididdles.org.

"Go Bananas"

Bananas unite! *(put hands together overhead)*
Bananas split! *(hands out to side)*
Go bananas! *(turn in circle, waving arms for next four lines)*
Go, go bananas!

Go bananas!
Go, go bananas!
Bananas to the left *(point left)*
Bananas to the right *(point right)*
Peel your banana and, mmmmm, take a bite! *(peel and bite
   banana)*

2. Sing "I'm **B**ringing Home a **B**aby **B**umblebee." (http://www.ki-
   diddles.com/lyrics/b002.html)

3. Play **b**all.

4. Take a walk around the neighborhood. Look for things that
   begin with B. A **b**ridge? Someone playing **b**aseball? A **b**lack cat?
   A **b**ench? Write everything down, and when you get home or
   back to the preschool, write down all the words. Have the children draw the pictures. Create a cover for their **B B**ook, punch
   three holes on the side, string yarn through, and, ta-dah! Each
   child has her very own **b**ook to take home and read.

5. Play "I Spy," asking only for things that begin with B, or a color
   that begins with B. Or, you can ask for the sounds of letters. "I
   Spy something that starts with the buh sound and we read it at
   story time." Or, with older children, you could actually spell it
   out. "I Spy something that is spelled b-o-o-k."

6. Have a treasure hunt. If this is at home, give your child a **b**ag.
   If it's at the preschool, assign one child to carry the **b**ag, while
   others explore the room, add to the **b**ag anything they can find
   that begins with the letter of the day. Possibilities are a **b**arrette,
   a **b**rown hat, a teddy **b**ear, a **b**attery, and so on.

7. Use the tune to "Farmer in the Dell," and make up B phrases:

Betty loves balloons,
Betty loves balloons,
Be be bop and buh buh buh,
Betty loves balloons.
Betty eats bananas,
Betty eats bananas,
Be be bop and buh buh buh,
Betty eats bananas.

8. For lunch, have peanut **b**utter sandwiches and **b**lueberries.

9. Blow bubbles. Sing the following rhyme, to the tune of "Row,
   Row, Row Your Boat":

Blow, blow, blow some bubbles,
Do the bubble hop. *(jump up and pop the bubbles)*
Jump so high, until they pop,
Then you have to stop.

10. Play the "Suitcase" game. This is a word game that requires a good memory. Someone starts with "I packed my suitcase and in it I put a ball." The next person says the same beginning, has to remember all the words that came before and add one on. So the sentence might get to "I packed my suitcase and in it I put a ball, a bat, a banana, a bear, a boat, and a boy."

11. Play "Here's My **B**ag." I intersperse this attention grabber throughout story time. I fill a bag with objects that begin with our featured letter, such as a toy **b**ee, a **b**anana, a ladybug **b**eetle puppet, and a **b**all. I sing the following:

Here's my bag with something inside.
What could it be?
I'll pull it out so you can look.
Tell me what you see.

Here's My Bag

Heather McNeil

Sometimes I give hints and they have to guess. "It's begins with the letter b, and it buzzes." Sometimes they are objects within objects, such as a **b**ean inside a small **b**ag being held by a **b**ear. It's amazing how this activity immediately quiets everyone down and refocuses them if they've gotten a little bit rowdy during story time.

12. If you're at home, wear clothes that begin with the letter, either in color or name, such as **b**lack shoes, **b**lue jeans, and a **b**elt. At the school or library, just point out whoever is wearing some-

thing that matches the letter of the day. Or you could play "If You're Wearing," to the tune of "Mary Had a Little Lamb":

If you're wearing blue today, blue today, blue today,
If you're wearing blue today, please stand up.

The child(ren) stands up, everyone claps, then you move on to something else that begins with B. "If you're feeling **b**rave today…" "If you have a teddy **b**ear…"

13. Sing "My **B**onnie Lies Over the Ocean." Begin with everyone sitting down. When a word begins with B, everyone stands up. The next time a word begins with B, everyone sits down. And so on, up and down throughout the song. It's harder than you think, and always makes young and old laugh a lot. You can listen to the tune at www.kididdles.org.

My **B**onnie *(stand)* lies over the ocean,
My **B**onnie *(sit)* lies over the sea.
My **B**onnie *(stand)* lies over the ocean,
Oh, **b**ring *(sit)* **b**ack *(stand)* my **B**onnie *(sit)* to me.
Bring *(stand)* **b**ack *(sit)*, **b**ring *(stand)* **b**ack, *(sit)*
Oh, **b**ring *(stand)* **b**ack *(sit)* my **B**onnie *(stand)* to me, to me.
Bring *(sit)* **b**ack *(stand)*, **b**ring *(sit)* **b**ack *(stand)*,
Oh, **b**ring *(sit)* **b**ack *(stand)* my **B**onnie *(sit)* to me.

14. After nap, **b**ounce **b**alloons.

15. Play "Belly Button" on the CD that accompanies the book *Philadelphia Chickens* by Sandra **B**oynton.

16. When you're out doing errands, play literacy games in the car. Look for the letter **b** on license plates, or road signs. Make up stories about the people in the next car, with everyone's name beginning with the letter **b**. "Do you see that **b**lue car? Inside are **B**obbity, his wife, **B**ippity, and their little boy, **B**oo. They're on their way to the **b**each so they can play **b**all and eat ____." If your child is old enough, pause there and see if she can offer an idea, such as "**b**agels!"

17. Play "Word Bird." Help your child decorate a box, basket, or bag to look like a bird. You sing the following, to the tune of "Frere Jacques":

What's the word
To feed Word Bird?

It starts with B
B sounds like Buh
It's round and it rolls
It's over by the chair,
What's the word
To feed Word Bird?

Your child guesses "Ball," and gets to "feed" the Word Bird by putting the ball in the container. You can make this more difficult as your child gets older and wiser:

What's the word
To feed Word Bird?
It ends with B
B sounds like Buh
It's where your sister sleeps
It's where you used to sleep,
What's the word
To feed Word Bird?

Your child guesses cri**b**. Of course, you can't put the "crib" into Word Bird, but you could write the word out on a card and your child gets to feed that into the container instead. (By the way, this is also a great game for phonological awareness, which you'll find in Chapter Five. Just change to a rhyming game. "What's the word/To feed Word Bird?/It rhymes with cat/It rhymes with rat?/I wear it on my head/It keeps my head warm/What's the word?/To feed Word Bird? Hat!)

18. Rename everyone and everything all day long by changing the first letter to B. For instance, toast becomes **b**oast. Amelia becomes **B**amelia. Grocery store becomes **b**rocery **b**ore. Dad becomes **B**ad! Harder than you think, but lots of silly fun.

19. Throughout the day read **b**ooks. Hooray! Some possibilities are *My Bear and Me* by Barbara Maitland, in which a curly haired girl describes all the reasons she loves her bear; *I Love Bugs* by Emma Dodd; *Ugh! A Bug* by Mary Bono after searching for bugs outside; or *Teeny Weeny Bop* by Margaret Read MacDonald, which is a cumulative tale of a lonely woman trading pets to find the right companion. I challenge you to keep a straight face as you read *Hello, My Name Is Bob* by Linas Alsenas, a tongue-in-cheek tale of a **b**oring **b**ear whose idea of a good time is to

Letter symbols and sounds are abstract and very easy to confuse. Offering varied, multisensory experiences that link each letter to its sound and having the child practice them over a long period of time leads to mastery of the letter-sound match that's essential to reading.

Hauser, Jill. *Wow! I'm Reading!,* p. 81. Charlotte, VT: Williamson Publishing Co., 2000.

count toothpicks and dust plants. And sit. And sit. "Sitting is fun, isn't it?"

20. Create the letter **B** in a variety of ways. Draw it with finger paint. Make it with several bodies lying on the floor. Create it with string. Trace it in pudding, then eat it up.

21. Make a collage. Cut out pictures of objects that begin with **b** from magazines and glue them into a giant **B** collage. Or, give the child an inexpensive disposable camera, have her take pictures all day, then get them printed to make the collage the next day.

22. Play with rhymes that have the letter **B** in them. Here's one I made up for the story time I do with toddlers, using the tune to the first two lines of "Twinkle, Twinkle, Little Star":

Bears, bears, everywhere bears.
Bears, bears, sitting on chairs,
Bears, bears, everywhere bears.
Bears, bears, climbing up stairs,
Bears, bears, everywhere bears.
Bears, bears, giving out stares.
Bears, bears, everywhere bears.
Bears, bears, combing their hairs,
Bears, bears, everywhere bears.
Bears, bears, everywhere bears.

23. Make up tongue twisters. **B**elinda **b**rought **b**ears **b**ouncy **b**alls and **b**lue **b**ubbles.

24. At home, take a **b**ath before **b**ed. While your child is in the water have him draw the letter **b** with **b**athtub paints.

25. Read *Bedtime for Bear* by Brett Helquist, a hilarious story of two raccoons determined to get their friend Bear outside to play before he begins sleeping for the winter.

26. A perfect lullaby to end the day would be anything with the word **b**aby, such as "Hush, Little Baby."

Select a few of the aforementioned activities for a day, not all of them. Otherwise, your child will hate that letter by the time you get through them all! Mix them up, and select different ones for different letters. Maybe you prefer "Letter of the Week," and you do just two each day, for seven days. Whatever works for you is what will make these activities successful in teaching a child letter knowledge.

STILL MORE FUN WITH LETTERS

Make a Word

In a classroom setting, have everyone wear headbands, or cards on craft sticks, decorated with letters of the alphabet (one letter per child). Then see if they can find other letters to make a word. When they do, they stand together. It would require assistance from the teacher for the younger ones. "I want to put together the word Frog. I need an F. Who has the F-F-F-F sound?" Keep at it until all four children have come together to create the word frog. For older preschoolers, they might be able to gather up the right people on their own, especially if the word is on the board for them to see.

Missing Letters

Try saying words with the first letter obviously missing. "Children, let's get ready for a nack." You might have to say it a few obvious times before finally someone will chime in, "No, not nack. Snack!" "That's right. What letter was missing?"

ABC Book

At home you can make a personal ABC book. Use a notebook, filled with 26 blank construction paper pages. Print one letter of the alphabet on each page. Then the child creates a collage, cutting out magazine pictures, or words from the newspaper, or stickers—anything that begins with that letter.

Month by Month

Read together *Jump for Joy: A Book of Months* by Megan Halsey. The book is extremely simple, with alliteration used for activities with each month, such as "Jump for joy in January" and "Do a dance in December." Now make up your own book together, highlighting the things you like to do each month in your family or school. "Make a mess in March," then draw pictures of stamping in mud puddles.

Sing and Pass

At preschool, make giant capital letters and attach them to a craft stick. Choose one letter and brainstorm lots of words that begin with that letter. Seat the children in a circle, and pass the letter around as you sing the following, to the tune of "Skip to My Lou":

A, A, the letter A,
A, A, sounds like "aah."
A, A, the letter A,
A is the letter for _____.

Whoever is holding the letter fills in the blank with a word that begins with the letter.

You'll find more ideas for games and activities in a publication found online called "America Reads Challenge: Read*Write*Now!: Activities for Reading and Writing Fun"; http://www2.ed.gov/Family/RWN/Activ97/index.html. This was a joint project of the U.S. Department of Education, the American Library Association, Pizza Hut, Inc., Scholastic Inc., and Reading Is Fundamental, Inc. The publication is in the public domain, is divided by grade level, from birth through grade six, and the activities are simple and inexpensive. Here are a few of the games I particularly recommend:

- **Same Sounds Game.** Write two sets of capital letters on index cards. Mix them up, then turn them face side down. Each person draws two cards, and identifies the sound of the letter. If the two match, you get to keep the cards. If not, the cards get mixed back into the pile. The goal of the game is to pick up all the cards (p. 19).

- **Letter-Sound Grab Bag.** Place some of the aforementioned letter cards that your child is familiar with in a paper bag. Say "Start," and the child reaches into the bag, pulls out one card, and says the sound. He keeps picking cards until one minute is up. If he doesn't know the sound, the letter goes back in the bag. The goal is to get more and more letters in one minute each time you play (p. 20).

- **Letter Swap.** Print out one simple word in large print. On another paper, print the same word, without the first letter. For instance, LOG on one paper, and __OG on the other. Now print a set of letters on cards that could fit onto the blank in front of OG. Place the word LOG above the word __OG. Explain to your child that she is to try and make new words with the letters you have printed out. She places them in the blank space, says the sound, and the new word. When this game becomes too simple, try doing the same with the end of the word, or the middle (p. 25).

MORE BOOKS TO CELEBRATE LETTERS

You can always find a book to feature whatever letter you are celebrating. If it's the letter G, select a story about a goose or a gorilla. If the letter is R, look for a rabbit or a rock. Those whose titles or characters feature alliteration make it even more obvious, such as some of the following titles.

HEATHER RECOMMENDS

52 Books to Celebrate the 26 Letters

A. Blackstone, Stella. *Alligator Alphabet.* This presents the entire alphabet, using animals for each letter.

A. Mwalimu. *Awful Aardvark.* Aardvark's snoring keeps everyone awake.

B. Mwenye Hadithi. *Baby Baboon.* This original African folktale features not only the B sound, but also lazy leopard and hopping hare.

B. Massie, Diane Redfield. *The Baby Beebee Bird.* A bird who sings all night long keeps the zoo animals awake.

C. Mockford, Caroline. *Cleo's Color Book.* Cleo the cat is looking for colors in this book just right for babies and toddlers.

C. Wilson, Karma. *The Cow Loves Cookies.* All the other farm animals eat what they're supposed to eat, but the cow only wants cookies.

D. Dodd, Emma. *Dog's Colorful Day.* Counting and colors are presented as Dog goes exploring.

D. Hindley, Judy. *Do Like a Duck Does.* A fox pretends he's a duck, but the mother duck is smart enough to out-trick him.

E. D'Amico, Carmelo. *Ella, the Elegant Elephant.* Ella thinks that wearing her grandmother's good luck hat will make her feel better on her first day of school.

E. McKee, David. *Elmer.* Most elephants are boring grey, but Elmer is different.

F. Bruce, Lisa. *Fran's Flower.* Fran and her dog Fred are trying to grow a flower.

F. Stevens, Janet, and Susan Stevens Crummel. *The Great Fuzz Frenzy.* What is the green round thing that has fallen into the prairie dogs' burrows?

G. Emberly, Ed. *Go Away, Big Green Monster.* Children absolutely love this classic story that proves that anyone can be brave enough.

G. Freedman, Claire. *Gooseberry Goose.* A goose is so busy having fun he doesn't realize that winter is coming.

H. Mwenye Hadithi. *Hungry Hyena.* Why does the hyena slink across the savanna while the eagle soars overhead?

H. Waddell, Martin. *The Happy Hedgehog Band.* Harry and Helen start up the hedgehog band, but pretty soon all the animals want to join in.

I. Lionni, Leo. *Inch by Inch.* An inchworm inches away from being eaten.

I. Mallett, David. *Inch by Inch: The Garden Song.* This is the classic song about the delight of growing a garden.

J. Blackstone, Stella. *Jump into January.* Short verses about each month lead readers to find hidden objects in the pictures.

J. Kalan, Robert. *Jump Frog Jump.* This cumulative tale about a fly, a frog, a snake, and more is perfect for encouraging independent reading.

K. Andreae, Giles. *K Is for Kissing a Cool Kangaroo.* Every page is full of alphabet fun.

K. Wild, Margaret. *Kiss Kiss.* Baby Hippo forgets to kiss his mama, until all the jungle sounds remind him.

L. Bright, Paul. *Nobody Laughs at a Lion!* All the animals are laughing at silly lion, until they find out what he can do better than anyone.

L. McQuinn, Anna. *Lola at the Library.* Lola loves going to the library.

M. Riley, Linea Asplind. *Mouse Mess.* Mouse makes quite a mess in the kitchen on his hunt for food.

M. Robbins, Maria Polushkin. *Mother, Mother, I Want Another.* A mother mouse and her child misunderstand each other when the youngster asks for "another."

N. Hartt-Sussman, Heather. *Noni Says No.* Noni has to learn that sometimes you have to say no, even to your best friend.

N. Walsh, Melanie. *My Nose, Your Nose.* Children have many things in common, in spite of their differences.

O. Gravett, Emily. *Orange Pear Apple Bear.* With only five words and clever illustrations, children will easily read on their own this simple story of a bear and three fruits.

O. Kraus, Robert. *Owliver.* Owliver the Owl has his own ideas about what he'll be when he grows up.

P. French, Jackie. *Too Many Pears.* Pamela the cow loves pears, until the day she eats 600.

P. Stevens, Janet. *Princess and the Pea.* The classic fairy tale is illustrated with animals as the characters.

Q. Carle, Eric. *The Very Quiet Cricket.* A cricket wants to make sounds like the other animals.

Q. Cumpiano, Ina. *Quinito, Day and Night/Quinito, dia y noche.* Written in both Spanish and English, this story of one boy's life teaches opposites.

R. Hills, Tad. *How Rocket Learned to Read.* A small yellow bird teaches a dog the wonders of reading.

R. Trapani, Iza. *Row, Row, Row Your Boat.* A family of bears have quite an adventure while rowing down the stream.

S. Edward, Pamela Duncan. *Some Smug Slug.* An abundance of words that begin with S tell this story of an innocent slug who climbs up what he thinks is a slope.

S. Wood, Audrey. *Silly Sally.* Rhyming text about a girl going to town, "walking backward, upside down."

T. Crimi, Carolyn. *Tessa's Tip-Tapping Toes.* A young mouse only wants to dance, dance, dance.

T. Mwenye Hadithi. *Tricky Tortoise.* Tortoise decides to teach elephant a lesson about stepping on others.

U. Parr, Todd. *Underwear Do's and Don'ts.* Parr gives hilarious examples of what you should and should not do with your underwear.

U. Wadsworth, Ginger. *Up, Up, and Away.* For older preschoolers, this is an excellent nonfiction story of the life of a spider.

V. Paye, Won-Ldy and Margaret H. Lippert. *The Talking Vegetables.* Spider won't help pick the vegetables, but when he tries to eat them he learns his lesson in this African folktale.

V. Sayre, April Pulley. *Vulture View.* This nonfiction book is best with older preschoolers since it is about the life of a vulture, but the magnificent illustrations and simple rhyming text make it fascinating.

W. Meschenmoser, Sebastian. *Waiting for Winter.* Hilarious antics of squirrel, hedgehog, and bear as they search for something "white and wet and cold and soft" make this simple tale a treasure.

It is easy to give your child a literacy-rich day just by celebrating one letter with books and activities. Emma already knows that reading a **b**ook to **b**aby sister Gina at **b**edtime is a great way to learn the letter **B**.

W. Seeger, Laura Vaccaro. *Walter Was Worried.* All the children's names match their feelings, such as "Priscilla was puzzled" and "Frederick was frightened."

X. McLerran, Alice. *Roxaboxen.* Children build the town of Roxaboxen with just their imagination and plenty of creativity.

X. Portis, Antoinette. *Not a Box.* A rabbit demonstrates all the things that can be done with a box.

Y. Raschka, Chris. *Yo! Yes?* Minimal text tells of two lonely children, one black and one white, who meet and become friends.

Y. Rosenthal, Amy Krouse. *Yes Day!* What would it be like if there was a special day when you got everything you asked for?

Z. Ernst, Lisa Campbell. *Zinnia and Dot.* Two competitive hens set aside their arguments to protect an egg from a weasel.

Z. Gay, Michel. *Zee.* Zee the Zebra needs a plan so he can wake up his parents and climb into bed with them.

I can't complete a chapter about letters without praising one particular book that is a classic and a masterpiece. *Chicka Chicka Boom Boom* by Bill Martin Jr. and John Archambault combines rhythm, jazz, comedy, and the alphabet to cleverly tell a story about baby letters wanting to climb up the coconut tree. Lois Ehlert's sharp, bright illustrations lend just the right motion and color to each page as all the letters climb the tree until it begins to bend, and eventually break, from their weight. "Skit skat skoodle doot./Flip flop flee" is just one of the many charming phrases that make this story a favorite that has lasted for more than 20 years, and will continue for many more.

BIBLIOGRAPHY

For Librarians, Teachers, and Parents

Hauser, Jill. *Wow! I'm Reading!* Charlotte, VT: Williamson Publishing Co., 2000.

For Children

Alsenas, Linas. *Hello, My Name Is Bob.* New York: Scholastic Press, 2009.
Andreae, Giles. *K Is for Kissing a Cool Kangaroo.* New York: Orchard Books, 2003.
Aylesworth, Jim. *Old Black Fly.* New York: Holt, 1992.
Aylesworth, Jim. *Little Bitty Mousie.* New York: Walker, 2007.
Baker, Keith. *LMNO Peas.* New York: Beach Lane Books, 2010.
Basher, Simon. *ABC Kids.* New York: Kingfisher, 2011.
Blackstone, Stella. *Jump into January.* Cambridge, MA: Barefoot Books, 2004.
Blackstone, Stella. *Alligator Alphabet.* Cambridge, MA: Barefoot Books, 2005.
Bono, Mary. *Ugh! A Bug.* New York: Walker, 2002.
Bottner, Barbara. *An Annoying ABC.* New York: Alfred A. Knopf, 2011.
Boynton, Sandra. *Philadelphia Chickens.* New York: Workman Pub., 2002
Bright, Paul. *Nobody Laughs at a Lion!* Intercourse, PA: Good Books, 2005.
Brown, Margaret Wise. *Sleepy ABC.* New York: HarperCollins Publishers, 2009.
Bruce, Lisa. *Fran's Flower.* New York: HarperCollins, 2000.
Carle, Eric. *The Very Quiet Cricket.* New York: Philomel Books, 1990.
Carle, Eric. *Eric Carle's ABC.* New York: Grosset & Dunlap, 2007.
Cousins, Lucy. *Maisy's ABC.* Somerville, MA: Candlewick Press, 2008.

Crimi, Carolyn. *Tessa's Tip-Tapping Toes.* New York: Orchard Books, 2002.

Cumpiano, Ina. *Quinito, Day and Night/Quinito, dia y noche.* San Francisco, CA: Children's Book Press, 2008.

D'Amico, Carmelo. *Ella, the Elegant Elephant.* New York: A. A. Levine Books, 2004.

Dodd, Emma. *Dog's Colorful Day: A Messy Story about Colors and Counting.* New York: Dutton Children's Books, 2000.

Dodd, Emma. *I Love Bugs.* New York: Holiday House, 2010.

Doyle, Charlotte. *The Bouncing, Dancing, Galloping ABC.* New York: G. P. Putnam's Sons, 2006.

Eastman, P. D. *The Alphabet Book.* New York: Random House, 2000.

Edward, Pamela Duncan. *Some Smug Slug.* New York: HarperCollins Publishers, 1996.

Emberly, Ed. *Go Away, Big Green Monster.* Boston, MA: Little, Brown, 1992.

Ernst, Lisa Campbell. *Zinnia and Dot.* New York: Viking, 1992.

Freedman, Claire. *Gooseberry Goose.* Wilton, CT: Tiger Tales, 2003.

French, Jackie. *Too Many Pears.* New York: Star Bright Books, 2003.

Gay, Michel. *Zee.* New York: Clarion Books, 2003.

Gravett, Emily. *Orange Pear Apple Bear.* New York: Simon & Schusters Books for Young Readers, 2007.

Mwenye Hadithi. *Hungry Hyena.* London: Hodder & Stoughton, 1994.

Mwenye Hadithi. *Tricky Tortoise.* London: Hodder Children's, 2004.

Mwenye Hadithi. *Baby Baboon.* London: Hodder Children's, 2005.

Halsey, Megan. *Jump for Joy: A Book of Months.* New York: Bradbury Press, 1994.

Hartt-Sussman, Heather. *Noni Says No.* Toronto: Tundra Books, 2011.

Helquist, Brett. *Bedtime for Bear.* New York: HarperCollins Publishers, 2011

Hills, Tad. *How Rocket Learned to Read.* New York: Schwarz & Wade Books, 2010.

Hindley, Judy. *Do Like a Duck Does.* Cambridge, MA: Candlewick Press, 2002.

Howland, Naomi. *ABCDrive: A Car Trip Alphabet.* New York: Clarion Books, 1994.

Kalan, Robert. *Jump, Frog, Jump.* New York: Greenwillow Books, 1981.

Katz, Susan B. *ABC, Baby Me.* New York: Robin Corey Books, 2010.

Kraus, Robert. *Owliver.* New York: Simon & Schuster Children's Publishing, 1987.

Lionni, Leo. *Inch by Inch.* New York: Mulberry Books, 1995.

MacDonald, Margaret Read. *Teeny Weeny Bop.* Morton Grove, IL: Albert Whitman, 2006.

Maitland, Barbara. *My Bear and Me.* New York: Margaret K. McElderry Books, 1999.

Mallett, David. *Inch by Inch: The Garden Song.* New York: HarperCollins, 1997.

Martin, Bill, Jr., and John Archambault. *Chicka Chicka Boom Boom.* New York: Simon & Schuster Books for Young Readers, 1989.

Massie, Diane Redfield. *The Baby Beebee Bird.* New York: HarperCollins Publishers, 2000.

McKee, David. *Elmer.* New York: Lothrop, Lee & Shepard Books, 1989.

McLerran, Alice. *Roxaboxen.* New York: Lothrop, Lee & Shepard, 1990.

McQuinn, Anna. *Lola at the Library.* Watertown, MA: Charlesbridge, 2006.

Meschenmoser, Sebastian. *Waiting for Winter.* Tulsa, OK: Kane Miller, 2009.

Mockford, Caroline. *Cleo's Color Book.* Cambridge, MA: Barefoot Books, 2006.

Munari, Bruno. *Bruno Munari's ABC.* San Francisco, CA: Chronicle Books, 2006.

Murray, Alison. *Apple Pie ABC.* New York: Disney Hyperion Books, 2011.

Mwalimu. *Awful Aardvark.* Boston, MA: Little, Brown, 1989.

Parr, Todd. *Underwear Do's and Don'ts.* Boston, MA: Little, Brown, 2000.

Paye, Won-Ldy, and Margaret H. Lippert. *The Talking Vegetables.* New York: Henry Holt, 2006.

Pearle, Ida. *A Child's Day: An Alphabet of Play.* Orlando, FL: Harcourt, 2008.

Pechter, Lesley Wynne. *Alligator Bear Crab: A Baby's ABC.* Victoria, BC: Orca Book Publishers, 2011.

Portis, Antoinette. *Not a Box.* New York: HarperCollins, 2006.

Priddy, Roger. *Happy Baby ABC.* New York: Priddy Books, 2003.

Priddy, Roger. *B Is for Bear.* New York: Priddy Books, 2007.

Rankin, Laura. *The Handmade Alphabet.* New York: Dial Books, 1991.

Raschka, Chris. *Yo! Yes?* New York: Orchard Books, 1993.

Riley, Linea Asplind. *Mouse Mess.* New York: Blue Sky Press, 1997.

Robbins, Maria Plushkin. *Mother, Mother, I Want Another.* New York: Knopf, 2005.

Rose, Deborah Lee. *Into the A, B, Sea: An Ocean Alphabet.* New York: Scholastic Press, 2000.

Rosenthal, Amy Krouse. *Yes Day!* New York: HarperCollins, 2009.

Sayre, April Pulley. *Vulture View.* New York: Henry Holt, 2007.

Seeger, Laura Vaccaro. *Walter Was Worried.* New Milford, CT: Roaring Book Press, 2005.

Sobel, June. *B Is for Bulldozer: A Construction ABC.* San Diego, CA: Harcourt, 2003.

Stevens, Janet. *Princess and the Pea.* New York: Holiday House, 1982.

Stevens, Janet, and Susan Stevens Crummel. *The Great Fuzz Frenzy.* Orlando, FL: Harcourt, 2005.

Trapani, Iza. *Row, Row, Row Your Boat.* Dallas, TX: Whispering Coyote Press, 1999.

Van Fleet, Matthew. *Alphabet.* New York: Simon and Schuster, 2008.

Waddell, Martin. *The Happy Hedgehog Band.* Cambridge, MA: Candlewick Press, 1994.

Wadsworth, Ginger. *Up, Up, and Away.* Watertown, MA: Charlesbridge, 2009.

Walsh, Melanie. *My Nose, Your Nose.* Boston, MA: Houghton Mifflin, 2002.

Werner, Sharon, and Sarah Forss. *Alphabeasties and Other Amazing Types.* Maplewood, NJ: Blue Apple Books, 2009.

Wild, Margaret. *Kiss Kiss.* New York: Simon & Schuster Books for Young Readers, 2004.

Wilson, Karma. *The Cow Loves Cookies.* New York: Margaret K. McElderry Books, 2010.

Wood, Audrey. *Silly Sally.* San Diego, CA: Harcourt Brace Jovanovich, 1992.

Yoyo Books. *Baby's First Library ABC.* New York: Sterling, 2006.

Zuckerman, Andrew. *Creature ABC.* San Francisco, CA: Chronicle Books, 2009.

WEBLIOGRAPHY

www.kididdles.org

http://www2.ed.gov/Family/RWN/Activ97/index.html

Chapter Seven

IT'S STORY TIME!

My first library job was in North Carolina. I was not yet a librarian; I just had a part-time job assisting here and there. It was determined that my skills were with children's literature, thanks to my mother who raised me on a steady diet of books, plus she was an amazing school librarian, and her sister was an amazing public librarian. So it was in my blood. Soon I was assisting with creating the summer reading program, doing puppet shows, and, eventually, occasional story times. I had absolutely no idea what I was doing, but I loved children's books and my background was in theater, so I used different voices and pacing. And I had a puppet.

He was a gray and white, full-bodied, realistic rabbit, and his name was Feffer, short for Hossenfeffer, which is the German word for rabbit stew (but I never told that to the puppet or the children). Feffer welcomed the children each week, and they hugged him with great energy. He did not talk, but he waved and moved about, he was soft and lifelike, and he could scratch, shake his head, rub his nose, and generally be charming. He was absolutely real to the children and they adored him. However, there was a problem. His name was Feffer, my name is Heather. It all got very muddled up in their mouths.

They called me Heifer.

(Now I have a sheep dog puppet who welcomes everyone, participates in the weekly tickle and closing song, and enjoys hugs from everyone at the end. His name is Winston, which is impossible to combine with mine.)

Over the years there have been many such delightful memories, as there are for all of us who are lucky enough to be children's librarians. There have been parents who tell me their child plays "Miss Heather" at home, reading aloud to stuffed animals. There are squished dandelions, glorious giggles, scribbled Valentines, and hundreds of hugs, all tucked safely into my heart for remembering.

I think back to how I began, with no experience, and no degree yet in library science. But, due to my mother and aunt, I had seen how books could be brought to life. From watching them, I knew that children could be mesmerized by a tale as deceptively simple as *Inch by Inch* by Leo Lionni, or caught up in the rhythm and rhyme of "12 little girls in two straight lines," from *Madeline* by Ludwig Bemelmans. From my grandfather, a professor of Shakespeare, I knew that speaking aloud great words of literature with energy and creativity made those words even more memorable. And I had what is most important, a passion for connecting children with books. You must have that passion as well, or you wouldn't be here, on this page, with me.

Now, 30 years later, I have learned a lot. I have made mistakes, I have gathered ideas from others, and I have come to a design that I believe leads to a successful story time. I hope these recommendations will be helpful as you create your own design, based on your own talents and skills.

THE WELCOME

Many years ago, I allowed only the children to come to story time, while the parents waited outside. Big mistake!! I highly recommend that families sit together. It might be uncomfortable for some, who are used to sending their five-year-old up to the front so they can sit in the back and not have to participate, not have to be engaged, not have to let themselves enjoy what you are doing. But I'm a firm believer that if you are prepared and having fun, everyone else will, too. Find gentle opportunities to remind parents that they are their child's first and most important teacher. If they all get up and do the Turkey Hokey Pokey, the child will remember and relish forever the memory of Dad flapping his wings as he tried to turn in a circle. There will, of course, be some who just won't join the fun. Don't embarrass them by forcing their participation. Perhaps they will do them at home. At the very least, they have seen other parents shaking their sillies out, or wiggling like jelly in the jar, and, one day, it just might seem like too much fun to avoid anymore.

There are additional reasons for having the parents in the room, with the child. That way they hear the stories and hopefully will talk about them with the child later. They'll hear the early literacy tips you weave in (more on that later). Best of all, they're observing you as a role model for how all of the components of story time are essential for growing a reader.

Begin by introducing yourself, welcoming everyone, asking who is a newcomer, and basically making everyone feel like they are one big story family who have come together to share 20–30 minutes of stories, songs, rhymes, and FUN. I have rhyme sheets available, and I encourage the adults to pick one up so they can participate in the rhymes and songs we will be doing. I also ask for the caregivers' help with crowd control, because I often have 80 or more at Toddlin' Tales, the highly active story time I do three times weekly for ages 18–36 months. If one child wanders up to climb on my lap, or play with the stuffed monkey I brought along, or peel the felt board pieces off, or eat any of my props, then it is extremely likely that 10 more toddlers will quickly follow. If one child is running back and forth in front of me, anxious to get the attention of mom and most everyone else, then several others are going to join in the hilarity, and soon story time is not story time, but rather a combination of playground, dance recital, and a game of catch-me-if-you-can. So here's what I say:

"During story time, if your child needs to get up and move about when we're not doing action rhymes, that is absolutely fine. But please keep them with you in your space, or at the back of the room. At the end of story time, I'll be inviting them up into my space, and that's when they get to play with the toys, dance to the music, look at the books, and, of course, hug Winston. But please wait for that until the end of story time so that I can continue with the stories, and everyone can see." It works. Parents bring their wandering children back, or take the active ones away from the front row to move about in the back. I rarely have to interrupt a story in order to tell a child to return to her caregiver, or to bring back my pig hat.

You might have a much smaller audience, and feel that it is unnecessary to make this announcement. Great! Do what is best for you to keep control. But do keep control. Story time is a time for listening to wonderful books, learning how to follow directions, and sharing special moments between caregiver and child. Yes, there are a few parents who want uncontrolled freedom for their child, but once they learn that there will be opportunities for the child to be creative and carefree with scarves or animal actions or movement rhymes, they will appreciate the more structured times of being focused on the book and the reader.

THE OPENING

Young children adore ritual. They want to know what comes first, next, and last. As they are making sense out of the world and all its occasional chaos, they enjoy having a place and time that is predictable, secure, and complete. That is story time. That is why the best story times begin and end with the same songs or rhymes every week, and have the same design in between.

There are hundreds of appropriate songs and rhymes you could use to begin story time. In fact, there are books where you can find plenty of choices.

HEATHER RECOMMENDS

Five Books of Story Time Rhymes

Briggs, Diane. *Toddler Storytimes II.* Lanham, MD: Scarecrow Press, 2008.

Cobb, Jane. *I'm a Little Teapot: Presenting Preschool Storytime.* Vancouver: Black Sheep Press, 1996.

Ernst, Linda L. *Baby Rhyming Time.* New York: Neal-Schuman Publishers, Inc., 2008.

MacMillan, Kathy. *A Box Full of Tales: Easy Ways to Share Library Resources through Story Boxes.* Chicago, IL: American Library Association, 2008.

MacMillan, Kathy, and Christine Kerker. *Storytime Magic: 400 Fingerplays, Flannelboards, and Other Activities.* Chicago, IL: American Library Association, 2009.

Here are a few story time openings I created or adapted and used over the years:

Read, Rhyme, and Romp—Opening

It's time for story time.
We'll read and romp and rhyme.
Time for books, time for songs,
Time to play along.
Let's clap for story time.
We'll read and romp and rhyme.
Time to hear, time to see,
So listen quietly.

Read, Romp and Rhyme--Opening

Heather McNeil

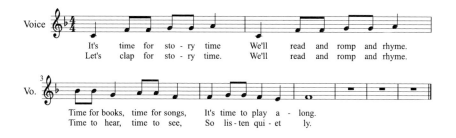

It's time for sto - ry time   We'll read and romp and rhyme.
Let's clap for sto - ry time.   We'll read and romp and rhyme.

Time for books, time for songs,   It's time to play a - long.
Time to hear, time to see,   So lis - ten qui - et ly.

Grab a Cloud (Tune: Old MacDonald)

I'm so glad you're here today. Everyone say hi. Hi!
Stand up tall, spread your wings,
Reach up, tickle the sky.
Tickle your ears, tickle your nose,
Tickle your knees, tickle your toes.
Now grab a cloud, float softly down,
Down to the ground. It's story time!

Story Time Is Here

Story time is here.
Give a great big cheer!
Songs and rhymes, a real good time.
Story time is here.
Story time is here.
Give a great big cheer!
Lots of fun, for everyone.
Story time is here.
Story time is here.
Give a great big cheer!
Bend your knees, give yourself a squeeze,
Story time is here.
Story time is here.
Give a great big cheer!
Turn around, sit on the ground,
Story time is here.
Story time is here.
Give a great big cheer!

Quietly, listen and see,
Story time is here!

Story Time Is Here

Heather McNeil   Traditional

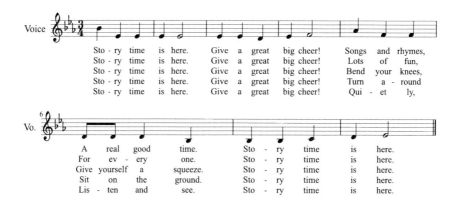

Sto - ry time is here. Give a great big cheer! Songs and rhymes,
Sto - ry time is here. Give a great big cheer! Lots of fun,
Sto - ry time is here. Give a great big cheer! Bend your knees,
Sto - ry time is here. Give a great big cheer! Turn a - round
Sto - ry time is here. Give a great big cheer! Qui - et ly,

A real good time. Sto - ry time is here.
For ev - ery one. Sto - ry time is here.
Give yourself a squeeze. Sto - ry time is here.
Sit on the ground. Sto - ry time is here.
Lis - ten and see. Sto - ry time is here.

Here We Are (Tune: The More We Get Together)

Here we are at story time, at story time, at story time.
Here we are at story time, at story time today.
We'll read books and sing songs,
We'll have fun and get along.
Here we are at story time,
At story time, HOORAY!

Let's March and March (Tune: When Johnny Comes Marching Home)

Let's march and march for story time,
Hooray! Hooray!
Let's march and march for story time,
Hooray, hooray!
Let's march and march for story time,
For silly songs and books that rhyme.
Let's march and march for story time, HOORAY!
Let's clap and clap...
Let's sit right down...

Hello, How Are You (Tune: Skip to My Lou)

Hello, how are you! Hello, how are you?
Hello, how are you? Soon it's story time.
Everybody clap their hands, *(repeat 3 times)*
Soon it's story time.
Everybody pat their knees…stomp their feet…
Everybody sit quietly down, quietly down, quietly down.
Everybody sit quietly down,
Now it's story time!

Patty Cake Story Time (Tune: First two lines of "Twinkle, Twinkle Little Star")

Patty cake, patty cake *(clap)*
Story time!
Read me a book, tell me a rhyme.
Patty cake, patty cake *(clap)*
Come along.
Read me a book, sing me a song.
Patty cake, patty cake *(clap)*
Everyone.
Read me a book, let's have fun!

THE STORY SONG

One of the best tips I can offer you is this one: have a song or rhyme that is repeated just before each story. That means if you are reading three stories, you will do it three times. The reason is because it tells your audience, "Now it's time for listening. We're done with the actions, or the talking or the singing. Now it's time for listening to a story." Plus, it's part of the routine and predictability of story time, which young children enjoy.

Here are three story songs I've created or adapted over the years:

It's Story Time for Me

My ears *(place hands beside ears)* are ready to hear. *(Clap! Clap!)*
My eyes *(encircle eyes with fingers)* are ready to see. *(Clap! Clap!)*
My hands will clap *(clap),* then in my lap *(place hands in lap).*
It's story time for me.

It's Storytime For Me

Heather McNeil   Heather McNeil

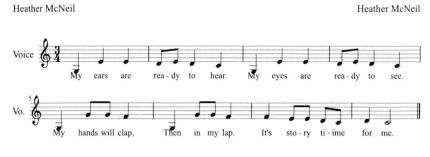

A Good Story

I do this one as a call and answer, which means I sing each line first, and then the audience repeats right after me.

It's time to sit *(audience repeats)*
It's time to see *(audience repeats; circle eyes with fingers)*
It's time to listen *(audience repeats; cup ears with hands)*
To a good story. *(audience repeats)*
So I'll clap my hands *(clap while audience repeats)*
Then quiet as can be *(whisper; audience repeats)*
I'll listen close *(audience repeats; cup ears with hands)*
To a good story.

A Good Story

Heather McNeil   Heather McNeil

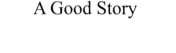

Sometimes I do all eight lines the first time, and only the first four lines before the next two stories. It depends on the audience, and whether they're actively participating.

ARE YOU KIDDING ME?

Most of my story times are energetic, hilarious, and simply fun. Most of the parents are supportive and engaged. But there was one situation that shall forever stick in my mind. It was the worst example of "Are you kidding me??!!"

I was in the middle of the second of three stories when I noticed a woman in the back of the room reach into a large bag and pull out a potty chair. Yes, an honest-to-goodness potty chair! She set it up, then turned to her son, and loudly whispered words of encouragement to him as she began to pull down his pants. He sat on the potty chair, she kept on whispering, and I was stunned, absolutely stunned. I knew that toilet training can be sensitive, so I didn't want to embarrass the child, but I also knew this could not continue. So I finished the story, and jumped right into the closing song, rather than doing the usual tickle and third story. Everyone looked a bit confused, but went along, singing "If You're Happy and You Know It." The room began to clear out, and I approached the woman who had now put the potty chair back into her bag. (I guess his efforts were unsuccessful.)

"Perhaps you didn't know that there is a bathroom in this meeting room," I said.

"Oh, yes, I know. But he's not very good with bathrooms, and this is the week I'm potty training him."

I almost couldn't speak. THE week? The one and only week? No further training next week? After this one week he'll be perfect? I didn't say any of this, of course. I just said, "Well, for sanitary reasons, you cannot be potty training during story time. Next week please take him to the bathroom, and then come back and join us."

Can't you just picture a story time with 25 children in the audience, all of them sitting on their potty seats, listening to their mother's encouraging words, while you read—try to read—a story? And just imagine when you ask them to stand up and do a movement rhyme!

READING ALOUD

Your first book should be the longest one, or the most complex. Here are five tips for a great reading:

1. Read with expression. Don't be afraid to truly blubber and wail when the bear wakes up and discovers all his friends had a party without him in *Bear Snores On* by Karma Wilson. Lower your voice

as the animals tiptoe behind the bee with the phrase, "Buzz! Buzz! Growl! Growl! Honk! Honk! Squeak! Squeak! Shh!" in *Where There's a Bear, There's Trouble* by Michael Catchpool. Be silly and obnoxious with the baby beebee bird's annoying call of "Beebee-bobbee beebeebobbee beebeebobbee" in *The Baby Beebee Bird* by Diane Redfield Massie. If at all possible, use different voices for different animals or characters. Children love it! Of course, if you do that, be consistent, and make sure that the grumpy, growly bear always sounds grumpy and growly.

2. Change the pacing. Sometimes speed up the words, sometimes slow down the words. Sometimes pause and wait. All of this keeps their attention on the story, wondering what will happen next.

3. Make sure everyone has a chance to see the pictures. I hold the book to my right to read the words, then pass the book slowly in front of me and to the audience on the left as I am saying the last sentence. Try to avoid long, silent periods while you pass the book; instead, draw out that last sentence so the passing of the book is still part of the reading of the story.

4. When appropriate, invite audience participation. If there is a repeating phrase, such as "Move over, Rover!" in the book by the same title by Karen Beaumont, encourage everyone to join in. You can either tell the audience about it before you begin the story, giving them a chance to practice, or, after you've read it twice in the story, invite them on the third repetition to say it with you. I often gesture with one hand or a nod of the head, so they know when to say the words or do the action. Or, I just say, "I'm sure you remember what the animals said. Let's say it together. 'Move over, Rover!'"

5. Don't be afraid to edit. With toddlers, I often skip a paragraph or a page, as long as the story still makes sense. However, *don't* be afraid to use unusual words, changing "reveled" to "liked." They should be able to understand the meaning of the word just by how you read it, or the expression on your face, or through the context of the story. It's important for them to hear these words that spark imagination and learning.

MOVEMENT RHYMES

After the first story, do a song or rhyme that invites action. And, by action, I don't mean just moving their fingers for the five little pumpkins sitting on a gate, or counting backward about five ladybugs who flew away, one by one. They've been sitting for about 8–10 minutes by now, and need a chance to stretch and wiggle. You can certainly do a finger rhyme, but follow that with an action rhyme, or the same rhyme done again while standing up and acting out the actions.

HEATHER RECOMMENDS

Nine Books of Action Songs and Rhymes

Cole, Joanna, and Stephanie Calmenson. *The Eentsy, Weentsy Spider: Fingerplays and Action Rhymes.* New York: William Morrow and Company, Inc., 1991.

Dowell, Ruth I. *Move Over, Mother Goose!: Finger Plays, Action Verses & Funny Rhymes.* Mt. Rainier, MD: Gryphon House, Inc., 1987.

Low, Elizabeth Cother. *Big Book of Animal Rhymes, Fingerplays and Songs.* Westport, CT: Libraries Unlimited, 2009.

MacMillan, Kathy. *Storytime Magic: 400 Fingerplays, Flannelboards, and Other Activities.* Chicago, IL: ALA, 2009.

Maddigan, Beth. *The Big Book of Stories, Songs, and Sing-Alongs: Programs for Babies, Toddlers and Families.* Westport, CT: Libraries Unlimited, 2003.

Orozco, Jose-Luis. *Diez Deditos: Ten Little Fingers & Other Play Rhymes and Action Songs from Latin America.* New York: Dutton Children's Books, 1997.

Schiller, Pam. *And the Cow Jumped Over the Moon!: Over 650 Activities to Teach Toddlers Using Familiar Rhymes.* Beltsville, MD: Gryphon House, Inc., 2006.

Scott, Barbara A. *1,000 Fingerplays & Action Rhymes: A Sourcebook & DVD.* New York: Neal Schuman Publishers, Inc., 2010.

Stetson, Emily, and Vicky Congdon. *Little Hands Finger Plays & Action Songs: Seasonal Rhymes & Creative Play for 2- to 6-Year Olds.* Charlotte, VT: Williamson Publishing, 2001.

The following movement songs are ones I've adapted and used frequently because they are simple to remember, and fun to do:

Reach Up, Touch Down

Reach up, touch down,
Stamp your feet and turn around.
Reach up, touch down,
Stamp your feet and sit back down.

Reach Up, Touch Down

Heather McNeil

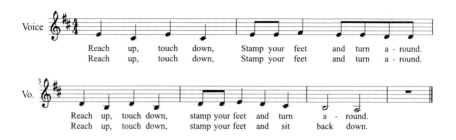

Reach up, touch down, Stamp your feet and turn a - round.
Reach up, touch down, Stamp your feet and turn a - round.

Reach up, touch down, stamp your feet and turn a - round.
Reach up, touch down, stamp your feet and sit back down.

I'm Gonna Hop

I'm gonna hop and I'll hop then I'll stop. *(everyone stops)*
I'm gonna hop and I'll hop, then I'll stop.
I'm gonna hop and I'll hop and I'll hop and I'll hop and I'll hop
    and I'll hop, then I'll stop.
(repeat, and when you get to the last line, change it to, "then I'll
    drop." Everyone sits back down.)

I'm Gonna Hop

Heather McNeil

I'm gon - na hop and I'll hop, then I'll stop. I'm gon - na hop and I'll hop,
I'm gon - na hop and I'll hop, then I'll stop. I'm gon - na hop and I'll hop,

then I'll stop. I'm gon - no hop and I'll hop and I'll hop and I'll hop
then I'll stop. I'm gon - na hop and I'll hop and I'll hop and I'll hop

and   I'll   hop   and   I'll   hop,   then   I'll   stop.
and   I'll   hop   and   I'll   hop,   then   I'll   drop.

Clap Your Hands (Tune: First line of M-I-C-K-E-Y-M-O-U-S-E)

Clap your hands, clap your hands, clap them just like me. *(loud)*
Tap your toes, tap your toes, tap them just like me. *(quiet)*
Clap your hands, clap your hands, clap them just like me. *(loud)*

Stretch up high, stretch up high, stretch up just like me. *(quiet)*
Clap your hands, clap your hands, clap them just like me. *(loud)*
Sit back down, sit back down, and listen quietly. *(quiet)*

Running, Running (Tune: Frere Jacques)

Running, running, running, running.
Hop, hop, hop. Hop, hop, hop.
Tippy tippy tiptoe, tippy tippy tiptoe.
Now we stop! Now we drop!

Shake, Shake, Shake (Tune: Turkey in the Straw)

I can jump like a frog, I can stretch like a cat.
I can hop like a bunny, I can flap like a bat.
I can wiggle like a worm, and slither like a snake.
I can be a wet dog, and shake, shake, shake!

The FAQ

Have you ever dealt with side conversations going on during story time from mothers who just have to share their recent experience at the playground while you're reading? Do cell phones go off during story time? Have you had a crying, screaming child that stays, and stays, and stays, so that you have to talk louder and louder and louder? All of us have dealt with interruptions and distractions; it's just part of having a group of children and adults. But I found a good way to control some of these situations, without having to stop the flow of story time or embarrass a parent or child in front of others. On the back of the rhyme sheet I hand out each week is the Story Time FAQ. It is a series of questions and answers that help make your expectations clear for a successful story time. Feel free to use any part or all, if it could be helpful for you. Here's what it says:

Welcome to Story Time!

We are so glad you have chosen to spend time at the library with your child, listening to stories. We want to make sure that our story times are enjoyable for all, so here are some answers to questions you might have.

Should I leave if my child gets noisy during story time?

Children have different listening skills, depending on their stage of development and personality. But sometimes a noisy or active child causes so much disturbance that others cannot hear or focus. So, if your child just doesn't want to listen today, you can leave the room briefly, and then rejoin us when your child is ready. Or perhaps you could try a different story time that is shorter. Baby Steps is 15 minutes, Toddlin' Tales is 25 minutes, and Preschool Parade is 30 minutes.

May I bring a snack for my child?

A small snack, such as a bag of cereal, is no problem. However, please do not bring out a variety of foods. It takes the focus away from the stories, plus other children might attack you!

Do I have to do all the songs and actions with the librarian?

When you sing along, or do a finger rhyme, you are showing your child that what we are doing is not only fun, but also important. All our story times promote early literacy skills, many of which you can duplicate at home. So don't worry about being silly; we're masters at it!

Is It OK to chat with my friend, or use my cell phone?

Unfortunately, your chatting becomes a distraction for others. Please turn off your cell phone and have personal conversations after story time is over. Then you can hang out and visit wherever you are comfortable for as long as you want.

Your schedule does not fit my schedule. May I bring my two-year-old to a story time for five-year-olds?

The programs are designed to fit the stage of development of the child, including listening, motor, and cognitive skill levels. So an older child might be bored at a story time for toddlers, and a toddler might be overwhelmed by the complexity of the stories for preschoolers. We'll never turn anyone away, and we certainly understand that a parent could bring more than one child. But if you want a recommendation, check in with library staff and discuss which session that does fit your schedule would be best.

Why all this information about early literacy?

Experts believe that reading, singing, and rhyming are the best activities parents can do with their young child to get them ready to learn how to read. Librarians do those every week at story time. So we take this opportunity to give you tips on what you can do, as well as model for you some of the fun ways to bring books alive.

IN-BETWEENS

Consider other activities in between stories. Use the "Here's My Bag" song to refocus attention; it's described on page 111. If you have a smaller group, invite some conversation about the book you just read, and ask simple questions about their own experience. Have you ever lost a favorite toy? (after reading *Tom's Rabbit* by Martin Waddell) What makes you feel grumpy? (after reading *Grump Groan Growl* by Bell Hooks) What is your favorite food? (after reading *Lunch!* by Denise Fleming) You can only do this with a small group so that everyone has a chance to speak; otherwise, there are hurt feelings, and some children will not stop trying to find the opportunity to tell you what they wanted to say.

CONTINUING ON

Now you're ready for another story. Do your story song or rhyme again, and read a second story, one that is a bit shorter. I recommend that the second one include audience participation, so that they remain focused on what is happening. Follow with another action rhyme.

TICKLES AND LAP BOUNCES

If you have babies or toddlers in your audience, a regular time for a tickle or a lap bounce can be a lot of giggly fun. I have it on the rhyme sheet, and I explain how to do it, demonstrating with Winston in my lap. Tickle and bounce time is his favorite time, so he gets everyone all excited about what's going to happen. Plus he laughs uproariously, which gets them comfortable and anxious to begin. We do the bounce or tickle together, twice. Again, you're not only modeling fun, loving activities with a child, which releases healthy serotonin to the brain and builds bonds with the caregiver, but you're also playing with rhyming words, which teaches phonological awareness. Do make sure that you remind parents to always be gentle with rhymes and bounces, and to stop whenever anyone says stop. I also remind the children that they can tickle mommy/daddy/grandma/babysitter, too!

Nursery rhymes make great lap bounces. Tickles can be created by using two lines from almost any relevant rhyme. Or just make it up! "Wiggly worm wiggles as quickly as can be./Wiggly worm wiggles and then he tickles me!"

LAST STORY

One more time, lead them in your Story Song, followed by your last story. This one should be the shortest. I often do a pop-up book, such as *The Scared*

Little Bear by Keith Faulkner, or one that is a familiar song, such as *The Itsy Bitsy Spider* by Lorianne Siomades. Now you're ready for the closing.

CLOSING SONG OR RHYME

A staff member once told me that she finished story time, but forgot to do her usual closing song, "If You're Happy and You Know It." She said, "It was so weird. I kept waving good-bye, and saying, 'Thanks for coming. See you next week.' But they just stood there, totally confused and frozen." Finally she realized what was missing, and she quickly started them up with the familiar clapping, stomping, and shouting "Hooray!" Only then were they willing to leave.

A closing ritual lets them know that it's time to move on to the next thing, maybe a craft, or a hug, or checking out books, or going outside for a snack in the park. It comfortably and securely brings story time to an end. Choose one that you enjoy doing week after week. Here are three I created:

Read, Rhyme, and Romp—Closing

We had our story time.
We read and romped and rhymed.
Time for books, time for friends,
But now it's at an end.
Now it's time to go.
Let's stand and jump just so.
Wave up high, wave down low,
Now it's time to go.

Read, Romp and Rhyme--Closing

Heather McNeil

We Heard Stories (Tune: This Old Man)

We heard stories, we made friends,
Now story time must come to an end.
So stand up tall, jump up high,
Hug yourself, and wave good-bye.

I'm Glad You Came (Tune: We Wish You a Merry Christmas)

I'm glad you came to story time,
I'm glad you came to story time,
I'm glad you came to story time,
But now you must go.
Let's all stand and clap like crazy, *(you can change this to match
    the theme of the day; for instance, stomp like elephants, flap like
    turkeys, etc.)*
Let's all stand and clap like crazy,
Let's all stand and clap like crazy,
And then you must go.
Let's all wave our hands up high,
Let's all wave our hands down low,
Let's all wave our hands to everyone,
And then you must go.

BABY STORY TIME

Long ago, in the day, it was not believed that babies should be present at story time. After all, they don't understand the vocabulary, they can't follow directions, and they frequently just fall asleep and never hear a word. But now we know that reading aloud to babies right from the beginning is essential for healthy brain development, as well as growing a reader. When you offer a story time for the youngest of listeners, what you're really doing is offering role modeling for the parent or care provider. They will be learning from you about the importance of having fun with words, learning rhymes, singing, and most important of all, bonding with a baby by hugging, tickling, snuggling, and through the comfort of the adult's voice, warmth, and heartbeat.

Another benefit of doing a story time for babies is that you are establishing the library habit. In a couple of years baby moves on to a toddler or preschool story time, but then along comes baby number two, and the cycle starts again. Parents or grandparents or babysitters are visiting the library once or twice a week, and what could be better than that?

Our "Baby Steps" story time at Deschutes Public Library is 15 minutes long. Each session includes three very, very short stories that are just right for babies; four or five nursery or finger rhymes; maybe a lap bounce or tickle; and the usual opening, story, and closing songs. At the end, we visit each baby and allow him or her to hug the puppet or stuffed animal that represents Baby Steps. (Mine is a big, soft, and squishy brown teddy bear named Jingles, because he has a jingle bell in his tail. And the name doesn't rhyme with Heather!) Sometimes there are soft toys for the babies to explore, as well as gentle, playful music. Then the adults stay as long as they want with their babies, often visiting for 30 minutes or more. In fact, that has become one of the biggest values of Baby Steps, allowing an opportunity for the parents to share stories or offer recommendations about parenting to other parents.

If you are new to the idea of including babies at story time be sure to look at *Baby Rhyming Time* by Linda Ernst, and *What'll I Do with the Baby-Oh: Nursery Rhymes, Songs and Stories for Babies* by Jane Cobb. Both include recommended songs, rhymes, and stories, as well as information on why baby story time is important and tips on how to plan and present the program.

HEATHER RECOMMENDS

44 Stories Just Right for Babies

Ayres, Katherine. *Matthew's Truck.* Matthew has many adventures with his toy truck.

Baker, Keith. *Big Fat Hen.* Count to 10 in this traditional nursery rhyme.

Barry, Frances. *Duckie's Splash.* Duckie takes a colorful walk home to a rainbow surprise.

Beaumont, Karen. *Baby Danced the Polka.* It's bedtime, but not for one busy baby.

Boynton, Sandra. *Moo, Baa, La, La, La.* Anything by Boynton is sure to make you giggle.

Butler, John. *Can You Growl Like a Bear?* Everyone can mimic animal sounds.

Charlip, Remy. *Sleepytime Rhyme.* A gentle rhyme about all the reasons to love baby.

Cronin, Doreen. *Bounce* and *Wiggle.* Both lead to plenty of fun.

Dodds, Siobhan. *Ting-a-Ling!* Tilly plays with her telephone until bath time.

Elffers, Joost. *Do You Love Me?* Adorable creatures called Snuzzles explore love.

Fleming, Denise. *Sleepy, Oh, So Sleepy.* Animal babies get ready for bed.

Fox, Mem. *Zoo-Looking.* Flora and her father visit the zoo.

van Genechten, Guido. *The Cuddle Book.* All animals have a special way to cuddle.

Godwin, Laura. *What the Baby Hears.* Rhyming text and loving words heard by animals and humans.

Greenspun, Adele Aron. *Ariel and Emily.* Beautiful photographs accompany a simple story of two baby girls who are best friends.

Henderson, Kathy. *Look at You! A Baby Body Book.* An exuberant book about all the things the body can do.

Hindley, Judy. *Baby Talk.* Rhyming text all about a baby's day.

Intrater, Roberta Grobel. *Peek-a-Boo, You!* One in a series of cardboard books with colorful photos of babies.

Katz, Karen. *Babies on the Bus.* An adaptation of the popular song featuring multicultural babies.

Katz, Karen. *Where Is Baby's Belly Button?* Lift the flaps and find baby's hands, eyes, and other parts in this multicultural book.

Katz, Susan. *ABC, Baby Me.* The busy days of babies, from A to Z.

Kubler, Annie. *Ten Little Fingers.* One in a series of cardboard books with adorable multicultural babies and very short nursery rhymes.

Macken, JoAnn Early. *Baby Says "Moo!"* According to baby, everyone says "moo."

Martin, David. *We've All Got Bellybuttons.* Fun with all our body parts.

McGee, Marni. *Sleepy Me.* Daddy carries his sleepy baby to bed.

Milord, Susan. *Love That Baby!* Flaps reveal what to do when baby is hungry, sad, scared, and so on.

Mockford, Caroline. *Cleo the Cat.* First in a series of simple stories about a cat and her world.

Morrow, Tara Jaye. *Mommy Loves Her Baby/Daddy Loves His Baby.* Turn the book upside down for two stories.

O'Connell, Rebecca. *The Baby Goes Beep.* Everyone makes fun sounds that entertain baby.

Oxenbury, Helen. *All Fall Down.* One in a series of cardboard books that feature multicultural babies and simple nursery rhymes.

Patricelli, Leslie. *Tubby.* A baby describes all the joys of bath time.

Ryder, Joanne. *Won't You Be My Kissaroo?* Rhyming text describes many kinds of kisses.

Simmons, Jane. *Quack, Daisy, Quack.* Daisy and little brother Pip explore the noisy world.

Siomade, Lorianne. *The Itsy Bitsy Spider.* Colorful and silly illustrations for the popular rhyme.

Sturges, Philemon. *How Do You Make a Baby Smile?* Animal parents use their best tricks to help their babies smile.

Tafolla, Carmen. *Fiesta Babies.* Spanish and English combine in a rhyming story about playful Mexican American babies.

Tafuri, Nancy. *The Big Storm: A Very Soggy Counting Book.* Animals find shelter in a hill hollow.

Walton, Rick. *Baby's First Year!* From birth to first birthday, a baby grows and learns.

Weeks, Sarah. *Overboard!* A baby discovers how fun it is to throw things overboard.

Wheeler, Lisa. *Jazz Baby.* Baby and his family make some jazzy music.

Whippo, Walt. *Little White Duck.* A duck, a frog, a bug, and a snake are all in the water.

Wilhelm, Hans. *Hugaboo, I Love You.* Flaps reveal all kinds of hugs.

Yolen, Jane. *Hush, Little Horsie.* Gentle, rhyming text and beautiful illustrations introduce different horses and their babies.

Yoon, Salina. *Peek-a-Love.* Flaps reveal what bees, butterfly, fish, and Mama loves.

EARLY LITERACY TIPS

It is important that occasionally during story time you voice a tip or two about early literacy. It doesn't need to be anything long or complicated. Saroj Ghoting, one of the American Library Association's original trainers on Every Child Ready to Read @ your library, has an excellent book filled with ideas of what you can say. *Early Literacy Storytimes @ Your Library: Partnering with Caregivers for Success* offers themes, songs, rhymes, titles, openings, and closings, as well as suggestions for what you can say so that parents appreciate and benefit from your knowledge about early literacy. You'll also find ideas on her website, www.earlylit.net.

There is no question that doing a teachable moment during the flow of story time can seem to make you lose your audience's attention, especially the children's. My tips are less than a minute long, intended only to help adults understand why you picked this particular book to read, or what is important about rhyming. For instance, after reading *Mama Cat Has Three Kittens* by Denise Fleming I would say, "This book is a perfect example of a story that children will soon be able to read all on their own because of its repetition and predictability. Plus all of Fleming's books are just right for toddlers, with simple stories, big text, and things hidden on pages to hunt for." That's all I'd say, and then we'd do an action rhyme to get out the wiggles. Here are a few other samples.

After reading *Bear Came Over to My House* by Rick Walton I might say, "Did you notice how I paused before the rhyme? That's a good way to encourage your child to 'read' all on his own, by looking at the pictures and guessing the next word that rhymes." (That's phonological awareness!)

After asking for them to join in on the reoccurring rhyme in *The Pout-Pout Fish in the Big-Big Dark* by Deborah Diesen, I would say, "The reason I asked for your participation is because that rhyme about being afraid of the dark could become one to repeat together with your child when something seems scary. Books can help children deal with their feelings." (That's loving books!)

After reading *The Feel Good Book* by Todd Parr I would say, "Today's craft will be making a 'feel good' book to take home. Your child gets to draw pictures of what makes her feel good, while you write out the words. Write the words in block letters, and as simply as possible, so the child will soon read them on her own." (That's knowing print!)

After reading *Ten on the Sled* by Kim Norman I would say, "Did you notice all the different words that described the way the animals left the sled? Spilled, hopped, shot, whirled, slipped, squeezed...Books introduce three times more rare words than conversation." (That's learning words!)

After reading *Some Smug Slug* by Pamela Duncan Edwards I would say, "What letter did most of the words begin with? Yes, S. Books are a great way to introduce children to letters of the alphabet, and the sounds they make. Choose a letter of the day next week when you come to story time, and I'll help you find a great book that uses that letter." (That's knowing letters!)

After acting out a rhyme such as "Five Little Mice," I would say, "Acting out stories like we just did with that rhyme teaches a child about the parts of a story—beginning, middle, end. It also encourages them to make up stories on their own, which is an important skill to have before learning to read." (That's storytelling!) Here's the rhyme, sung to the tune of "One Elephant Went Out to Play."

Five little mice went out to play,
Tiptoeing quietly on their way. *(tiptoe)*

Out came a pussycat, sleek and black. *(crouch and extend one arm out, then the other, as if stalking like a cat)*
Squeak! Four little mice went scampering back. *(run)*
Four…three…two…one little mouse went out to play…way…
No little mice went scampering back.

USING PROPS

There's a very simple rule about whether or not to use props. If the prop enhances the story, and is easy to add, then it's a good prop. But if the prop just adds confusion, or detracts from the story, or is difficult to handle, then put the prop away.

I once saw a story reader present a story that involved a box. Every so often she would stop the story, set the book down, bend forward, and pull a toy out of the box. She'd talk about the toy, then set it beside her, then pick up the book again and say things like, "Now, where were we?" or "Do you remember what just happened?" Her bending and stopping and extra conversation was very confusing to everyone, plus the young ones in her audience just wanted to grab the toys that came out of the box.

Make sure that the props you are using truly add to the story, and that you can keep control of them once they appear. When I do a song like "Old MacDonald Had a Farm," I frequently have a large duffle bag filled with stuffed animals. But *before* I begin the song I'll explain, "Old Mac-Donald's animals, and a few surprises are in my bag. I'm going to pull them out as we sing the song. *At the end of story time* everyone can come up and play with the animals. Until then, they need to stay with Old Mac-Donald." As soon as the song is over, I put the animals back in the bag, but at the end of story time I pull them out again so everyone can play with them.

Some stories invite using a bag full of props, but make sure you don't need to bend over, and that the props really enhance the story. Do you need to hold up a ball just because there is a ball in the story? Or is the ball part of the surprise and encourages participation? When I tell the story *Lunch* by Denise Fleming, I use a mouse puppet and the stuffed food available from Childcraft (www.childcraft.com). I have the children guess what might be the food, based on the description, such as "sweet yellow—", then I pause, and they guess "corn." Then I pull out the corn, mouse loudly munches and chews and then I throw the corn away by tossing it over my shoulder as he gulps. The children find this throwing of food hilarious! (By the way, you'll need to tell them *before* the story begins that they don't need to worry about picking anything up from the floor until you ask for their help at the end.)

BOOK SELECTION

Story time is the time to introduce the best in children's literature. Movie characters, television stars, and didactic tales of why-you-should-behave-like-this do not belong. Instead, search out the unusual, the playful, the hilarious, and the ones that create a sense of awe.

Usually, story times are done by theme—pets, winter, elephants, and so on. I'm listing them by the eight categories that I think make books memorable, and then you can fit them in with your theme:

- Stories of creativity and imagination
- Stories of growing up
- Stories that make you feel good or create a mood
- Stories with surprises
- Stories that make children (and care providers) laugh
- Stories that invite participation
- Stories that play with words
- Stories of all the world

These books are not necessarily in the mainstream of popularity, but have been story time favorites with myself and the amazingly talented and dedicated children's librarians at Deschutes Public Library. They might be out of print, but hopefully will still show up in some library collections. I've indicated the interest level, but you know your audience best. If you choose what you like, they'll like it, too.

HEATHER RECOMMENDS

20 Stories of Creativity and Imagination

Encourage young children to explore the fine arts and their own imagination with these tales of music, painting, and other forms of creative expression.

Beaumont, Karen. *I Ain't Gonna Paint No More!* A mischievous child just can't give up painting, and adorns his world with color. (preschool)

Bently, Peter and Helen Oxenbury. *King Jack and the Dragon.* Three children create their castle and imagine the beasts and dragon they must fight. (toddler/preschool)

Craig, Lindsey. *Dancing Feet.* All the animals are dancing to the beat, from slappity ducks to thumpity bears. (baby/toddler)

Crimi, Carolyn. *Tessa's Tip-Tapping Toes.* Nothing can stop Tessa the mouse from dancing and Oscar the cat from singing. (preschool)

Fuge, Charles. *I Know a Rhino.* A little girl has a rhino for tea, an ape to dance with, and more. (toddler/preschool)

Gravett, Emily. *Monkey and Me.* A pigtailed girl and her monkey become the animals from the zoo. Read this one standing up so everyone can participate. (toddler/preschool)

Hager, Sarah. *Dancing Matilda.* A young kangaroo just cannot stop dancing. (preschool)

Hall, Michael. *Perfect Square.* After you read the story of a square who is much more than a square, hand the children squares of paper and see what they create. (preschool)

Heap, Sue. *What Shall We Play?* Two girls and a boy use their imagination to be trees, cars, cats, and even jello. (toddler)

Henkes, Kevin. *My Garden.* What if you could grow seashells in your garden? (toddler/preschool)

Keats, Ezra Jack. *Regards to the Man in the Moon.* This classic multicultural story shows just how creative children can be when they build a spaceship with what they find in the city. (preschool)

Lowery, Linda. *Twist with a Burger, Jitter with a Bug.* All kinds of people do all kinds of dancing. (all ages)

Manning, Maurie J. *Kitchen Dance.* Two Hispanic American children sneak out of bed for some family fun as they join their parents dancing and singing in the kitchen. (preschool)

Na, Il Sung. *The Thingamabob.* An elephant finds something that he's never seen before. (preschool)

Nikola-Lisa, W. *Setting the Turkeys Free.* An African American boy figures out how to help his handmade turkeys escape from Foxy the fox. (preschool)

Schaefer, Carole Lexa. *Squiggle.* An Asian American girl shows her class that a string is not just a string, but an invitation to the imagination. (preschool)

Schotter, Roni. *Captain Bob Sets Sail.* A young boy in the bath imagines himself the captain of the seas. (preschool)

Symes, Ruth. *Harriet Dancing.* A joyful hedgehog discovers that anyone can dance, no matter what the butterflies say. (preschool)

Tafolla, Carmen. *What Can You Do with a Paleta?* Children describe all the creative ways to use a delicious, fruity, ice-cold paleta. (preschool)

Tafolla, Carmen. *What Can You Do with a Rebozo?* A young girl and her family show all the things that can be done with a rebozo, a traditional Mexican woven shawl. (preschool)

HEATHER RECOMMENDS

14 Stories of Growing Up

Children love stories that help them understand there are others with the same frustrations as they have about being too small, as well as give them comfort that someday they will know more and be bigger.

Bates, Ivan. *All by Myself.* An elephant is determined to show his mother what he can do without any help. (preschool)

Bedford, David. *Touch the Sky, My Little Bear.* A young polar bear learns from his mother all the amazing things he will do when he gets bigger. (toddler/preschool)

Best, Cari. *Red Light, Green Light, Mama and Me.* An African American girl is finally old enough to walk with her mother to the library and help her at work. (preschool)

Bynum, Janie. *Kiki's Blankie.* A small monkey never goes anywhere without her blanket, until the day it is blown away. (toddler)

Chodos-Irvine, Margaret. *Ella Sarah Gets Dressed.* Ella Sarah pays no attention to everyone's advice when she chooses her own clothes. (toddler)

Cuyler, Margery. *The Biggest, Best Snowman.* Nell's big sisters like to tell her what she can't do, but Nell and her forest friends find out just how amazing she is. (preschool)

Gorbachev, Valeri. *Chicken Chickens.* Two little chickens try to find the courage to go down the slide. (toddler/preschool)

Pfam, LeUyen. *Big Sister, Little Sister.* The Vietnamese author wrote and illustrated this for her younger sister, celebrating their differences. (preschool)

Reidy, Jean. *Too Purpley!* A young girl expresses her strong feelings about clothes. (toddler)

Simmons, Jane. *Come Along, Daisy.* Daisy the duckling learns a valuable lesson about staying with Mama Duck. (toddler)

Soto, Gary. *Big Bushy Mustache.* Ricky, a Mexican American boy, wants to look just like his father, including the mustache. (preschool)

Stein, David Ezra. *Pouch.* A joey begins to discover the world outside of his mother kangaroo's pouch, and finds there are wonders and surprises. (toddler)

Thompson, Lauren. *Little Quack.* Four little ducklings get brave enough to paddle in the water, but Little Quack is not so sure. (toddler/preschool)

Wild, Margaret and Ann James. *Little Humpty.* A curious and endearing young camel begins to explore his world, hoping to find a friend. (preschool)

HEATHER RECOMMENDS

30 Stories That Make You Feel Good or Create a Mood

Quiet, gentle stories are important to introduce, too, so that parents can hear how a soft voice and a lovely tale will quickly bring peace. Others in this list were chosen just because there will be "feel good" atmosphere in the room when you finish the last word.

Appelt, Kathi. *Incredible Me!* A red-headed girl is exuberant about all the joys of being herself. (toddler/preschool)

Bajaj, Varsha. *How Many Kisses Do You Want Tonight?* Mommies and daddies count all the kisses for their young animals. (toddler)

Bang, Molly. *All of Me! A Book of Thanks.* Bold illustrations and loving words tell of a biracial child who is thankful for everything he can do. (toddler/preschool)

Banks, Kate. *Close Your Eyes.* If ever a story can lull a child to sleep this gentle tale of a young tiger and his mother will be the one. (toddler/preschool)

Berger, Barbara. *Grandfather Twilight.* Imagination soars in this simple tale of an old man, a pearl, and how the moon appears in the sky. (preschool)

Church, Caroline Jayne. *One More Hug for Madison.* An adorable mouse avoids going to sleep by asking his mother for "one more thing." (toddler/preschool)

Cooke, Trish. *So Much.* An African American family has so much love to give to their toddler child. (toddler/preschool)

Cruise, Robin. *Little Mama Forgets.* A Mexican American girl notices that her grandmother forgets some things, but always remembers what's important with her granddaughter. (preschool)

Dorros, Arthur. *Mama and Me.* A bilingual girl creates a special and colorful surprise for her mother. (preschool)

Fox, Mem. *Time for Bed.* The author's rhythmic words and Nancy Tafuri's elaborate illustrations present a lullaby tale of animals preparing for sleep. (toddler/preschool)

Gleeson, Libby. *Cuddle Time.* When the sun shines, it's time to be brave and get past the bed monster for a cuddle. (baby/toddler)

Goodhart, Pippa. *Pudgy: A Puppy to Love.* A lonely girl and a bad puppy find each other. (baby/toddler)

Greenfield, Eloise. *Honey, I Love.* An African American girl describes all the things she loves, from her cousin's speech to her mother's arm. (preschool)

Henkes, Kevin. *Kitten's First Full Moon.* Kitten is convinced that the moon is a bowl of warm milk. (toddler/preschool)

Joosse, Barbara. *Papa, Do You Love Me?* A boy learns about unconditional love from his Masai father. (preschool)

Katz, Karen. *Counting Kisses.* What could be better than counting kisses, and babies? (baby/toddler)

Krauss, Ruth. *And I Love You.* A mother cat reassures her kitten that there will always be her love, no matter what challenges life brings. (toddler/preschool)

Lieshout, Maria van. *Hopper and Wilson.* A toy elephant and mouse travel all the world to find each other. (preschool)

Mayhew, James. *Who Wants a Dragon?* An adorable baby dragon finally finds someone to love him. (baby/toddler)

Murphy, Mary. *I Kissed the Baby!* All the animals are excited about the new baby in the barnyard. (baby/toddler)

Nakamura, Catherine Riley. *Song of Night: It's Time to Go to Bed.* Parents prepare their young animals for bed. (toddler)

Parr, Todd. *The I Love You Book.* There are many kinds of love for many reasons. (all ages)

Ray, Mary Lyn. *Red Rubber Boot Day.* There are so many ways to enjoy a rainy day. (toddler)

Rowe, John A. *I Want a Hug.* Elvis the hedgehog wants a hug, but everyone thinks he's too "prickly." (toddler)

Scanlon, Liz Garton. *Noodle & Lou.* Lou the worm has a "rain-cloudy heart," but his friend Lou the blue jay helps him find joy. (toddler/preschool)

Smalls, Irene. *Jonathan and His Mommy.* An African American boy and his mother enjoy together different ways of walking through the neighborhood. (preschool)

Stojic, Manya. *Rain.* All the senses reveal to the animals that rain is coming on the African savannah. (toddler/preschool)

Tillman, Nancy. *Tumford the Terrible.* A cat who always seems to be in trouble just can't seem to be able to say, "I'm sorry." (preschool)

Willis, Jeanne. *Never Too Little to Love.* A mouse and a giraffe have a very special relationship. (toddler/preschool)

Yolen, Jane. *Owl Moon.* Join a young girl and her father as they walk on a cold night under a full moon, in search of owls. (preschool)

HEATHER RECOMMENDS

25 Stories with Surprises

It's such fun to hear a giggle or gasp of amazement when what they thought was true is something else all together.

Averbeck, Jim. *Except If.* An egg might not be just an egg when it hatches into something else. (toddler/preschool)

Brett, Jan. *The Mitten: A Ukranian Folktale.* Animals climb inside a mitten that keeps growing bigger until a sneeze is just too much. (preschool)

Brown, Ken. *The Scarecrow's Hat.* Chicken wants the scarecrow's hat and has to figure out how to make a trade. (preschool)

Cleminson, Katie. *Magic Box.* Eva is given a special box on her birthday that leads her on a journey of imagination that might be more real than not. (preschool)

Donaldson, Julia. *The Gruffalo.* A clever mouse manages to trick his way to safety, until the real monster appears. (preschool)

Ehlert, Lois. *Snowballs.* It's amazing what can be used to make a snow family. (toddler/preschool)

French, Vivian. *Henny Penny.* A new ending to an old tale makes this folktale fun for young listeners. (preschool)

Gilani-Williams, Fawzia. *Nabeel's New Pants: An Eid Tale.* Everyone says they're too busy to shorten Nabeel's new pants. What a surprise when he puts them on to celebrate the holiday of Eid! (preschool)

Gravett, Emily. *Dogs.* A deceptively simple story and delightful illustrations of all kinds of dogs lead to the discovery of who really likes dogs. (all ages)

Grimm, Jakob, and Wilhelm Grimm. *The Elves and the Shoemaker.* Jim La Marche's adaptation and stunning illustrations make this classic tale just right for story time. (preschool)

Hall, Michael. *My Heart Is Like a Zoo.* Give the children plenty of time to discover all the hearts that make up all the animals. (all ages)

Horacek, Petr. *Butterfly Butterfly.* Peek-a-boo holes reveal a girl's discoveries in the garden, including a gorgeous pop-up butterfly at the end. (toddler)

Klassen, Jon. *I Want My Hat Back.* This is a deceptively simple story of a bear searching for his hat, and a rabbit wearing a hat. (preschool)

Kulka, Joe. *Wolf's Coming!* All the animals are hiding from Wolf, but your audience won't guess why. (toddler/preschool)

Luthardt, Kevin. *Flying!* An African American boy has many questions for his father, most of which begin with "Why?" (preschool)

Portis, Antoinette. *Not a Box.* A rabbit explores all the things one can make from a box that is not just a box. (all ages)

Rohmann, Eric. *Clara and Asha.* Clara's friend is a giant fish who plays with her in the snow and in the sky. (preschool)

Sanderson, Ruth. *Goldilocks.* The traditional folktale is enhanced with the addition of blueberry muffins. (preschool)

Sattler, Jennifer. *Sylvie.* Sylvie is a flamingo who discovers she can change colors, but eventually decides that being herself is best. (toddler/preschool)

Schwarz, Vivian. *There Are Cats in This Book.* Three cats are guaranteed to bring chuckles with their excitement about pillows, fish,—and the reader! (preschool)

Seeger, Laura Vaccaro. *Lemons Are Not Red.* This introduction to colors helps children think about what they think they know. (all ages)

Smee, Nicola. *Splish-Splash.* A dog, cat, pig, duck, and horse share a boat. (toddler)

Tanaka, Beatrice. *The Chase: A Kutenai Indian Tale.* All the animals run when they see the rabbit run, but why is the rabbit running? (toddler/preschool)

Tullet, Herve. *Press Here.* Instructions are given on how to create more or less dots just by pressing here and there. (toddler/preschool)

Waring, Richard. *Hungry Hen.* The really young won't quite get the punch line at the end, but older preschoolers (and their parents) will love the big surprise about hen and fox, and will immediately say, "Read it again!" (preschool)

HEATHER RECOMMENDS

18 Stories to Make Children (and Their Care Providers) Laugh

The truth is, children will always remember the books that made them laugh out loud, and they'll want to hear them again and again.

Alborough, Jez. *Where's My Teddy?* A big bear with a big teddy bear and a little boy with a little teddy bear get all mixed up with each other one day in the forest. (toddler/preschool)

Andersen, Hans Christian. *The Princess and the Pea.* Janet Stevens's adaptation of this folktale is very simple, and the illustrations of a dancing elephant, a tiptoeing hippo, and a soggy tiger are absolutely hilarious. (preschool)

Catchpool, Michael. *Where There's a Bear, There's Trouble!* This one never fails to make everyone laugh as a bee, a bear, two geese, and three mice tiptoe their way toward disaster. (toddler/preschool)

Dodd, Emma. *Meow Said the Cow.* A clever cat mixes up everyone's voice on the farm. (preschool)

Fore, S. J. *Tiger Can't Sleep.* A tiger in the boy's closet is causing all kinds of trouble as he munches potato chips, bounces a ball, plays band instruments, and does all that he can to keep from sleeping. (preschool)

Harris, Robie. *Maybe a Bear Ate It!* There's plenty of exaggerated drama in this tale of a kitten who loses her favorite book and looks for it everywhere. (preschool)

Ketteman, Helen. *Goodnight, Little Monster.* Cold worm juice and baked beetle bread are just right for a little monster preparing for bed. (toddler/preschool)

Kimmel, Eric. *Anansi and the Moss-Covered Rock.* This is the first in a series of hilarious stories about the West African trickster spider. (preschool)

Lee, Spike, and Tonya Lewis Lee. *Please, Baby, Please!* It will be the parents who laugh delightedly at the antics of the world's most charming African American child. (baby/toddler)

Lloyd, Sam. *What Color Is Your Underwear?* Lift the flaps to find out what kind of underwear each animal wears. (toddler/preschool)

MacDonald, Margaret Read, and Nadia Jameel Taibah. *How Many Donkeys?: An Arabic Counting Tale.* Smart children will figure out the foolishness of the father who can't count his donkeys. (preschool)

McDonnell, Flora. *Splash!* It's a baby elephant that figures out how to help everyone cool off. (baby/toddler)

Melling, David. *Hugless Douglas.* Douglas the bear wakes up wanting a hug, but no one seems willing to give him one. (preschool)

Miranda, Anne. *To Market, to Market.* There's chaos in the kitchen as farm animals ruin a woman's plans to bring home food from the market. (toddler/preschool)

Salley, Coleen. *Epossumondas.* Hilarious illustrations by Janet Stevens make this classic tale of a confused possum even funnier. (preschool)

Shannon, David. *Duck on a Bike.* Every illustration is funnier than the next in this tale of farm animals and bicycles. (preschool)

Shea, Bob. *New Socks.* There's nothing you can't do if you just have bright orange new socks. (toddler/preschool)

Willems, Mo. *Don't Let the Pigeon Drive the Bus.* What could be funnier than a pigeon having a temper tantrum about not being allowed to drive a bus? (preschool)

HEATHER RECOMMENDS

28 Stories That Invite Participation

Whenever there is a repeating phrase or sound, invite your audience to join in with you by either practicing before the story, or identifying a gesture from you that tells them when. They'll love and remember the story even more!

Axtell, David. *We're Going on a Lion Hunt.* Children join in on all the sounds and actions of hunting for a lion. (toddler/preschool)

Brown, Ken. *What's the Time, Grandma Wolf?* A surprise ending and a repeating shout of "What's the time, Grandma Wolf?" make this a hit every time. (toddler/preschool)

Cabrera, Jane. *Here We Go Round the Mulberry Bush.* This is one in a series of nursery rhymes given new verses and plenty of fun in colorful illustrations by Cabrera. (toddler/preschool)

Dodd, Emma. *Dog's Colorful Day.* Children can join in on guessing the colors and numbers in this story of a white dog with one black ear. (toddler/preschool)

Durango, Julia. *Cha Cha Chimps.* Everyone will enjoy the chorus of monkey sounds and counting mischievous monkeys, as well as the surprise ending. (toddler/preschool)

Fleming, Denise. *Mama Cat Has Three Kittens.* "Boris naps" repeats throughout the story in this simple and delightful tale of kitten capers. (toddler)

Fox, Mem. *Where Is the Green Sheep?* Children will "read" this one all on their own in no time because of its repetition, rhythm, rhyme, and predictability. (toddler/preschool)

Gershator, Phillis. *Moo, Moo, Brown Cow, Have You Any Milk?* Children can join in on the phrase, "Yes, sir, yes, sir," in this expanded version of "Baa, Baa, Black Sheep." (toddler)

Hillenbrand, Will. *Down by the Station.* Everyone gets to puff, choo choo, and join in on a chain of animal sounds in this story of a train gathering animals for the zoo. (toddler/preschool)

Hort, Lenny. *Seals on the Bus.* To the tune of "Wheels on the Bus," this is the story of noisy animals on a chaotic bus. (toddler/preschool)

Kirk, Daniel. *Keisha Ann Can!* The African American girl is older than your preschool audience, but she will be a role model as she makes her way through a day at school. Plus everyone can shout out, "Keisha Ann can!" (preschool)

Long, Ethan. *The Croaky Pokey!* Hilarious frogs demonstrate their own version of the "Hokey Pokey." (toddler/preschool)

MacDonald, Margaret Read. *A Hen, a Chick and a String Guitar.* This Chilean cumulative folktale begins with a chick, and ends up with 16 pets and a very catchy song. (preschool)

McDonald, Megan. *Is This a House for Hermit Crab?* A crab searches for just the right shell to protect him from the prickle-pine fish. "Scritch-scratch, scritch-scratch" repeats throughout the story. (preschool)

Patten, Brian, and Nicola Bayley. *The Big Snuggle-up.* A scarecrow and a variety of animals take refuge from a storm. Rhymes and cumulative repetitions make this perfect for participation. (preschool)

Polacco, Patricia. *Oh, Look!* Three goats and a girl go on a journey with plenty of sounds and actions, much like "Goin' on a Bear Hunt." (preschool)

Rueda, Claudia. *Let's Play in the Forest while the Wolf Is Not Around.* A rollicking song helps relieve the tension as the hungry wolf comes closer and closer. (toddler/preschool)

Scade, Susan, and Jon Buller. *The Noisy Counting Book.* When a boy goes fishing, he hears all kinds of animal noises. (baby/toddler)

Silverman, Erica. *Don't Fidget a Feather.* Duck and Gander have a contest that almost leads to disaster when Fox realizes they are not moving. See if your audience can stay as still as the two birds. (preschool)

Stevens, Janet. *The Three Billy Goats Gruff.* Janet Stevens adapted this traditional folktale with hilarious illustrations, including the biggest billy goat in a leather jacket, and a troll with a nose as long as a zucchini. (preschool)

Thomas, Jan. *Is Everyone Ready for Fun?* Be prepared for lots of giggles as children jump, dance, and wiggle with the cows. (toddler/preschool)

Thomson, Pat. *Drat That Fat Cat!* Everyone joins in on the animal sounds, plus "No, he was not!" as the fat cat tries to fill his belly. (preschool)

Vamos, Samantha. *The Cazuela That the Farm Maiden Stirred.* Spanish words are sprinkled throughout this cumulative tale similar to "The House That Jack Built." (preschool)

van Kampen, Vlasta. *It Couldn't Be Worse!* A family learns that their noisy house is not so bad after all. (preschool)

Walker, Anna. *I Love to Dance.* A young zebra loves to dance like jelly, twirl, and hop, and everyone else can, too. (toddler)

Wilson, Karma. *The Cow Loves Cookies.* The farmer knows what all the animals like to eat, but the cow only wants cookies. (toddler/preschool)

Wong, Janet S. *Buzz.* A boy's day begins and he notices all the things that buzz, from bee to hair dryer. (toddler/preschool)

Zimmerman, Andrea, and David Clemesha. *Trashy Town.* Mr. Gilly travels around town gathering trash, and your listeners join in on the delightful refrain, "Dump it in, smash it down, drive around the Trashy Town!" (toddler/preschool)

HEATHER RECOMMENDS

17 Stories That Play with Words

You can help children explore the wonders of language by reading stories that present ways to play with words.

Cabrera, Jane. *Kitty's Cuddles.* A kitten explores the many kinds of cuddles, from teeny-weeny to squidgy, quidgy. (baby/toddler)

Crebbin, June. *Cows in the Kitchen.* Pigs are in the pantry, sheep are on the sofa, and hens are on the hat stand in this silly sing-along. (toddler/preschool)

Doyle, Malachy. *Sleepy Pendoodle.* A little girl can't quite remember the words she is supposed to say to make her new puppy wake up. (preschool)

Gordon, Gaelyn. *Duckat.* What do you get when you combine a cat with a duck? A duck that chases mice! (preschool)

Hubbard, Patricia. *My Crayons Talk.* All the colors of the crayon box have something to say. (toddler/preschool)

Jenkins, Steve, and Robin Page. *Move!* Animals swing, dance, float, leap, and slide. (toddler/preschool)

Lester, Julius. *Sam and the Tigers.* This new telling of an old tale introduces Sam-sam-sa-mara whose cleverness turns five tigers into butter. (preschool)

MacDonald, Alan. *Snarlyhissopus.* Remember the game of telephone, where a circle of friends whisper to the next what they thought they heard from the one before? That's what happens one day in the jungle as the word spreads about a terrible monster. (preschool)

MacDonald, Margaret Read. *Teeny Weeny Bop.* A silly woman wants a pet so she trades for a pig, a cat, a hamster, and even a slug, but nothing works out quite right. (preschool)

Montgomery, Tamara, and Jodi Parry Belknap. *When the Cassowary Pooped: A Tale of New Guinea.* A colorful tale that invites participation, with the rhyme, "Gotta catch a cassowary,/Cassowary, cassowary. /Gotta catch a cassowary,/Where can he be?" (preschool)

Newbery, Linda. *Posy.* A scruffy kitten is a "whiskers wiper, crayon swiper./Playful wrangler, knitting tangler." (toddler/preschool)

Pomerantz, Charlotte. *The Piggy in the Puddle.* This is such fun to read aloud with all the "fiddle faddle" and "mooshy sqooshy" words. Unfortunately, the book is small so you might consider a flannel board presentation while you read. (preschool)

Root, Phyllis. *The Rattletrap Car.* Will the rattletrap car that clanks, pops, brums, and booms get the family to the lake? (preschool)

Ruddell, Deborah. *Who Said Coo?* Words that rhyme with "coo" cleverly fill this story of a pig trying to sleep. (toddler)

Schaefer, Carole Lee. *Dragon Dancing.* A multicultural group of children help Mei Lin celebrate her birthday by making dragons with "boink-boink eyes" and "ricky-rack backs." (toddler/preschool)

Wheeler, Lisa. *Bubble Gum Bubble Gum.* Chewy-gooey, icky-sticky bubble gum is melting in the road and causes all kinds of problems. (preschool)

Yolen, Jane. *Off We Go!* Rhyme and repetition combine in this animal tale with fun words such as "tip-toe, tippity toe" and "Dig deep, diggity deep." (toddler/preschool)

HEATHER RECOMMENDS

21 Stories of All the World

Be sure to include books that represent different ethnicities, cultures, and families, so that children will have a better understanding of all the joyous differences in the world.

Baker, Keith. *Who Is the Beast?* The animals are afraid of the tiger, but he helps them understand that we are all alike in many ways. (toddler/preschool)

Dey, Joy Morgan and Nikki Johnson. *Agate.* Unusual words and illustrations enhance this story of a moose who thinks he is worthless, but all the other animals help him realize he is a gem like everyone else. (preschool)

Fox, Mem. *Ten Little Fingers and Ten Little Toes.* Adorable illustrations of babies around the world exemplify how love is universal. (all ages)

Hamanaka, Sheila. *All the Colors of the Earth.* Joyous children of all colors celebrate the beauty of earth. (toddler/preschool)

Isadora, Rachel. *Friends.* One word per page and illustrations of all ethnicities make this a perfect introduction to the world. (baby/toddler)

Isadora, Rachel. *Happy Belly, Happy Smile.* A young Chinese boy in Chinatown explores his grandfather's restaurant and enjoys a meal with his African American friend. (preschool)

Kasza, Keiko. *A Mother for Choco.* An unusual bird is adopted by a bear, who already has children that are a hippo and a tiger. (toddler/preschool)

Katz, Karen. *The Colors of Us.* All shades of skin colors, from cinnamon to peach, are highlighted. (preschool)

Kostecki-Shaw, Jenny Sue. *Same, Same but Different.* Two boys, one from America, the other from India, compare their lives. (preschool)

Lin, Grace. *Round Is a Mooncake.* A Chinese American girl explores the shapes that make up her world. (toddler/preschool)

Marshall, Linda Elovitz. *Talia and the Rude Vegetables.* Talia can't understand why her grandmother wants rude vegetables for Rosh Hashanah stew. (preschool)

Otoshi, Kathryn. *One.* Colors and numbers are the characters in this powerful story about bullies and friendship. (preschool)

Otoshi, Kathryn. *Zero.* Zero learns that everyone has value. (preschool)

Parr, Todd. *The Family Book.* All kinds of families are presented in Parr's colorful, happy style. (all ages)

Perlman, Willa. *Good Night, World.* The world is getting ready for bed. (toddler/preschool)

Pinkney, Sandra L. *A Rainbow All Around Me.* Photos of multicultural children depict the repeating phrase, "Colors are you, colors are me." (preschool)

Rotner, Shelley and Sheila M. Kelly. *Shades of People.* Children are not black and white, but all shades of all colors. (toddler/preschool)

Tingle, Tim. *When Turtle Grew Feathers.* This hilarious Choctaw variant of the Aesop fable teaches that working together leads to success, while only wanting to win can lead to disaster. (preschool)

Tyler, Michael. *The Skin You Live in.* Feel free to do a little editing if the rhyming story gets too long, but this is a great book for children to understand the joys of differences. (preschool)

Velthujis, Max. *Frog and the Stranger.* A mouse has joined the neighborhood, and it's up to the frog to show the others that the rodent is not dangerous. (preschool)

Wong, Janet S. *This Next New Year.* A Chinese American boy talks about the traditions of the Chinese New Year, and how all his friends from other ethnicities celebrate. (preschool)

Emma and her grandmother come to my Toddlin' Tales story time every week. Emma is an imaginative and outgoing girl with a mop of curly brown hair and sparkly brown eyes. She loves books. No, she LOVES books! Each week she and Nancy, her grandma, fill up a book bag as they wander through the shelves, especially focusing on the new ones. Emma always brings a stuffed animal to story time, and together they do the tickles and actions. Before story time, she peeks into the dog house easel, where I hide my welcoming puppet, to see if it's the usual Winston, or someone new, such as Sapphire the cat, or Yippers the fox. After story time, we search each other out for a hug, or maybe a peek-a-boo game as we circle around the pyramid-shaped bookshelves. And, like Jeff of many years ago, she is quite disgruntled if I take a vacation and miss story time. Nancy recently told me that when Emma had to stay at home with a cold, she said, "What will Miss Heather do without me?" And she's absolutely right; Toddlin' Tales that day was an ice cream sundae without the whip cream and cherry on top.

Emma's parents and grandparents have immersed her in literature and language since the day she was adopted into their loving family. She knows

Regular attendance at story time exposes children to unusual words, fun songs, and the best books. Emma has been coming to Toddlin' Tales since before she was two, and I can't imagine story time without her.

Credit: Used with permission of Leaetta Mitchell. Photography by Leaetta, http://www.photographybyleaetta.com/.

Sitting in chairs creates a formal setting. I prefer as many as possible on the floor because it's relaxed, children can cuddle in laps, and everyone will participate more readily. Make sure parents sit with their children!

Be sure to hold the book so everyone has a chance to see the pictures. The theme of Toddlin' Tales story time this week was trains and I'm reading *Down by the Station* by Will Hillenbrand.

Credit: Used with permission of Leaetta Mitchell. Photography by Leaetta, http://www.photographybyleaetta.com/.

Introducing story time each week with a puppet creates a special bond with the children and gives them a reason to visit with you and the puppet afterward. Winston is the real star of Toddlin' Tales!

I use the "Here's My Bag" song as an opportunity to increase vocabulary by bringing out objects that relate to the theme, or begin with the same letter, or rhyme with each other. At the train story time, I brought out a conductor's hat, a whistle, and two stuffed trains.

Before the stories and songs begin, remind your audience of the help you need to assure story time success. I'm asking parents to turn off cell phones, keep their children close by, and have a rhyme sheet so they can follow along and participate.

Children will remember and love the books even more if you have fun with expressive faces, effective pauses, and different voices.

Pointing out words, whether written on the board or in the book, helps young children begin to understand the importance of print. Behind me is a repeating phrase from *Hey, Mr. Choo Choo, Where Are You Going?* by Susan Wickberg. I wrote the words on the board so everyone would remember and join in.

Credit: Used with permission of Leaetta Mitchell. Photography by Leaetta, http://www.photographybyleaetta.com/.

Introduce each story with the same song or rhyme so the children know it's time to listen. I'm singing the call-and-answer story song, "A Good Story."

every Todd Parr book by heart, thinks that Eric Litwin's *Pete the Cat: I Love My White Shoes* is the best book ever, recognizes each character of literature that we have decorating the room, and effortlessly selects and checks out her books by herself. At story time she never holds back, eagerly doing every movement song, commenting on the books, and leading the pack at the end to hug Winston. Emma is the kind of child who affirms for me each week that what children's librarians do at the library, and what the library has for her, is not just important, but essential.

I dread the day she begins kindergarten and story time no longer includes Emma.

BIBLIOGRAPHY

For Librarians, Teachers, and Parents

Briggs, Diane. *Toddler Stoytimes II.* Lanham, M`D: Scarecrow Press, 2008.

Cobb, Jane. *I'm a Little Teapot: Presenting Preschool Storytime.* Vancouver: Black Sheep Press, 1996.

Cobb, Jane. *What'll I Do with the Baby-Oh: Nursery Rhymes, Songs and Stories for Babies.* Vancouver: Black Sheep Press, 2006.

Cole, Joanna, and Stephanie Calmenson. *The Eentsy, Weentsy Spider: Fingerplays and Action Rhymes.* New York: William Morrow and Company, Inc., 1991.

Dowell, Ruth I. *Move Over, Mother Goose!: Finger Plays, Action Verses & Funny Rhymes.* Mt. Rainier, MD: Gryphon House, Inc., 1987.

Ernst, Linda L. *Baby Rhyming Time.* New York: Neal-Schuman Publishers, Inc., 2008.

Ghoting, Saroj. *Early Literacy Storytimes @ Your Library: Partnering with Caregivers for Success.* Chicago, IL: American Library Association, 2006.

Low, Elizabeth Cother. *Big Book of Animal Rhymes, Fingerplays and Songs.* Westport, CT: Libraries Unlimited, 2009.

MacMillan, Kathy. *A Box Full of Tales: Easy Ways to Share Library Resources through Story boxes.* Chicago, IL: American Library Association, 2008.

MacMillan, Kathy, and Christine Kerker. *Storytime Magic: 400 Fingerplays, Flannelboards, and Other Activities.* Chicago, IL: American Library Association, 2009.

Maddigan, Beth. *The Big Book of Stories, Songs, and Sing-Alongs: Programs for Babies, Toddlers and Families.* Westport, CT: Libraries Unlimited, 2003.

Orozco, Jose-Luis. *Diez Deditos: Ten Little Fingers & Other Play Rhymes and Action Songs from Latin America.* New York: Dutton Children's Books, 1997.

Schiller, Pam. *And the Cow Jumped Over the Moon!: Over 650 Activities to Teach Toddlers Using Familiar Rhymes.* Beltsville, MD: Gryphon House, Inc., 2006.

Scott, Barbara A. *1,000 Fingerplays & Action Rhymes: A Sourcebook & DVD.* New York: Neal Schuman Publishers, Inc., 2010.

Stetson, Emily, and Vicky Congdong. *Little Hands Finger Plays & Action Songs: Seasonal Rhymes & Creative Play for 2-to-6-Year Olds.* Charlotte, VT: Williamson Publishing, 2001.

For Children

Alborough, Jez. *Where's My Teddy?* Cambridge, MA: Candlewick Press, 1995.

Andersen, Hans Christian. *The Princess and the Pea.* New York: Holiday House, 1982.

Appelt, Kathi. *Incredible Me!* New York: HarperCollins, 2002.

Averbeck, Jim. *Except If.* New York: Atheneum Books for Young Readers, 2011.

Axtell, David. *We're Going on a Lion Hunt.* New York: Holt, 2000.

Ayres, Katherine. *Matthew's Truck.* Cambridge, MA: Candlewick Press, 2005.

Bajaj, Varsha. *How Many Kisses Do You Want Tonight?* New York: Little, Brown and Co., 2004.

Baker, Keith. *Who Is the Beast?* San Diego, CA: Harcourt Brace Jovanovich, 1990.

Baker, Keith. *Big Fat Hen.* San Diego, CA: Harcourt Brace & Company, 1997.

Bang, Molly. *All of Me! A Book of Thanks.* New York: Blue Sky Press, 2009.

Banks, Kate. *Close Your Eyes.* New York: Frances Foster Books, 2001.

Barry, Frances. *Duckie's Splash.* Cambridge, MA: Candlewick Press, 2006.

Bates, Ivan. *All by Myself.* New York: HarperCollins, 2000.

Beaumont, Karen. *Baby Danced the Polka.* New York: Dial Books for Young Readers, 2004.

Beaumont, Karen. *I Ain't Gonna Paint No More!* Orlando, FL: Harcourt, 2005.

Beaumont, Karen. *Move over, Rover!* Orlando, FL: Harcourt, 2006.

Bedford, David. *Touch the Sky, My Little Bear.* Brooklyn, NY: Handprint Books, 2001.

Bently, Peter, and Helen Oxenbury. *King Jack and the Dragon.* New York: Dial Books for Young Readers, 2011.

Berger, Barbara. *Grandfather Twilight.* New York: Philomel Books, 1984.

Best, Cari. *Red Light, Green Light, Mama and Me.* New York: Orchard Books, 1995.

Boynton, Sandra. *Moo, Baa, La, La, La.* New York: Little Simon, 1995.

Brett, Jan. *The Mitten: A Ukranian Folktale.* New York: Putnam, 1989.

Brown, Ken. *The Scarecrow's Hat.* Atlanta, GA: Peachtree Publishers, 2001.

Brown, Ken. *What's the Time, Grandma Wolf?* Atlanta, GA: Peachtree, 2001.

Butler, John. *Can You Growl Like a Bear?* Atlanta, GA: Peachtree, 2007.

Bynum, Janie. *Kiki's Blankie.* New York: Sterling, 2009.

Cabrera, Jane. *Kitty's Cuddles.* New York: Holiday House, 2007.

Cabrera, Jane. *Here We Go Round the Mulberry Bush.* New York: Holiday House, 2010.

Catchpool, Michael. *Where There's a Bear, There's Trouble.* Wilton, CT: Tiger Tales, 2002.

Charlip, Remy. *Sleepytime Rhyme.* New York: Greenwillow Books, 1999.

Chodos-Irvine, Margaret. *Ella Sarah Gets Dressed.* San Diego, CA: Harcourt, 2003.

Church, Caroline Jayne. *One More Hug for Madison.* New York: Orchard Books, 2010.

Cleminson, Katie. *Magic Box: A Magical Story.* New York: Disney/Hyperion, 2009.

Cooke, Trish. *So Much.* Cambridge, MA: Candlewick Press, 1994.

Craig, Lindsey. *Dancing Feet.* New York: Alfred A. Knopf, 2010.

Crebbin, June. *Cows in the Kitchen.* Cambridge, MA: Candlewick Press, 2003.

Crimi, Carolyn. *Tessa's Tip-Tapping Toes.* New York: Orchard Books, 2002.

Cronin, Doreen. *Wiggle.* New York: Atheneum Books for Young Readers, 2005.

Cronin, Doreen. *Bounce.* New York: Atheneum Books for Young Readers, 2007.

Cruise, Robin. *Little Mama Forgets.* New York: Farrar, Straus and Giroux, 2006.

Cuyler, Margery. *The Biggest, Best Snowman.* New York: Scholastic, 1998.

Dey, Joy Morgan, and Nikki Johnson. *Agate: What Good Is a Moose?* Duluth, MN: Lake Superior Port Cities, Inc., 2007.

Diesen, Deborah. *The Pout-Pout Fish in the Big-Big Dark.* New York: Farrar Straus Giroux, 2010.

Dodd, Emma. *Dog's Colorful Day: A Messy Story about Colors and Counting.* New York: Dutton Children's Books, 2001.

Dodd, Emma. *Meow Said the Cow.* New York: Arthur A. Levine Books, 2011.

Dodds, Siobhan. *Ting-a-Ling!* New York: DK Pub., 1999.

Donaldson, Julia. *The Gruffalo.* New York: Dial Books for Young Readers, 1999.

Dorros, Arthur. *Mama and Me.* New York: Rayo, 2011.

Doyle, Malachy. *Sleepy Pendoodle.* Cambridge, MA: Candlewick Press, 2002.

Durango, Julia. *Cha Cha Chimps.* New York: Simon & Schuster Books for Young Readers, 2006.

Edwards, Pamela Duncan. *Some Smug Slug.* New York: HarperCollins Publishers, 2006.

Ehlert, Lois. *Snowballs.* San Diego, CA: Harcourt Brace, c1995

Elffers, Joost. *Do You Love Me?* New York: Bowen Press, 2009.

Faulkner, Keith. *The Scared Little Bear.* New York: Orchard Books, 2000.

Fleming, Denise. *Lunch!* New York: Henry Holt and Co., 1992.

Fleming, Denise. *Mama Cat Has Three Kittens.* New York: Henry Holt, 1998.

Fleming, Denise. *Sleepy, Oh, So Sleepy.* New York: Holt, 2010.

Fore, S. J. *Tiger Can't Sleep.* New York: Viking, 2006.

Fox, Mem. *Time for Bed.* San Diego, CA: Harcourt Brace, 1993.

Fox, Mem. *Zoo-Looking.* Greenvale, NY: Mondo Pub., 1996.

Fox, Mem. *Ten Little Fingers and Ten Little Toes.* Orlando, FL: Harcourt, 2008.

Fox, Mem. *Where Is the Green Sheep?* Boston, MA: Sandpiper, 2010.

French, Vivian. *Henny Penny.* New York: Bloomsbury Children's Books, 2006.

Fuge, Charles. *I Know a Rhino.* New York: Sterling, 2002.

Genechten, Guido van. *The Cuddle Book.* New York: HarperCollins Publishers, 2005.

Gershator, Phillis. *Moo, Moo, Brown Cow, Have You Any Milk?* New York: Random House Children's Books, 2011.

Gilani-Williams, Fawzia. *Nabeel's New Pants: An Eid Tale.* Tarrytown, NY: Marshall Cavendish Children, 2010.

Gleeson, Libby. *Cuddle Time.* Cambridge, MA: Candlewick Press, 2004.

Godwin, Laura. *What the Baby Hears.* New York: Hyperion Books for Children, 2002.

Goodhart, Pippa. *Pudgy: A Puppy to Love.* New York: Scholastic, 2003.

Gorbachev, Valeri. *Chicken Chickens.* New York: North-South Books, 2001.

Gordon, Gaelyn. *Duckat.* New York: Scholastic, 1991.

Gravett, Emily. *Monkey and Me.* New York: Simon & Schuster Books for Young Readers, 2008.

Gravett, Emily. *Dogs.* New York: Simon & Schuster Books for Young Readers, 2010.

Greenfield, Eloise. *Honey, I Love.* New York: HarperCollins Publishers, 2003.

Greenspun, Adele Aron. *Ariel and Emily.* New York: Dutton Children's Books, 2003.

Grimm, Jakob, and Wilhelm Grimm. *The Elves and the Shoemaker.* San Francisco, CA: Chronicle Books, 2003.

Hager, Sarah. *Dancing Matilda.* New York: HarperCollins Publishers, 2005.

Hall, Michael. *My Heart Is Like a Zoo.* New York: Greenwillow Books, 2010.

Hall, Michael. *Perfect Square.* New York: Greenwillow Books, 2011.

Hamanaka, Sheila. *All the Colors of the Earth.* New York: Morrow Junior Books, 1994.

Harris, Robie. *Maybe a Bear Ate It!* New York: Orchard Books, 2008.

Heap, Sue. *What Shall We Play?* Cambridge, MA: Candlewick Press, 2002.

Henderson, Kathy. *Look at You! A Baby Body Book.* Cambridge, MA: Candlewick Press, 2006.

Henkes, Kevin. *Kitten's First Full Moon.* New York: Greenwillow Books, 2004.

Henkes, Kevin. *My Garden.* New York: Greenwillow Books, 2010.

Hillenbrand, Will. *Down by the Station.* San Diego, CA: Harcourt Brace, 1999.

Hindley, Judy. *Baby Talk.* Cambridge, MA: Candlewick Press, 2006.

Hooks, Bell. *Grump Groan Growl.* New York: Hyperion Books for Children, 2008.

Horacek, Petr. *Butterfly Butterfly.* Cambridge, MA: Candlewick Press, 2007.

Hort, Lenny. *Seals on the Bus.* New York: Henry Holt, 2000.

Hubbard, Patricia. *My Crayons Talk.* New York: Henry Holt, 1996.

Intrater, Roberta Grobel. *Peek-A-Boo, You!* New York: Scholastic, Inc., 2002.

Isadora, Rachel. *Friends.* New York: Greenwillow Books, 1990.

Isadora, Rachel. *Happy Belly, Happy Smile.* Boston, MA: Harcourt Children's Books, 2009.

Jenkins, Steve, and Robin Page. *Move!* Boston, MA: Houghton Mifflin, 2006.

Joosse, Barbara. *Papa, Do You Love Me?* San Francisco, CA: Chronicle Books, 2005.

Kampen, Vlasta van. *It Couldn't Be Worse!* Toronto: Annick Press, 2003.

Kasza, Keiko. *A Mother for Choco.* New York: Putnam, 1992.

Katz, Karen. *The Colors of Us.* New York: Holt, 1999.

Katz, Karen. *Where Is Baby's Belly Button?* New York: Little Simon, 2000.

Katz, Karen. *Counting Kisses.* New York: Little Simon, 2003.

Katz, Karen. *Babies on the Bus.* New York: Henry Holt, 2011.

Katz, Susan. *ABC, Baby Me.* New York: Robin Corey Books, 2010.

Keats, Ezra Jack. *Regards to the Man in the Moon.* New York: Four Winds Press, 1981.

Ketteman, Helen. *Goodnight, Little Monster.* New York: Marshall Cavendish, 2010.

Kimmel, Eric. *Anansi and the Moss-Covered Rock.* New York: Holiday House, 1988.

Kirk, Daniel. *Keisha Ann Can!* New York: G. P. Putnam's Sons, 2008.

Klassen, Jon. *I Want My Hat Back.* Somerville, MA: Candlewick Press, 2011.

Kostecki-Shaw, Jenny Sue. *Same, Same but Different.* New York: Henry Holt, 2011.

Krauss, Ruth. *And I Love You.* New York: Scholastic Press, 2010.

Kubler, Annie. *Ten Little Fingers.* Auburn, ME: Child's Play, 2003.

Kulka, Joe. *Wolf's Coming!* Minneapolis, MN: Carolrhoda Books, 2007.

Lee, Spike, and Tonya Lewis Lee. *Please, Baby, Please!* New York: Simon & Schuster Books for Young Readers, 2002.

Lester, Julius. *Sam and the Tigers.* New York: Dial Books for Young Readers, 1996.

Lieshout, Maria van. *Hopper and Wilson.* New York: Philomel Books, 2011.

Lin, Grace. *Round Is a Mooncake: A Book of Shapes.* San Francisco, CA: Chronicle Books, 2000.

Lloyd, Sam. *What Color Is Your Underwear?* New York: Scholastic, 2004.

Long, Ethan. *The Croaky Pokey!* New York: Holiday House, 2011.

Lowery, Linda. *Twist with a Burger, Jitter with a Bug.* Boston, MA: Houghton Mifflin, 1994.

Luthardt, Kevin. *Flying!* Atlanta, GA: Peachtree, 2009.

MacDonald, Alan. *Snarlyhissopus.* Wilton, CT: Tiger Tales, 2002.

MacDonald, Margaret Read. *A Hen, a Chick and a String Guitar.* Cambridge, MA: Barefoot Books, 2005.

MacDonald, Margaret Read. *Teeny Weeny Bop.* Morton Grove, IL: Albert Whitman, 2006.

MacDonald, Margaret Read, and Nadi Jameel Taibah. *How Many Donkeys?: An Arabic Counting Tale.* Morton Grove, IL: Albert Whitman, 2009.

Macken, JoAnn Early. *Baby Says "Moo!"* New York: Disney/Hyperion Books, 2011.

Manning, Maurie J. *Kitchen Dance.* New York: Clarion Books, 2008.

Marshall, Linda Elovitz. *Talia and the Rude Vegetables.* Minneapolis, MN: Kar-Ben, 2011.

Martin, David. *We've All Got Bellybuttons.* Cambridge, MA: Candlewick Press, 2005.

Massie, Diane Redfield. *The Baby Beebee Bird.* New York: HarperCollins Publishers, 2000.

Mayhew, James. *Who Wants a Dragon?* New York: Orchard Books, 2004.

McDonald, Megan. *Is This a House for Hermit Crab?* New York: Orchard Books, 1990.

McDonnell, Flora. *Splash!* Cambridge, MA: Candlewick Press, 2003.

McGee, Marni. *Sleepy Me.* New York: Simon and Schuster Books for Young Readers, 2001.

Melling, David. *Hugless Douglas.* Wilton, CT: Tiger Tales, 2010.

Milord, Susan. *Love That Baby!* Boston, MA: Houghton Mifflin, 2005.

Miranda, Anne. *To Market, to Market.* Orlando, FL: Harcourt, 2007.

Mockford, Caroline. *Cleo the Cat.* New York: Barefoot Books, 2001.

Montgomery, Tamara, and Jodi Parry Belknap. *When the Cassowary Pooped: A Tale of New Guinea.* Honolulu, HI: Calabash Books, 2009.

Morrow, Tara Jaye. *Mommy Loves Her Baby/Daddy Loves His Baby.* New York: HarperCollins, 2003.

Murphy, Mary. *I Kissed the Baby!* Cambridge, MA: Candlewick Press, 2005.

Na, Il Sung. *The Thingamabob.* New York: Alfred A. Knopf, 2010.

Nakamura, Catherine Riley. *Song of Night: It's Time to Go to Bed.* New York: Blue Sky Press, 2002.

Newbery, Linda. *Posy.* New York: Atheneum Books for Young Readers, 2009.

Nikola-Lisa, W. *Setting the Turkeys Free.* New York: Hyperion Books for Children, 2004.

Norman, Kimberly. *Ten on the Sled.* New York: Sterling, 2010.

O'Connell, Rebecca. *The Baby Goes Beep.* Brookfield, CT: Roaring Book Press, 2003.

Otoshi, Kathryn. *One.* Mill Valley, CA: KO Kids Books, 2008.

Otoshi, Kathryn. *Zero.* San Rafael, CA: KO Kids Books, 2010.

Oxenbury, Helen. *All Fall Down.* New York: Aladdin Books, 1987.

Parr, Todd. *The Feel Good Book.* Boston, MA: Little Brown, 2002.

Parr, Todd. *The Family Book.* New York: Little, Brown, 2003.

Parr, Todd. *The I Love You Book.* New York: Little, Brown and Co., 2009.

Patricelli, Leslie. *Tubby.* Somerville, MA: Candlewick Press, 2010.

Patten, Brian, and Nicola Bayley. *The Big Snuggle Up.* Tulsa, OK: Kane Miller, 2011.

Perlman, Willa. *Good Night, World.* New York: Beach Lane Books, 2011.

Pfam, LeUyen. *Big Sister, Little Sister.* New York: Hyperion Books for Children, 2005.

Pinkney, Sandra L. *A Rainbow All Around Me.* New York: Scholastic, 2002.

Polacco, Patricia. *Oh, Look!* New York: Philomel Books, 2004.

Pomerantz, Charlotte. *The Piggy in the Puddle.* New York: Macmillan, 1974.

Portis, Antoinette. *Not a Box.* New York: HarperCollins, 2006.

Ray, Mary Lyn. *Red Rubber Boot Day.* San Diego, CA: Harcourt Brace, 2000.

Reidy, Jean. *Too Purpley!* New York: Bloomsbury Children's Books, 2010.

Rohmann, Eric. *Clara and Asha.* New Milford, CT: Roaring Book Press, 2005.

Root, Phyllis. *The Rattletrap Car.* Cambridge, MA: Candlewick Press, 2001.

Rotner, Shelley, and Sheila M. Kelly. *Shades of People.* New York: Holiday House, 2009.

Rowe, John A. *I Want a Hug.* New York: Minedition, 2007.

Ruddell, Deborah. *Who Said Coo?* New York: Beach Lane Books, 2010.

Rueda, Claudia. *Let's Play in the Forest while the Wolf Is Not Around.* New York: Scholastic Press, 2006.

Ryder, Joanne. *Won't You Be My Kissaroo?* Orlando, FL: Harcourt, 2007.

Salley, Coleen. *Epossumondas.* San Diego, CA: Harcourt, 2002.

Sanderson, Ruth. *Goldilocks.* New York: Little, Brown, 2009.

Sattler, Jennifer. *Sylvie.* New York: Random House, 2009.

Scade, Susan, and Jon Buller. *The Noisy Counting Book.* New York: Random House Children's Book, 2010.

Scanlon, Liz Garton. *Noodle & Lou.* New York: Beach Lane Books, 2011.

Schaefer, Carole Lee. *Dragon Dancing*. New York: Viking Children's Books, 2007.

Schaefer, Carole Lexa. *Squiggle*. New York: Crown Publishers, 1996.

Schotter, Roni. *Captain Bob Sets Sail*. New York: Atheneum Books for Young Readers, 2000.

Schwarz, Vivian. *There Are Cats in This Book*. Cambridge, MA: Candlewick Press, 2008.

Seeger, Laura Vacarro. *Lemons Are Not Red*. Brookfield, CT: Roaring Book Press, 2004.

Shannon, David. *Duck on a Bike*. New York: Blue Sky Press, 2002.

Shea, Bob. *New Socks*. New York: Little, Brown, 2007.

Silverman, Erica. *Don't Fidget a Feather*. New York: Maxwell Macmillan International, 1994.

Simmons, Jane. *Come Along, Daisy*. Boston, MA: Little, Brown, 1998.

Simmons, Jane. *Quack, Daisy, Quack*. Boston, MA: Little Brown, 2002.

Siomades, Lorianne. *The Itsy Bitsy Spider*. Honesdale, PA: Boyds Mills Press, 2001.

Smalls, Irene. *Jonathan and His Mommy*. Boston, MA: Little, Brown, 1992.

Smee, Nicola. *Splish-Splash*. Bel Aire, CA: Boxer Books, 2011.

Soto, Gary. *Big Bushy Mustache*. New York: Knopf, 1998.

Stein, David Ezra. *Pouch!* New York: G. P. Putnam's Sons, 2009.

Stevens, Janet. *The Three Billy Goats Gruff*. San Diego, CA: Harcourt Brace Jovanovich, 1987.

Stojic, Manya. *Rain*. New York: Crown, 2000.

Sturges, Philemon. *How Do You Make a Baby Smile?* New York: HarperCollins, 2007.

Symes, Ruth. *Harriet Dancing*. New York: Chicken House/Scholastic, 2008.

Tafolla, Carmen. *What Can You Do with a Rebozo?* Berkeley, CA: Tricycle Press, 2008.

Tafolla, Carmen. *What Can You Do with a Paleta?* Berkeley, CA: Tricycle Press, 2009.

Tafolla, Carmen. *Fiesta Babies*. Berkeley, CA: Tricycle Press, 2010.

Tafuri, Nancy. *The Big Storm: A Very Soggy Counting Book*. New York: Simon & Schuster Books for Young Readers, 2009.

Tanaka, Beatrice. *The Chase: A Kutenai Indian Tale* New York: Crown, 1991.

Thomas, Jan. *Is Everyone Ready for Fun?* New York: Beach Lane Books, 2011.

Thompson, Lauren. *Little Quack*. New York: Simon & Schuster Books for Young Readers, 2003.

Thomson, Pat. *Drat That Fat Cat!* New York: Arthur A. Levine Books, 2003.

Tillman, Nancy. *Tumford the Terrible*. New York: Feiwel & Friends, 2011.

Tingle, Tim. *When Turtle Grew Feathers*. Atlanta, GA: August House LittleFolk, 2007.

Tullet, Herve. *Press Here*. San Francisco, CA: Chronicle Books, 2011.

Tyler, Michael. *The Skin You Live in*. Chicago, IL: Chicago Children's Museum, 2005.

Vamos, Samantha. *The Cazuela That the Farm Maiden Stirred*. Watertown, MA: Charlesbridge, 2011.

Velthujis, Max. *Frog and the Stranger*. London: Andersen Press, 2005.

Waddell, Martin. *Tom Rabbit*. Cambridge, MA: Candlewick Press, 2001.

Walker, Anna. *I Love to Dance*. New York: Simon & Schuster Books for Young Readers, 2011.

Walton, Rick. *Bear Came over to My House*. New York: Putnam, 2001.

Walton, Rick. *Baby's First Year!* New York: G. P. Putnam's Sons, 2011.

Waring, Richard. *Hungry Hen*. New York: HarperCollins Publishers, 2001.

Weeks, Sarah. *Overboard!* Orlando, FL: Harcourt, 2006.

Wheeler, Lisa. *Bubble Gum Bubble Gum*. New York: Little, Brown and Co., 2004.

Wheeler, Lisa. *Jazz Baby*. Orlando, FL: Harcourt, 2007.

Whippo, Walt. *Little White Duck*. Boston, MA: Little Brown, 2000.

Wickberg, Susan. *Hey, Mr. Choo-Choo, Where Are You Going?* New York: G. P. Putnam's Sons, 2008.

Wild, Margaret, and Ann James. *Little Humpty*. Vancouver: Simply Read Books, 2004.

Wilhelm, Hans. *Hugaboo, I Love You*. New York: Scholastic, 2009.

Willems, Mo. *Don't Let the Pigeon Drive the Bus*. New York: Hyperion Books for Children, 2003.

Willis, Jeanne. *Never Too Little to Love*. Cambridge, MA: Candlewick Press, 2005.

Wilson, Karma. *The Cow Loves Cookies*. New York: Margaret K. McElderrry Books, 2010.

Wong, Janet S. *Buzz*. San Diego, CA: Harcourt, 2000.

Wong, Janet S. *This Next New Year*. New York: Frances Foster Books, 2000.

Yolen, Jane. *Owl Moon*. New York: Philomel Books, 1987.

Yolen, Jane. *Off We Go!* Boston, MA: Little, Brown, 1999.

Yolen, Jane. *Hush, Little Horsie*. New York: Random House, 2010.

Zimmerman, Andrea, and David Clemesha. *Trashy Town*. New York: HarperCollins Publishers, 1999.

WEBLIOGRAPHY

www.earlylit.net
www.childcraft.com
http://www.photographybyleaetta.com/

Chapter Eight

WHAT'S SO IMPORTANT ABOUT READING ALOUD: WHAT THE RESEARCH TELLS US

It is doubtful that there is any research that says reading aloud to your child is harmful, or that intimacy between caregiver and child does not lead to healthy brain development. In fact, research proves, again and again, that:

- Reading aloud to your child increases bonding and the release of serotonin.
- Synapses in the brain connect constantly and quickly when a child is stimulated through conversation, positive experiences, and nurturing.
- Reading books to your child leads to a broader vocabulary that enhances social skills.
- Reading aloud every day for at least a total of 20 minutes right from birth will, most likely, result in raising a reader.
- Reading aloud from the beginning increases the likelihood of academic success.

But perhaps you need sound bites for an ad, or data to motivate an organization to donate books, or research that states clearly the impact that reading aloud has on a child's kindergarten readiness. Research is sprinkled throughout this book, clearly marked with the words "Facts 'n Stats." In addition, I've arranged more research in this chapter by the following categories:

- The Importance of Reading Aloud
- The Development of Learning to Read
- Books in the Home
- Language Development
- Kindergarten Readiness
- Screen Time

THE IMPORTANCE OF READING ALOUD

I asked Bridget, the parent of now 12-year-old twins, why they are such avid readers and book lovers. She gave the answer I expected, "Because I always read to them, right from the start. One of my favorite memories is of lying on my back, with one baby on each side of my head. I would hold the book up in the air so they could both see it, and read aloud to them. They always listened." When they were 11, she read aloud all 7 of the Harry Potter books to them in one year! "It was exhausting, and I'd want a break. But as soon as I finished one they'd say, 'Let's start the next one.'" Which just confirms what I've always believed, you're never too old to have a book read aloud to you.

It doesn't really take research to convince anyone of the importance of reading aloud. Reading aloud results in very special memories and moments. It is also the great equalizer. Parents who were not given exposure to literature when they were children, nor talked to with frequency and engagement, will find it to be an easy way to improve their child's chances for academic success, increase their vocabulary, and, most importantly, build a bond of intimacy and trust through the lap-time and loving that occurs during story time.

Here's what research says about the importance of reading aloud:

1. "The single most important activity for building the knowledge required for eventual success in reading is reading aloud to children...The benefits are greatest when the child is an active participant, engaging in discussions about stories, learning to identify letters and words, and talking about the meanings of words."

   (National Academy of Education. *Becoming a Nation of Readers: The Report of the Commission on Reading,* p. 33. National Academy of Education, 1985.)

2. "Parents play roles of inestimable importance in laying the foundation for learning to read. Parents should informally teach preschool children about reading and writing by reading aloud to

them, discussing stories and events, encouraging them to learn letters and words and teaching them about the world around them. These practices help prepare children for success in reading."

(National Academy of Education. *Becoming a Nation of Readers: The Report of the Commission on Reading,* p. 67. National Academy of Education, 1985.)

THE DEVELOPMENT OF LEARNING TO READ

Think about it. Think about all that it takes to decode this amazing process called reading. Experts agree that it would never just happen. It is a process that begins at birth when a baby hears sounds. Later, sounds become words, and the words have meanings. The child learns to repeat those words and use them in the right context. Then those words transfer to scribbles on paper. Every scribble must be deciphered to determine its meaning and sound. There are phonemes and punctuation and weird spellings, all of which have to be figured out. It's truly a miracle, one that only humans can claim.

Here's what research says about the development of learning to read:

1. "According to research, here are the basic principles of emergent literacy.

    1. Literacy is a social process. It occurs in the context of children's interactions with other children and adults.

    2. Literacy begins at birth. From an infant's first observations of human behaviors and her resulting imitations of adult sounds and social cues, literacy is developing.

    3. All aspects of literacy—listening, speaking, reading, writing, and thinking—develop interdependently.

    4. Literacy develops along a continuum just like intellectual and physical growth. Children will develop literacy at their own pace. Slow times are often times when internalization is occurring."
    (Schiller, Pam. *Creating Readers,* p. 13. Gryphon House, Inc., 2001.)

2. "To Sum Up:

    1. Reading takes knowing about letters and words (print awareness).

    2. It requires ear training (recognizing sounds in words) and eye training (recognizing letter symbols).

3. Link symbols to sounds (phonics), and a child can figure out most words written in our alphabetic code.

4. Those words only have meaning (comprehension) if they relate back to an experience the child has been given language to define and appreciate (concept and language development)."

(Hauser, Jill Frankel. *Wow! I'm Reading,* p. 9. Charlotte, VT: Williamson Publishing Co., 2000.)

3. "The Department of Education (July 2001) says that scientific research shows that there are five essential components of reading that children must be taught in order to learn to read. These five important elements in learning to read include the ability to:

1. Hear the phonemes, or sounds, in words,

2. Recognize words used often,

3. Take apart words phonetically—phonics are important,

4. Recognize the alphabet, and

5. Make sense of what was read through discussion and rereading."

(Silberg, Jackie. *Reading Games for Young Children,* p. 12. Gryphon House, Inc., 2005.)

4. "[T]he emerging pre-reader sits on 'beloved laps,' samples and learns from the full range of multiple sounds, words, concepts, images, stories, exposure to print, literacy materials, and just plain talk during the first five years of life. The major insight in this period is that reading never just happens to anyone. Emerging reading arises out of years of perceptions, increasing conceptual and social development, and cumulative exposures to oral and written language."

(Wolf, Maryanne. *Proust and the Squid,* p. 115. Harper, 2007.)

5. "*Early literacy* encompasses *language readiness* (knowing how oral language works); *background knowledge* (as children develop word knowledge, they also develop world knowledge based on their experiences), which supports comprehension; and *print components* (understanding that print has meaning and that print relates to what is spoken). Early literacy is what children know about reading and writing before they actually learn to read and write."

(Ghoting, Saroj. *Early Literacy Storytimes @ Your Library*, p. 6. Chicago, IL: American Library Association, 2006.)

6. "As you begin to understand the true building blocks for reading—vocabulary, storytelling, phonological awareness, and deciphering the written code—you'll see how children gradually discover important aspects of literacy as they reach certain milestones on their reading journey. These milestones include distinguishing between pictures in a book and real objects, identifying letters from squiggles and designs, and learning how to sound out printed words."

(Hirsh-Pasek, Kathy, and Roberta Michnick Golinkoff. *Einstein Never Used Flash Cards: How Our Children REALLY Learn—And Why They Need to Play More and Memorize Less*, p. 99. Rodale, 2003.)

BOOKS IN THE HOME

Many studies have been done that prove the importance of books being readily available to young children, as well as the importance of caregivers making sure that they find time to read what they enjoy themselves. Children must be able to ask for books, handle books, and see reading as a valuable part of every day. Of course, that doesn't mean having to *buy* books, since they are free at the public library. The child's books that can be chewed, explored, and loved should be easily accessible in a basket or a low shelf. I like to recommend encouraging the child to decorate a box, and then the adult prints in big, block letters, "JAMIE'S BOOK BOX." Books that require gentler treatment can be placed on a higher shelf until the child is old enough to understand. When a child is treating a book improperly, rather than shouting out, "NO! Don't eat the book!," try interacting in a more positive manner as you carefully remove the book from her mouth. "I see you have *Baby Talk*. We love that book, don't we? Let's sit together and I'll read it to you. You can lift the flaps."

Here's what research says about the importance of books in the home:

1. "Within the U.S., access to books is essential to reading development: the only variable that directly correlates with reading scores is the number of books in the home. However, most recent data describes a profound, even shocking gap: while the ratio of books to children in middle-income neighborhoods is approximately 13 books to 1 child, the ratio in low-income neighborhoods is 1 book to 300 children."

(Neuman, Susan B., and David K. Dickinson, ed. *Handbook of Early Literacy Research,* Vol. 2, p. 31. New York: Guilford Press, 2006.)

2. "Over 80 percent of childcare centers serving low-income children lack age-appropriate books." (www.theliteracysite.com.)

3. "Children from low-income families have been exposed to an average of only 25 hours of one-on-one reading time compared to an average of 1,000 to 1,700 hours for children from middle-class families."(www.theliteracysite.com.)

4. A study, "Children's Access to Print Material and Education-Related Outcomes" (August, 2010), was commissioned by Reading Is Fundamental (RIF) and conducted by Learning Point Associates, "a nonprofit education research and consulting organization and affiliate of American Institutes for Research (AIR)."

The analysis found that access to print materials

- *"Improves children's reading performance.* Findings from the rigorous studies suggest that providing children with print materials helps them read better. Among the studies reviewed, kindergarten students showed the biggest increase in reading performance.

- *Proves instrumental in helping children learn the basics of reading.* Providing children with reading materials allows them to develop basic reading skills such as letter and word identification, phonemic awareness, and completion of sentences.

- *Causes children to read more and for longer lengths of time.* Giving children print materials leads to more shared reading between parents and children. Children receiving books also read more frequently and for longer periods of time.

- *Produces improved attitudes toward reading and learning among children.* Children with greater access to books and other print materials—through either borrowing books or receiving books to own—express more enjoyment of books, reading, and academics."

(http://www.rif.org/us/about/literacy-issues/giving-children-access-to-print-materials-improves-reading-performance.htm. Used with permission from RIF.)

LANGUAGE DEVELOPMENT

Talk, talk, talk. Talk to your baby, your toddler, your preschooler. Talk about your day, your thoughts, your plans. Talk about what you see and what you feel. Ask questions, and listen to your child's responses. If the word is incorrect, such as "I goed to the liberry," you repeat and correct in a positive way so as to encourage more conversation. "Yes, you went to the library. What did you find over by the window?" "Bears!" "Yes, they had lots of teddy bears. One was very big. What did we do with him?" "Read tory." "Yes, we read a story about a silly chicken. What else did you do at the library?" "Puter!" "Yes, you played the Dr. Seuss game on the computer." The more your child hears, the more she learns. The more words she has when she begins school, the more comfortable she'll feel about making friends and participating in class.

Reading books to your child is a simple way to increase her vocabulary, as previously discussed in Chapter Three. So if you, as a parent, are uncomfortable at first with all that talking, simply make time to read, read, read to your baby, your toddler, your preschooler. She'll hear unusual words that you would never use in normal conversation, and you'll have the story to talk about as it relates to your own lives. "Remember the book we read last night called *Thunder Cake* by Patricia Pollaco? It's going to rain today, so let's read it again, and then we can make thunder cake, just like in the book."

Here's what research says about language development:

1. "Consider that by the age of 18 months, 'most children can pronounce four-fifths of the English phonemes and use 9 to 20 words..' [B]etween their second and third birthdays, toddlers' vocabularies expand from 300 to 1,000 words!"

   (Bennet-Armistead, V. Susan. *Beyond Bedtime Stories: A Parent's Guide to Promoting Reading, Writing and Other Literary Skills from Birth to 5*, p. 66. New York: Scholastic Teaching Resources, 2007.)

2. "When one realizes that children have to learn about 88,700 written words during their school years, and that at least 9,000 of these words need to be learned by the end of grade 3, the huge importance of a child's development of vocabulary becomes crystal-clear."

   (Wolf, Maryanne. *Proust and the Squid: The Story and Science of the Reading Brain*, p. 123. New York: Harper, 2007.)

3. A study focused on four-year-olds attending Head Start and their mothers or primary caregivers revealed a significant correlation between the age when shared reading began, and the

language scores of the child. Between 12 and 18.5 percent of the differences in those scores are attributed to the "home literacy environment." A full report can be found in the article "The Role of Home Literacy Environment in the Development of Language Ability in Preschool Children from Low-Income Families," written by Adam Payne, Grover Whitehurst, and Andrea Angeli, and published by *Early Childhood Research Quarterly,* and available at http://www.sciencedirect.com/science/article/pii/0885200694900183.

4. "Studies show that babies who are talked to from the start have 300 more words in their vocabulary at age two than children who do not have adults who communicate with them. Just hearing language on TV or grown-ups talking to each other doesn't do the trick. One-on-one interactions between babies and their caregivers are key to developing the brain and language skills."

(Oppenheim, Joanne. *Oppenheim Toy Portfolio's Read It! Play It! With Babies and Toddlers: Building Literacy Through Reading and Play,* p. vii. New York: Oppenheim Toy Portfolio, 2006.)

5. "Reading books to children is a much more effective way to build vocabulary than family conversations or speech heard on TV or videos. Typically an adult will use only 9 'rare' words per 1,000 when speaking to a child under age 5. We find three times as many of those rarer words in children's books. Regular family conversations will take care of the basic vocabulary, but when you read to the child you leap into the rare words that help the most when it's time for school and formal learning."

(From Trelease, Jim. *The New Read-Aloud Handbook.* New York: Viking Penguin, 1989. Copyright © 1979, 1982 1985, 1989 by Jim Trelease. Used by permission of Viking Penguin, a division of Penguin Group (USA) Inc.)

6. "The average vocabulary for 3-year-olds is about 900 words, four-year-olds know between 3,000 and 8,000 words, and one year later the number of words known, for the average 6-year-old, is around 13,000. It is no wonder that when a child moves beyond the toddler stage, linguistic ability moves to an entirely different level."

(Nevills, Pamela, and Patricia Wolfe. *Building the Reading Brain, PreK-3,* p. 59. Thousand Oaks, CA: Corwin Press, 2009.)

7. Candy Schulman, in her article "I Love Reading"(*American Baby,* October 1998), quotes William Staso, PhD, an educational psychologist and the author of *What Stimulation Your Baby Needs to*

Become Smart, published by Great Beginnings, 1995. Staso states that developing an "extensive, relevant vocabulary . . . affects the development of more academic skills than any other type of learning."

8. A comprehensive study on language development, done by Betty Hart and Todd R. Risley, was published in their book, *Meaningful Differences in the Everyday Experience of Young American Children.* Among the findings of their important research: "[I]n a year children in professional families heard an average of 11 million words, while children in working class families heard an average of 6 million words and children in welfare families heard an average of 3 million words. By kindergarten, a child from a welfare-recipient family could have heard 32 million words fewer than a classmate from a professional family." The book description states, "By giving children positive interactions and experiences with adults who take the time to teach vocabulary, oral language concepts, and emergent literacy concepts, children should have a better chance to succeed at school."

9. Jim Trelease, in the 2006 edition of his classic *The Read-Aloud Handbook,* described a study entitled *Meaningful Differences in the Everyday Experience of Young American Children,* conducted by Betty Hart and Todd Risley at the University of Kansas, and published in 1996. The study involved children from three socioeconomic groups identified as welfare, working class, and professional. The study projected the daily number of words for each group of children for 4 years, and found that the welfare child will have heard 32 million fewer words than the child from a professional family.

KINDERGARTEN READINESS

When a child enters kindergarten, he is not expected to be able to read. It's more important that the child be familiar with books, and how they work. He should have a vocabulary of approximately 8,000–10,000 words. He should know the letters of the alphabet and their sounds. And if he already enjoys rhymes, and knows how to play with words, then learning to read will progress much more quickly and comfortably.

Here's what the research says about kindergarten readiness:

1. "Primary prevention of reading difficulties during the preschool years involves ensuring that families and group care settings for young children offer the experiences and support that make these

language and literacy accomplishments possible. Parents and other caregivers should spend time in one-on-one conversation with young children, read books with them, provide writing materials, support dramatic play that might incorporate literacy activities, demonstrate the uses of literacy, and maintain a joyful, playful atmosphere around literacy activities. For most children, these primary prevention efforts will ensure that they are ready for formal reading instruction."

(Snow, Catherine E., M. Susan Burns, and Peg Griffin. *Preventing Reading Difficulties in Young Children,* pp. 170–171. Washington, DC: National Academy Press, 1998.)

2. "The relationship between the skills children possess when entering school and their later academic performance is remarkably stable. Research has shown that there is nearly a 90 percent probability that a child who is a poor reader at the end of the fourth grade started out a poor reader at the end of first grade. Knowing alphabet letters when beginning kindergarten is a strong predictor of reading ability in the tenth grade. G. Reid Lyon (testimony U.S. Senate, Committee on Labor and Human Resources, April 28, 1998)"

(Ghoting, Saroj. *Early Literacy Storytimes @ Your Library,* p. 11. Chicago, IL: American Library Association, 2006.)

SCREEN TIME

Books good, television bad. That's what many of us have heard, yet the reality is that television, as well as computer time, is part of our daily lives, and can offer relief during a busy day. Setting time limits for screen time, turning off the television when no one is watching, and watching with your child, so you can interact about what you're seeing, are all simple ways to keep the negative addiction of screen time under control. It's all about balance, except for the very young child. According to the American Pediatric Association, screen time is not recommended for children age two and under. Why would an 18-month-old need to be propped in front of a television, staring at a screen that doesn't interact and has no warmth? What skills will an infant learn about computer use? Those first years are the years to cuddle and play and talk and bond. There is absolutely no proof that a child will be a better reader, or more academically successful, just because he watched "make-your-baby-a-genius" videos, or had index cards flashed in front of his face, or labels on everything in his home. There is proof that intimacy, reading aloud, and conversation will lead to those qualities, as well as make memories that are irreplaceable and priceless.

Here's what research says about screen time:

1. According to their parents, children six and under spend an average of about two hours a day with screen media (1:58), and three times as much time as they spend reading or being read to (39 minutes) (p. 4).

The American Academy of Pediatrics recommends that children under two not watch any television, and that all children over two be limited to one to two hours of educational screen media a day. Despite these recommendations, in a typical day, 68 percent of all children under two use screen media (59% watch TV, 42% watch a video or DVD, 5% use a computer, and 3% play video games), and these youngsters will spend an average of two hours and five minutes in front of a screen. Indeed, according to their parents, 43 percent of all children under two watch TV every day, and one-quarter (26%) have a TV in their bedroom. Seventy-four percent of all infants and toddlers have watched TV before age two. (p. 5)

Children in heavy TV households are also less likely to read every day (59% vs. 68%), and when they do read or are read to, it is for a shorter amount of time than for children in nonheavy TV households. In fact, these children are less likely to be able to read at all: according to their parents, 24 percent of children over the age of two in heavy TV households can read, compared to 36 percent of children in other homes. This difference is even more pronounced among the four- to six-year-old group, where 34 percent of those in heavy TV homes can read, compared to 56 percent of those in nonheavy TV homes, according to their parents (p. 6).

(Rideout, Victoria J., Elizabeth A. Vandewater, and Ellen A. Wartella. *Zero to Six: Electronic Media in the Lives of Infants, Toddlers and Preschoolers.* This information was reprinted with permission from the Henry J. Kaiser Family Foundation. The Kaiser Family Foundation is a nonprofit private operating foundation, based in Menlo Park, California, dedicated to producing and communicating the best possible analysis and information on health issues. http://www.kff.org/entmedia/upload/Zero-to-Six-Electronic-Media-in-the-Lives-of-Infants-Toddlers-and-Preschoolers-PDF.pdf.)

2. "On average, children spend only forty-nine minutes with books per day compared with two hours and twenty-two minutes in front of a TV or computer screen. Want above-average kids? Read."

(Straub, Susan, and K. J. Dell'Antonia. *Reading with Babies, Toddlers and Twos:* A Guide to Choosing, Reading and Loving Books Together, p. ix. Naperville, IL: Sourcebooks, Inc., 2006.)

3. "This updated policy statement provides further evidence that media—both foreground and background—have potentially negative effects and no known positive effects for children younger than 2 years. Thus, the AAP reaffirms its recommendation to discourage media use in this age group. This statement also discourages the use of background television intended for adults when a young child is in the room. Although infant/toddler programming might be entertaining, it should not be marketed as or presumed by parents to be educational."

(American Academy of Pediatrics. "Media Use by Children Younger than 2 Years." *Pediatrics: Official Journal of the American*

Research confirms that reading aloud to children is the most important activity a parent can do to ensure academic success. Bridget found that reading *Corduroy* by Don Freeman to her twin babies, Emily and Jack, while lying on the floor allowed them to both see the pictures.

Academy of Pediatrics, October 17, 2011, http://pediatrics.aap-publications.org/content/128/5/1040.full#sec-7.)

BIBLIOGRAPHY

Bennet-Armistead, V. Susan. *Beyond Bedtime Stories: A Parent's Guide to Promoting Reading, Writing and Other Literary Skills from Birth to 5.* New York: Scholastic Teaching Resources, 2007.

Freeman, Don. *Corduroy.* New York: Viking Press, 1968.

Ghoting, Saroj. *Early Literacy Storytimes @ Your Library.* Chicago, IL: American Library Association, 2006.

Hauser, Jill Frankel. *Wow! I'm Reading.* Charlotte, VT: Williamson Publishing Co., 2000.

Hirsh-Pasek, Kathy, and Roberta Michnick Golinkoff. *Einstein Never Used Flash Cards: How Our Children REALLY Learn—And Why They Need to Play More and Memorize Less.* Emmaus, PA: Rodale, 2003.

National Academy of Education. *Becoming a Nation of Readers: The Report of the Commission on Reading.* Washington, D.C.: National Academy of Education, 1985.

Neuman, Susan B., and David K. Dickinson. *Handbook of Early Literacy Research.* Vol. 2. New York: Guilford Press, 2006.

Nevills, Pamela, and Patricia Wolfe. *Building the Reading Brain, PreK-3.* Thousand Oaks, CA: Corwin Press, 2009.

Oppenheim, Joanne. *Oppenheim Toy Portfolio's Read It! Play It! With Babies and Toddlers: Building Literacy through Reading and Play.* New York: Oppenheim Toy Portfolio, 2006.

Schiller, Pam. *Creating Readers: Over 1000 Games, Activities, Tongue Twisters, Fingerplays, Songs, and Stories to Get Children Excited About Reading.* Beltsville, MD: Gryphon House, 2001.

Schulman, Candy. "I Love Reading," *American Baby,* October, 1998.

Silberg, Jackie. *Reading Games for Young Children.* Beltsville, MD: Gryphon House, 2005.

Snow, Catherine E., M. Susan Burns, and Peg Griffin. *Preventing Reading Difficulties in Young Children.* Washington, D.C.: National Academy Press, 1998.

Straub, Susan, and K. J. Dell'Antonia. *Reading with Babies, Toddlers and Twos: A Guide to Choosing, Reading and Loving Books Together.* Naperville, IL: Sourcebooks, Inc., 2006.

Trelease, Jim. *The New Read-Aloud Handbook.* New York: Viking Penguin, 1989.

Wolf, Maryanne. *Proust and the Squid: The Story and Science of the Reading Brain.* New York: Harper, 2007.

WEBLIOGRAPHY

http://www.kff.org/entmedia/upload/Zero-to-Six-Electronic-Media-in
    the-Lives-of-Infants-Toddlers-and-Preschoolers-PDF.pdf   www.the
    literacysite.com

http://pediatrics.aappublications.org/content/128/5/1040.full#sec-7

http://www.rif.org/us/about/literacy-issues/giving-children-access-to
    print-materials-improves-reading-performance.htm

http://www.sciencedirect.com/science/article/pii/0885200694900183

Chapter Nine

READ MORE, LEARN MORE: PRINT RESOURCES, WEBSITES, AND EARLY LITERACY PROGRAMS

I have browsed my way through many books about early literacy and brain development, and activities that promote them. Some are highly technical, written for the expert or the doctoral student, and some are mundane. The ones I selected to review in this chapter are those that I found most helpful, user friendly, and/or fun. But these aren't just book reviews; I've also highlighted samples of the best activities and ideas in each book, in hopes of leading you to selecting titles that will teach you more about what you want to learn.

HEATHER RECOMMENDS

20 Print Resources about Early Literacy, Brain Development, and the Importance of Reading Aloud

Bennett-Armistead, V. Susan, Nell K. Duke, and Annie M. Moses. *Beyond Bedtime Stories: A Parent's Guide to Promoting Reading, Writing, and Other Literacy Skills from Birth to 5.* New York: Scholastic, 2007.

Filled with ideas about creating a literacy-rich environment for children, this book is extremely useful for parents. First of all, there is a very clever A to Z list of 26 "wonderful things for children to read," and explanations of each, from **A**lphabet and Other Concept Books to **Z**any

---

Books, with other media such as **D**irections and **K**itchen Magnets in between.

There is another helpful list of age-appropriate accomplishments associated with books and literacy, as well as "The Home Literacy Behavior Checklist." The author also describes creative ways to make every room in the house, even the bathroom, full of opportunities to promote early literacy. There are answers to common questions about reading aloud, such as "What if my child is always on the move?" and "Do read-alouds have to take place at bedtime?" Bennett-Armistead offers a chart of examples of what to say while reading in order to build various comprehension skills, such as forming opinions, predicting, and linking to writing. There is practical advice about the television, and how to keep it from becoming a default activity, while still enjoying its benefits, and a checklist for parents to assure that the care environment they choose is also literacy rich.

> Bickart, Toni S., and Diane Trister Dodge. *Reading Right from the Start: What Parents Can Do in the First Five Years.* Washington, DC: Teaching Strategies, 2000.

This is an excellent resource for parents who are new to the idea of reading, singing, and rhyming with their infant, toddler, or preschooler. It is available online in both Spanish and English (http://www.teaching-strategies.com/book/0045_ReadingFromStart.cfm) at reduced prices for large quantities, so it's a perfect gift to the parents at workshops. The small, brief paperback has all the basic information in an easy-to-read format. Particularly useful are the charts at the end of each age division that clearly outline simple activities parents can do to increase literacy. For instance, with a toddler, "When you walk to the playground or in your neighborhood you might make up silly rhymes—'See see, see the tree. Tree, tree, taller than my knee.' This helps your toddler hear the small sounds in words" (p. 37).

> Blakemore, Caroline J., and Barbara Weston Ramirez. *Baby Read-Aloud Basics: Fun and Interactive Ways to Help Your Little One Discover the World of Words.* New York: AMACOM, 2006.

Blakemore's book has abundant advice for parents with babies. The authors provide tips on read-aloud stages, managing TV, and how to read aloud. There are interviews with parents, recommended titles, and answers to frequently asked questions. I especially like the research that is offered, such as a study of 205 low-income multicultural families with 5- to 11-month old babies. Half of the families were given books and encouragement about reading aloud, the other half were not. For the families who received books and advice, the parents read more often and changed their attitude about the importance of reading aloud. The study also recorded a "40 percent increase in…words babies understand but may not yet speak" in those families, as opposed to a 16 percent increase for the other families (p. 19). There is a very helpful chart on pages 38–41, which recommends specific kinds of books based on the age and language and physical characteristics of the baby, beginning with nursery rhymes for "the listener" at 0 months and progressing to books with interesting language, concepts, and feelings for the "phrase maker" at 18–24 months.

Codell, Esme Raj. *How to Get Your Child to Love Reading.* Chapel Hill, NC: Algonquin Books of Chapel Hill, 2003.

Beginning with a story about potatoes, and how they led this teacher to dedicating herself to bringing literature into her students' lives every single day, Codell's passion for all things books abounds in this volume of recommended titles and activities. Chapters with titles such as "Magic Piece of Background Knowledge Number One: Read-Aloud Works Every Time" lead the reader to a multitude of tips on why children must have books in their lives from the very beginning. Abundant graphics, book covers, lists, and suggestions make this book extremely useful and downright fun to read.

Dollins, Cynthia. *The ABCs of Literacy: Preparing Our Children for Lifelong Learning.* Nashville, TN: Cumberland House, 2008.

This is a wonderful introduction to the art of book selection, choosing the right book for the right child at the right time. Chapters include information on why we read aloud, what to read aloud, how to read aloud, and ways to promote early literacy. Dollins gives a concise comparison of phonemic awareness and phonics, which clearly outlines the difference between the auditory and the visual. She explains how to enhance literacy through a multiple intelligences approach, using activities such as cooking, art, or drama.

Throughout the book, the author recounts her personal experiences with her daughter, Heather, and how they brought books into her life.

"We read to her so that she may become wiser. We read to her so that she may become better" (p. 3).

Fox, Mem. *Reading Magic: Why Reading Aloud to Our Children Will Change Their Lives Forever.* New York: Harcourt, 2001.

Mem Fox is an early literacy expert out of Australia, well-loved for her delightful children's books that promote early reading through the use of rhyme, rhythm, and repetition. *Reading Magic* describes how simple it is to encourage a child to begin reading, and what great rewards will follow. The book is perfect for busy parents with its short chapters, wide margins, and humorous, as well as endearing, stories of children who suddenly discovered the miracle of reading.

Ghoting, Saroj Nadkarni, and Pamela Martin-Diaz. *Early Literacy Storytimes @ Your Library: Partnering with Caregivers for Success.* Chicago, IL: American Library Association, 2006.

Ghoting was one of the original trainers for the American Library Association's nationwide program "Every Child Ready to Read @ your library." The book begins with an abundance of research concerning topics such as brain development, television, family economics, and the six early literacy skills. The rest of the book offers story time themes, with recommended titles, action rhymes and songs, openings and closings, as well as what to say to the adults during story time about early literacy. There are also tips on assessing story times, and how to promote early literacy outside of the library.

Gopnik, Alison, Andrew N. Meltzoff, and Patricia K. Kuhl. *The Scientist in the Crib: Minds, Brains, and How Children Learn.* New York: William Morrow and Company, Inc., 1999.

Although there is little in this book that specifically relates to reading aloud or learning to read, this is an insightful collection of questions, research, and discoveries about the process of learning. Chapter Six, "What Scientists Have Learned About Children's Brains," provides a simple description of how the brain changes due to experience, thus implicating why it is so important to expose infants, toddlers, and preschoolers to vocabulary and the world of books. Since young children progress from 2,500 synapses at birth to a peak of 15,000 synapses per neuron at two to three years of age, the authors state that the brains of preschool children are, "more active, more connected, and much more flexible" than adults.

Hauser, Jill Frankel. *Wow! I'm Reading! Fun Activities to Make Reading Happen.* Charlotte, VT: Williamson Publishing Co., 2000.

When I first picked up this book, I thought I would browse through and find a few new activities to use in early literacy workshops. Instead, I found hundreds! Every page is full of creative ideas that I hadn't found anywhere else. The sections follow the same basic early literacy skills promoted by the first edition of Every Child Ready to Read @ your library, plus writing. Each activity uses inexpensive materials and involves interaction between adult and child.

I particularly like how Hauser describes a literacy-rich day: "A child starts out in the morning immersed in a pile of books, then moves on to scribbling with crayons and pens. A grown-up includes her in writing a shopping list. Once on the road, letters and words on signs they pass are pointed out, discussed, and read. Reading labels and identifying familiar products in the store is part of shopping; so is talking about all those delicious, colorful fruits and vegetables. They play rhyming games on the drive back. Next comes listening to a favorite nursery rhyme CD and singing together back home. A grown-up comments on the magazine he's reading while the child plays with alphabet magnets on the refrigerator door. The grand finale involves listening to a wonderful bedtime story read aloud." (Hauser, Jill. *Wow! I'm Reading.* Charlotte, VT: Williamson Publishing Co., 2002. p. 12. Used with permission.)

Hirsh-Pasek, Kathy, and Roberta Michnick Golinkoff. *Einstein Never Used Flash Cards: How Our Children REALLY Learn—And Why They Need to Play More and Memorize Less.* Emmaus, PA: Rodale, 2003.

Just the title alone made me love this book. In Chapter 5, "Literacy: Reading Between the Lines," the coauthors emphasize over and over that the parents' role in encouraging a child to read is to make reading fun, to be a role model for reading, and to always allow for play. Experiences such as "being read to, drawing, scribbling, and engaging in lots of dialogue" are what they believe is the parents' job. Other topics covered in this encouraging book include brain development, learning about numbers, language development, and social intelligence.

Hunt, Gladys. *Honey for a Child's Heart: The Imaginative Use of Books in Family Life.* Grand Rapids, MI: Zondervan Books, 2002.

Some books are comfort food. You read them because they reassure you, or they entice you to explore what you've always known you've wanted to explore, or they make you sigh with contentment when you finish the last page. *Honey for a Child's Heart* is all of those, and more. Hunt writes about all the joys that abound as families share wonderful books together. She reminds parents that the best parents, including the fathers, read the best books aloud to their children. She encourages them to pause and reflect and converse about what they have discovered in a book. And she recommends hundreds of titles, from classics to poetry to spiritual to genre to simple favorites.

Lee Pesky Learning Center. *Every Child Ready to Read: Literacy Tips for Parents.* New York: Ballantine Books, 2004.

Short, simple, concise, and useful. Those are the words to describe this less-than-one-hundred page guide to basic information about early literacy, and activities to enhance the skills. The book emphasizes the parent's role as the child's first teacher, and the importance of "activities of home, family, and community life to help your child start school ready to learn to read" (p. xvi). The activities are very basic and easy, promoting fun and interaction, such as singing songs about whatever you're doing. "This is the way we change your diaper, change your diaper, change your diaper. This is the way we change your diaper. And now you're clean and dry—hey!" (p. 12). Each chapter features activities appropriate for the child's age (infant, toddler, preschooler), as well as a section on learning disabilities.

Nevills, Pamela, and Patricia Wolfe. *Building the Reading Brain PreK-3,* 2nd ed. Thousand Oaks, CA: Corwin Press, 2009.

Nevills and Wolfe's book is more technical than most of the others I have selected, but for those who are interested in pursuing brain basics, how language develops, and breaking the reading code, this is an excellent guide. I particularly liked "A Child's Brain and Reading: A Dozen Key Learnings." These pages, from 176 to179, are a wealth of information about how the brain figures out the incredibly complicated process called reading, as well as the necessary skills needed to learn to read. You won't find recommended books or activities, but you will find clear explanations of the necessity for parental involvement and encouragement.

Oppenheim, Joanne, and Stephanie Oppenheim. *Read It! Play It! With Babies and Toddlers: Building Literacy through Reading and Play!* New York: Oppenheim Toy Portfolio, Inc., 2006.

Very, very simple activities are what make this a good choice for families who are just getting used to the idea of interacting with their child through play, song, and crafts. Arranged chronologically, each page begins with a recommended book, followed by activities that explore further. For instance, the book *I Can* by Helen Oxenbury is enhanced with making a book that includes photos of things your baby can do, such as "Emily climbing" or "Emily bathing." Later in the book, the activities are more advanced for the toddler. *Read It! Play It!* has the same format, but focuses on books for preschoolers and early elementary school age.

Ozma, Alice. *The Reading Promise: My Father and the Books We Shared.* New York: Grand Central Publishing, 2011.

What we do matters. It especially matters when what we're doing involves a child. Ozma and her father agreed he would read aloud to her for 100 nights, no matter what. But when they achieved their goal, they found they didn't want to stop, and managed to continue until she left for college. He was an elementary school librarian, and he passed along his love of books to his daughter with books as wide-ranging as *Superfudge* by Judy Blume and *Skeleton Man* by Joseph Bruchac. This memoir is not just a listing of recommended titles, but rather a testament to the everlasting power of books and of spending time with your children. It is a love story, and you *must* read it.

Ruethling, Ann, and Patti Pitcher. *Under the Chinaberry Tree: Books and Inspirations for Mindful Parenting.* New York: Broadway Books, 2003.

I wish this book was updated more frequently because it is the most delightful book about parenting and books you will ever read. The essays are absolutely heartwarming and inspirational, from the first one of "Dailiness: Making It through the Day" to the last chapter "Surrendering the Day: Bedtime." You'll laugh, your heart will be touched, and you'll know, without any doubt, that weaving books throughout every day with your child will make a positive and never-ending difference. One of my favorite chapters is "Traditions: The Threads That Weave Our Lives Together." I have always been a strong believer in the importance of traditions, and I love the authors' perspective of how they evolve, sometimes from an accidental moment, sometimes from a purposeful celebration.

Ruethling and Pitcher recommend books that match their chapter themes of laughter, life's challenges, language, friends and family, and more. Their writings and reviews are astute, clever, and wise. Don't miss this book, and give it as a gift to every family you know. And be sure to visit their website www.chinaberry.com so you can order their catalog for books, toys, and other "treasures for the whole family."

Schiller, Pam. *Creating Readers: Over 1000 Games, Activities, Tongue Twisters, Fingerplays, Songs and Stories to Get Children Excited about Reading.* Beltsville, MD: Gryphon House, 2001.

Schiller is simply a wealth of ideas about early childhood education. With more than 30 books written about creative activities to do with children, as well as several CDs of songs, she has obviously dedicated herself to getting the word out about how to make learning fun. This particular volume focuses on the "Letter of the Day" approach to literacy, and offers all the categories listed in the title of the book for each letter. So if you're celebrating the letter M you'll find the song "Mister Moon" (an adaptation of "Mister Sun"), nursery rhymes such as "One Misty" and "Moisty Morning," fingerplays such as "Miss Mary Mack," patterns for a magnet story of "This Old Man," activities such as mixing a milkshake or pretending to be monkeys, a word list, and, of course, some recommended titles. I guarantee you won't get through this book without finding ideas you can use or adapt.

Be sure to check out http://www.schillereducationalresources.com, and see what other valuable resources Schiller has to offer.

Silberg, Jackie. *Reading Games*. Beltsville, MD: Gryphon House, 2005.

Just like Schiller, "Miss Jackie" has an amazing array of publications to choose from, including ones on brain games, the "I Can't Sing Book," and large volumes of rhymes, songs, activities, dances, games, and so on. She also has CDs, workshops, and a website, www.jackiesilberg. com. Miss Jackie is a favorite with preschool and kindergarten teachers. This particular volume is filled with creative games for the classroom, several of which I have mentioned previously. All of them are easily learned, and based on making learning fun.

Straub, Susan, and K. J. Dell'Antonia. *Reading with Babies, Toddlers and Twos: A Guide to Choosing, Reading and Loving Books Together*. Naperville, ILL: Sourcebooks, 2006.

Parents, read this book! The book lists are absolutely wonderful, leading you to excellent titles for you to share with your child. Topics cover almost any subject you might encounter during your child's first five years, such as "Happy Birthday Books," "Ten Books That Play to Common Toddler Obsessions," "Thirteen Books for Bedtime Troubles," and "Daddy: The Modern Version." I especially enjoyed "Ten Picture Books We Dare You Not to Enjoy" and "Well, WE Think These Are Funny." There are practical and simple tips on how you can select books that best fit the stages and behavior of your child(ren). Lists range from "Art Activities with Readers 0–3" to "Story Telling and Fairy Tales." Testimonials from parents give real-life examples of how books can calm, enchant, entertain, and influence children.

The advice is practical, supporting the first time, frightened parent, or the family who really needs to occasionally use the television to entertain the child, or the parent who is overwhelmed by all the choices. After all, the author, Susan Straub, is the founder of the Read to Me program, which targets teen mothers but is easily adapted to other populations. Learn more at www.readtomeprogram.org.

Here are some wise words from Straub for the parent who might not be as enthusiastic about books as librarians and teachers are: "The stories may be brilliant, but not everyone finds conveying them easy. It's normal and fair to feel awkward about reading aloud, even to the least demanding of audiences. After all, until you had a baby, the last time you read aloud was probably in an English classroom full of your peers, alternately critical, bored or inattentive. Your baby will be none of those things. She'll be delighted, enchanted, and enthralled, however you do it" (p. 69).

> Wolf, Maryanne. *Proust and the Squid: the Story and Science of the Reading Brain.* New York: HarperCollins Publishers, 2007.

If you wish to read one technical volume, a book that is based on research and uses many words never used in daily conversation, choose this one. Wolf does an excellent job of making the story and science of the brain readable. She begins with the history of writing, proceeds to how the brain works to decipher codes and eventually read, and ends with current research and discoveries about dyslexia. Although there certainly are technical and academic concepts expressed in the book, it is still readable. Much like Carl Sagan used to be able to fill us with the wonder of outer space and its "billions and billions of stars," Wolf makes it clear that learning to read is an amazing process that literally changed the world.

EARLY LITERACY PROGRAMS: 18 PLACES TO EXPLORE ON THE WEB

Why reinvent the wheel? If others have come up with programs that promote the skills, offer tips on activities, or explain the research, then use what they already know for your own purposes. What you'll find is some repetition from one website to the next, as well as some original ideas. We all have the same goal—to increase bonding, improve a child's academic skills, and promote the love of literature and reading.

Born Learning. www.bornlearning.org.
> This is an excellent site to wander through. There are video clips about parenting skills, as well as information on the importance of play. On the Ages and Stages page, you can click on the age of your child and it will give you information on topics such as nutrition, sleep, and growth development, as well as how to nurture your child with literacy activities.

Born to Read. http://www.ala.org/alsc/issuesadv/borntoread.
> The American Library Association created this website for librarians to find the information and resources they need to "help expectant

and new parents to become aware that reading to a baby from birth is critical to every baby's growth and well being." Using the slogan "It's Never Too Early to Start," Born to Read (BTR) offers brochures, information about story times and funding sources, booklists, talking points, and ideas for creating partnerships in the community.

Colorado Libraries for Early Literacy. www.clel.org.

Links to early literacy services and information on the early literacy skills are just the beginning. The best is the blog, where you'll find ideas from librarians and others about how to have fun with literacy through crafts and props. StoryBlocks is a series of videos demonstrating songs and rhymes, some in Spanish.

Every Child Ready to Read @ your library. http://www.everychildreadytoread.org/.

This is a joint project of the Public Library Association and the Association for Library Service to Children. It features the early literacy skills necessary for a child to learn to read, a list of research studies related to literacy and brain development, and materials needed to lead your own workshops, such as posters, scripts, and handouts. There are also translations in Chinese, French, Korean, Russian, and Spanish.

First Book. www.firstbook.org.

Citing the research that indicates the ratio of books to children in middle-income neighborhoods is 13 books to 1 child, vs. the ratio in low-income neighborhoods which is 1 book to 300 children, First Book's mission is "to provide a steady stream of new free or low cost books to elevate educational programming and improve access to reading materials." You can buy books from their website at very low prices, as well as register for free books if your program serves at least 80% children from low-income families.

Get Ready to Read. www.getreadytoread.org.

Get Ready to Read provides a screening tool for educators, child care providers, and parents "in order to help them prepare all children to learn to read and write." The online or print screening tool will reveal the child's progress toward mastering three core areas of early literacy—print knowledge, emergent writing, and linguistic awareness. There are also animated online games, activity cards, and checklists to create a "literacy friendly home or classroom." I particularly liked their idea of using a puppet to encourage exploration of and knowledge about books. The puppet invites help from the child to hold the book correctly, find the title page, figure out where to begin reading, and so on. Another is "Build Your Name," where you put plastic letters in a bag. The child reaches in and pulls one out. You ask if the letter is in his or her name, and, together, you build the name.

Get Set 4 K. www.getset4k.org.
This is Charlotte Mecklenburg Library's website for parents on kindergarten skills development, getting ready to read, and health and wellness. There are monthly tips about skills and development, as well as related activities and recommended books.

Hennepin County Library. www.hclib.org/BirthTo6.
Many libraries offer information about early literacy. Hennepin County in Minneapolis, Minnesota, does an excellent job with recommended titles and basic information about the skills. Particularly impressive is the many translations of "Tips for Reading to Young Children"—Amharic, Arabic, Cambodian, Chinese, French, German, Hindi, Hmong, Japanese, Lao, Oromo, Russian, Somali, Spanish, and Vietnamese.

International Reading Association. www.reading.org.
It's not necessary to join this organization in order to get helpful information. The section on Parent Resources provides printable brochures such as Getting Your Child Ready to Read and Supporting Your Beginning Reader. You'll also find a link to Choices, which are recommendations from children, teachers, and librarians of favorite books.

Jumpstart. www.jstart.org.
"Jumpstart is a national early education organization that helps these children (from low income neighborhoods) develop the language, literacy, and social skills they need to be successful in school, setting them on a path to close the achievement gap before it is too late." Click on "Our Programs," select "Jumpstart to Kindergarten," and sign up for monthly information and tips on literacy, as well as social, emotional, cognitive, and physical developments.

The Literacy Site. www.theliteracysite.com.
In partnership with First Book and Room to Read, The Literacy Site makes books available to children around the world. Each click helps provide a book through the sponsors listed on the site.

Milestone Moments: Learn the Signs. Act Early. http://www.cdc.gov/ncbddd/actearly/downloads.html.
This online publication by the Centers for Disease Control and Prevention lists stages of development from two months to five years.

Each stage describes what to watch for in the areas of emotional, language, cognitive, and movement development, as well as what the caregiver should be doing to encourage optimum growth. Related to literacy, there are tips such as reading books every day at six months, singing songs with actions at one year, and doing art projects together at two years.

National Association for the Education of Young Children (NAEYC). www.naeyc.org.

Calling itself the "world's largest organization working on behalf of young children," NAEYC offers an abundance of resources, including their position statements concerning topics such as "Learning to Read and Write" and "Technology and Young Children." You'll also find their report on "Developing Kindergarten Readiness and Other Large-Scale Assessment Systems," as well as many other publications available for sale. Membership in NAEYC gives you discounted rates, as well as online access to their periodical *Young Children* and annual conferences.

National Center for Family Literacy (NCFL). www.famlit.org.

NCFL promotes its mission as "Inspiring and engaging families in the pursuit of learning together." The website includes resources such as an early literacy calendar of monthly activities (http://www.famlit.org/wp-content/uploads/2010/08/celebrate-literacy-calendar.pdf), and free podcasts about parent involvement. Particularly useful are Early Literacy Initiative videos and posters, which you can download or order (http://www.famlit.org/free-resources/what-works/).

National Institute of Child Health & Human Development (NICHD). www.nichd.nih.gov.

Go to the Publications link, and select "literacy" as the keyword. Several publications will appear that are free to order, or download and print. These were done by the National Institute for Literacy (NIFL) and include "A Child Becomes a Reader," "Literacy Begins at Home: Teach Them to Read," "Shining Stars: Toddlers Get Ready to Read," and "Shining Stars: Preschoolers Get Ready to Read." If you're really interested in their research, go to "Research" and type in "early literacy." More than 200 links to documents will appear.

National Reading Panel (NRP). www.nationalreadingpanel.org.

The NRP, appointed by the NICHD, completed several years of research and the assessment of approaches to reading instruction. The members continue to present the NRP findings at various confer-

ences and organizational meetings. NICHD has formed a partnership with the NIFL and the U.S. Department of Education (ED) to
work on continuing to disseminate and implement research-based
reading practices. Be sure to download their publications, "Put
Reading First: The Research Building Blocks" and "Put Reading
First: Helping Your Child Learn to Read."

Oregon Statewide Early Literacy Initiative. http://www.oregon.gov/OSL/
LD/youthsvcs/earlylit/.
The Oregon State Library hosts a webpage that features information on the importance of early literacy, ideas of what libraries can
be doing to support that importance, and additional resources that
offer book suggestions, programming, songs, games, and more. It
also gives a summary of the statewide initiative made possible by an
LSTA grant awarded to Multnomah County libraries to "give library
staff the tools to implement the best evidence-based practices."

Parents' Action for Children. www.parentsaction.org.
Formerly I Am Your Child, this organization was founded by Rob
and Michele Reiner in an effort to inform parents about "the critical
importance the prenatal period through the first early years plays in
a child's healthy brain development." Advocacy is a primary focus, as
well as the production and sale of videos and booklets. Their DVD,
"Ready to Learn: Essential Tips for Early Literacy" is an excellent
resource to use at workshops.

Reach Out and Read. www.reachoutandread.org.
Reach Out and Read involves pediatricians giving parents advice about
the importance of reading aloud, as well as giving them new books for
their children. According to their website, the "3.9 million children
served by Reach Out and Read enter school with a six month developmental edge." Their Developmental Milestones, available in English,
Spanish, Chinese and Vietnamese, are clear and useful guidelines for
parents who might not be as familiar with why and when their child
does what he does. There is also a state-by-state chart of data as to the
percentage of parents who read aloud to their child(ren).

The Read to Me Program. www.readtomeprogram.org.
The goal of this organization is to "get mothers to read books to their
babies." The series of workshops is focused on teen mothers, but easily adapted for other populations. Promoted activities include visiting the library, making books, and, of course, reading books. Tips
are given on starting your own local program, including potential

partnerships, funding, and training. There are lists of recommended authors and titles, FAQs about child behavior, and a store for ordering the related books and DVDs.

Reading for Healthy Families (RFHF). http://www.oregon.gov/OSL/LD/youthsvcs/rfhf.home.page.shtml.
> "RFHF was a statewide early literacy project managed by Oregon Commission on Children and Families and Oregon State Library, funded by grants from the Oregon Community Foundation and the Paul G. Allen Family Foundation." The website includes research, how to plan a story time, finding good deals for buying books, tips on creating partnerships, and much more.

Reading Rockets. www.readingrockets.org.
> Advertised as "Teaching kids to read and helping those who struggle," this website overflows with information for parents, teachers, and librarians. There are videos and podcasts, booklists, tips on helping struggling readers, free reading guides, and topics from A to Z that offer help. Parents will find plenty here to help them understand, overcome, and interact. Librarians will love the Top 12 Resources, including dozens of themed booklists, hundreds of research-based articles, and a literacy calendar with ways to celebrate every month. Teachers will find plenty of ideas for classroom activities, tips on building strong parent–teacher relationships, and professional development resources. And it's all available in Spanish, too! Be sure to subscribe to the Reading Rockets newsletter.

Reading Is Fundamental (RIF). www.rif.org.
> Described as "the largest children's literacy nonprofit in the United States," RIF's vision is "a literate America in which all children have access to books and discover the joys and value of reading." They provide free books to those who need them the most. If you go to "Literacy Resources" and click on "Activities," you'll find a printable monthly calendar with simple and inexpensive literacy-based activities between caregiver and child for each day. They offer a multicultural booklist and articles for parents about reading aloud.

Starting Points: Meeting the Needs of Our Youngest Children. http://carnegie.org/fileadmin/Media/Publications/PDF/Starting%20Points%20Meeting%20the%20Needs%20of%20Our%20Youngest%20Children.pdf.
> This is an abridged version of the 1994 book by the same title, authored by the Carnegie Task Force on Meeting the Needs of Young

Children. Its focus is on identifying the "Quiet Crisis" that exists in the United States, which includes inadequate attention to prenatal care, and the need for quality child care, community support, and funding. Although literacy is not specifically mentioned in the abstract, it does highlight the importance of brain development during the infant years, and states, "Infants' early experiences also provide the building blocks for intellectual competence and language comprehension. Touching, holding, and rocking a baby, as well as talking and reading, seem most effective for later development" (pp. 3–4).

Washington Learning Systems. www.walearning.com.

"Our programs show educators and parents ways to 'power-up' everyday interactions with young children to promote language development, literacy, and learning." Click on "Literacy Resources," and you'll find free, reproducible activities for infants and preschoolers, in Spanish and English. Each activity is followed by tips for success and ways to make it more challenging. You'll also find "on-the-go" activities for parents to do in the car, or on a walk, and those are translated into Spanish, Mandarin, Vietnamese, Somali, Russian, and Burmese. The activities are simple, practical ways to give your child a day full of opportunities to grow literacy and language skills.

Zero to Three. www.zerotothree.org.

Zero to three is a national, nonprofit organization that "informs, trains, and supports professionals, policymakers, and parents in their efforts to improve the lives of infants and toddlers." I love the "Baby Brain Map," where you get to choose the age of the child, and the part of the brain that you want to understand better. In the section "Behavior and Development," you will find the "Tips and Tools" about early language and literacy, including the Beginnings of Literacy; Learning to Write and Draw; Tips for Choosing Books, Songs, Rhymes, and Fingerplays in Spanish and English; and information about how children learn multiple languages.

It's not always easy as a parent to know the best way to raise a child, but taking time out of every day to share books is guaranteed to be the right thing to do. Tracy read aloud to Lily and Jack from the very beginning, visited the library every week, and made sure they always had books to enjoy.

Chapter Ten

A PARENT, TWO TEACHERS, AND A LIBRARIAN: THOUGHTS ABOUT EARLY LITERACY

"There really is a light bulb. Those are good moments, when a child suddenly realizes, 'Hey, I just read that!'" (Ann, preschool teacher)

"You plant your seeds. Do they all sprout and grow at the same time? No. But, all of a sudden, they get it, when they're ready. I'd say, 'Wait a minute. You just read that!' And they are amazed." (Virginia, kindergarten teacher)

"I made reading part of every day, even when they were infants. I built a routine that included books—during bath time, before bed, while I was giving them a massage....It was very special to me when I saw Lily, age 4, reading aloud to Jack, age 2." (Tracy, parent)

Miss Ann (a.k.a. Ann Williams) was my daughter's preschool teacher. She owns Mudpies and Lullabies Preschool in Bend, Oregon. It is a gentle place, full of reassurance, creativity, color, play, and learning. I remember teachers singing quiet reminders of tasks to be completed, celebrating birthdays with treats and crowns, and a final graduation that featured a production of "Old MacDonald's Farm," with bright red bandanas tied around all the preschoolers' necks as they sang songs about geese and cows and pigs.

I asked Miss Ann what she sees as essential for making a reader. "Lots and lots of books should be available," she answered. "Children need to be able to pick up books and handle them. They need to hear different types of books because every child is different. We do Super Silent Reading, when every child 'reads' on his or her own each day. They need the confidence to believe they can read."

Other literacy-based activities at Mudpies and Lullabies include:

- Author's Month. Teachers read aloud books by their favorite authors, and they bring in a librarian to present a special story time. Children become authors and create their own books, based on titles such as *It's OK to Be Different* by Todd Parr.

- Each day pointing out the words for days of the week and the weather. "Today is Tuesday. What's the weather like? Sunny!"

- Handwriting without Tears. A multisensory curriculum developed by an occupational therapist, to teach writing by using songs, visual cues, sounds, and workbooks.

- Creative play. "Creative play comes from their hearts," said Miss Ann. "There are no boundaries. It leads to language development because they can have the conversations they want to have, and be whoever they want to be."

- Songs. "Singing is soothing, and it captures their attention. It touches a place in every child's heart. I make up silly songs all the time, and it works. They respond."

- Letter of the week. Children practice writing the letter, they brainstorm words that begin with the letter, they put pictures on the wall of objects that begin with the letter, and whoever has a name that starts with that letter gets to sit on the Letter Table and spell his or her name.

- Drawing books. "The teacher might read *The Snowy Day* by Ezra Jack Keats. Then she gives a starter sentence to the children, such as, 'On a snowy day I like to…' The child draws the pictures, the teacher writes the words, and it makes a very special and personal book to keep."

- Rhyming. "I say a word, and take it apart into its letter sounds. H-O-T. They spell it and read it with me. Then we go on to another word that rhymes. P-O-T."

After our interview, I realized that everything she had described was included in the title of this book—Read, Rhyme, Romp. That's what it takes to grow a reader who loves to read.

Virginia Nelson, my daughter's kindergarten teacher, was one of those rare and special teachers who knew how to make learning fun. Her high energy, willingness to be silly, and dedication to her "kiddos" made every day playful as well as educational. The school, Highland Elementary at Kenwood, follows the Scottish Storyline Method, in which teachers and students take on the role of characters in a "story" in order to immerse themselves in learning through a wide variety of techniques and sensory experiences. Parents are very involved. Virginia later transferred to a school where the population was more transient, included many who were non-English speaking, and where, as she described it, "conversation at home is about survival, not about what involves children."

I asked Virginia what makes the difference in creating a reader. "Give them (the children) the gift of time. Talk to them, talk to them!" Besides the obvious need for reading aloud books, Virginia also recommended that parents encourage reading what is real in their world. "Read ads, or plan a menu together."

What experts believe children should know *before* they begin kindergarten usually includes at least 8,000 words, familiarity with the alphabet and sounds of letters, and maybe how to spell a few words, including his or her name. But Virginia's observations are more basic about what is needed to make kindergarten and the development of reading successful:

- Children need to be aware of their environment, so they can make connections when they hear a story.
- Children need to be able to sit, not bother others, and listen to someone else.
- Children need "open hearts and willing ears."

Like Miss Ann, Virginia offered early literacy activities—she calls it "subversive teaching"—including writing, letter of the week, and journaling. What I remember most about her class was hearing giggles as she led 20 kindergarteners through the nonsense words and silly actions of the song "Mama Goony Bird," as well as seeing true belief and pride on the student's faces when they received a park ranger's badge after 6 weeks of learning about national parks, or succeeded at completing all the tasks necessary to be a lighthouse keeper after a story line about lighthouses. She led them to learning through the use of imagination in a story and the exploration of facts in books.

I have written about Jack and Lily earlier in this book because they are examples of what happens when children are given the joys of literature every day in many ways. Their mother, Tracy, and I shared Pad Thai at a local restaurant, and talked about favorite books and special memories of early literacy.

"I memorized *The Big Red Barn* by Margaret Wise Brown," Tracy said with a roll of her eyes. "I read it to them so-o-o-o many times. They loved any books that rhymed. Also anything by Eric Carle, Dr. Seuss, Kevin Henkes. They loved the silly poems and illustrations by David Catrow, like *Are You Quite Polite?*. I reinforced their personal interests or school subjects by visiting the library and checking out books on those topics. If we watched Reading Rainbow on TV, then we checked out the books."

What I observed with this family was how they always had plenty of time at the library. It was never, "Come on, hurry up and pick your books because then we have to go do blah-blah-blah." They arrived with an empty bag, and left one or two hours later with the bag more than full. They visited my office, played on the computers, searched for books, and kept bringing them to their Mom. "Look at this one!" "Here's one by Kevin Henkes that we haven't read!" "I want one about superheroes."

When it was Chinese New Year they read *D Is for Dancing Dragon: A China Alphabet* by Carol Crane. When they wanted to learn about Oregon, they read *B Is for Beaver: An Oregon Alphabet* by Marie Smith. And when Jack watched the animated movie Hercules he needed to know more, so they read *Z Is for Zeus: A Greek Mythology Alphabet* by Helen L. Wilbur. "Now he knows everything about the Greek heroes," stated Tracy. "The other day at the book store Jack (who is now 6) was telling someone else, much older than he is, all about Cerberus, the three-headed dog that guards Hades."

Tracy admits she was not much of a reader herself. "It's hard for me to stick with a long book. But children's books were short and fun. Plus I would let myself be goofy and silly with the voices, and they loved that."

Here are just some of the many activities Tracy described that encouraged early literacy with her children:

- "We made sure that getting their own library card was a BIG DEAL! They understood the importance and responsibility, we got the special cord from the librarian so they could wear it around their neck, and we really celebrated it as something very grown up."

- "When we visit the library the rule is that everyone gets to pick books, including Mom."

- "We came to story times so we would discover new authors from the librarians. That's how we learned about Keith Baker, and they still love his books because of all there is to explore in the illustrations."

- "Any special day deserves a book as a gift. Father's Day, birthday, any celebration."

- "We made books. The Me Book. The Color Book."

It was Tracy who introduced me to *When the Cassowary Pooped: A Tale of New Guinea* by Tamara Montgomery. It has become one of my favorites for demonstrating rhythm and rhyme. Tracy and I often shared titles we liked, and I tried to remember to pull new construction machinery books for Jack. Best of all, Tracy continues to share delightful tales about her children and their relationship with books.

When Lily was in kindergarten, each child was to come up with a word that began with the letter assigned to them. Lily's letter was C. Would it be car? Cat? Crayon? No, it was Chrysanthemum, from Kevin Henkes's delightful tale of a mouse who has always loved her flower name until she begins school. Later, when the entire class was studying the letter M, and everyone was offering M words, Lily's was "molecular." Why? Because she'd recently read a book about molecules, of course.

When Jack is telling his mother a story that he is absolutely sure is the absolute truth, he states, "And that's nonfiction, Mom."

Lily began keeping a journal before kindergarten. She read the first two Harry Potter books in second grade. She writes plays.

Tracy read aloud a book about dinosaurs, and the archaeologists who learn about them by digging up what remains. Later, the two children, about age three and five, were in the back seat of the car, and, like all siblings, they were having a disagreement about something or other. Suddenly Jack called out, "Mom! Lily just called me copralite, and that's fossilized dinosaur poop!"

Lily must have been truly captivated by the idea of digging up copralite because, for a while, she wanted to be an archaeologist. Then she decided she would be an artist. Next came the idea of being a pilot, and then a pet shop owner. At age seven, Lily decided she will be a librarian. Why? "Because I will be book wealthy," says Lily.

But my favorite story is about the nook. Recently, eight-year-old Lily announced, "Mom, I need a nook." Tracy couldn't believe her daughter even knew about e-books, and she was devastated that book-loving Lily would want this technological device, eliminating the touch of paper, the swish of turning pages, the smell of ink, the centuries-old charm of HOLDING a book.

A few hours later she was called into Lily's room. There, between the closet door and the wall, was a space about 2' by 3'. There was a small pillow taped to the wall, just right for Lily to lean against, and a blanket, just right for snuggling under. Handwritten motivational posters covered the wall, with words such as "To Read Is to Paint Your Mind." "Look!," Lily announced proudly. "Now I have a nook."

A book nook.

The world of reading is no longer found just in books. Technology is changing even as I write these words. I embrace all that has been created in my lifetime, from avatar to zip drive. Smart boards, e-books, and social networks present opportunities we never imagined.

HOWEVER...

Touching the screen of any computer device only provides what I call "flash and crash" entertainment, making things appear and disappear. Does it teach creativity? Language development that leads to social skills? An understanding of how print works so that you can eventually handle a book and read from beginning to end?

At Toddlin' Tales story time recently a father brought in his two-year-old. I'm always happy to see a father at story time, and looked forward to seeing him have fun with his daughter. Instead, he spent the entire 25 minutes tapping his iPhone. Never spoke to the child, sang a song, looked at the book, nothing.

I am reminded of a story passed along from teller to teller.

A television was brought into a village that had never before seen one. For a week everyone was mesmerized, watching whatever was on, laughing at new images, listening to whatever was said. The second week, the people would occasionally glance at the TV, watch for a bit, then wander away to listen to a story from their storyteller. By the third week, the television interested only a few, and by the end of the month it sat, unnoticed, collecting dust. However, the storyteller had a crowd, and everyone was singing, laughing, participating, with the story being told. The one who had introduced the television asked a person in the village, "Why aren't you watching the television anymore? It knows many more stories than your storyteller will ever know." "Yes," agreed the person, "the television knows many stories, but the storyteller knows *me.*"

When you hold a child in your lap, and you read to them of mice getting ready for bed, or a dragon looking for his mother, you are giving them more than just a wondrous tale. You are sharing the warmth of your skin, and the beat of your heart. That feeling of intimacy and security becomes connected to that object called "book," and that mysterious process called "reading." The child's brain not only identifies the words you are voicing, but also the love you are expressing by giving of yourself.

When you read aloud to a room of children who have open hearts and willing ears, you are offering them more than a story. You are introducing them to exploration and discovery, wonder and understanding, giving and receiving. Together, you are all journeying toward the acknowledgment that books lead to an awakening of senses and a broader perspective of the world. You learn from each other, and you teach them that reading is the beginning to everything.

Every day at the library I have the distinct privilege of connecting children, parents, and teachers with books that answer their questions, challenge their minds, help them learn, or laugh or listen. Every week I have

Lily and Jack visited the library weekly from the time they were toddlers, and regularly attended story times and other programs. Now they're both excellent readers in elementary school, and they still enjoy reading and cuddling with the bears at the Downtown Bend Library.

The library becomes a magical place to a young child when they regularly attend story times, and create a bond with the librarian who brings the books alive. Emma loves the library, Toddlin' Tales, and, most of all, Winston.

Reading aloud to a child should continue for as long as possible because it is a chance to fill part of every day with love and laughter. Jamie is 11 in this photo, and we're enjoying *A Horse of Her Own* by Annie Wedekind. At the time of writing this book she is 13, reading *Hunger Games* by Suzanne Collins by herself and *The Arabian Nights* with me each evening before bedtime. We still enjoy read-aloud time together and we always will.

the absolute joy of presenting story times to toddlers and their care providers who are open to hearing the best literature. And every day at home I have the rewarding challenge of connecting my own daughter with books, stories, rhymes, and songs that will open her heart and mind to all that is possible. I can't imagine a better life.

Giving time to our children is what builds the intimate bonds between care provider and child. Talking to the child and playing with words build the brain and connect the dots. "Being goofy and silly" charms children into the worlds of imagination and play, which builds language and the ability to create a story. And loving books is what makes book lovers and readers.

Guaranteed.

BIBLIOGRAPHY

Brown, Margaret Wise. *The Big Red Barn*. New York: Harper & Row, 1989.

Catrow, David. *Are You Quite Polite? Silly Dilly Manners Songs*. New York: Margaret K. McElderry Books, 2006.

Collins, Suzanne. *Hunger Games*. New York: Scholastic Press, 2008.

Crane, Carol. *D Is for Dancing Dragon: A China Alphabet.* Chelsea, MI: Sleeping Bear Press, 2006.

Henkes, Kevin. *Chrysanthemum.* New York: Greenwillow Books, 1991.

Keats, Ezra Jack. *The Snowy Day.* New York: Viking Press, 1962.

Montgomery, Tamara. *When the Cassowary Pooped: A Tale of New Guinea.* Honolulu, HI: Calabash Books, 2009.

Parr, Todd. *It's Okay to Be Different.* Boston, MA: Little, Brown, 2001.

Smith, Marie. *B Is for Beaver: An Oregon Alphabet.* Chelsea, MI: Sleeping Bear Press, 2003.

Wedekind, Annie. *A Horse of Her Own.* New York: Feiwel and Friends, 2008.

Wilbur, Helen L. *Z Is for Zeus: A Greek Mythology Alphabet.* Chelsea, MI: Sleeping Bear Press, 2008.

INDEX